Collaborative Electronic Resource Management

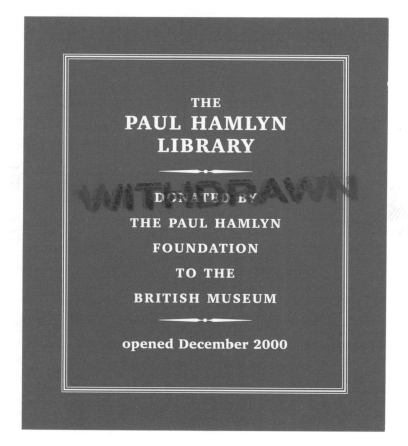

Collaborative Electronic Resource Management

From Acquisitions to Assessment

Joan E. Conger

LIBRARIES
UNLIMITED
A Member of the Greenwood Publishing Group

Westport, Connecticut • London

Library of Congress Cataloging-in-Publication Data

Conger, Joan E.
    Collaborative electronic resource management : from acquisitions to assessment /
Joan E. Conger.
        p.   cm.
    Includes bibliographical references and index.
    ISBN 1–59158–114–1 (pbk. : alk. paper)
    1. Libraries–Special collections–Electronic information resources. 2. Electronic
information resources–Management. 3. Library administration. I. Title.
    Z692.C65C67 2004
    025.17'.4—dc22   2004048925

British Library Cataloguing in Publication Data is available.

Library of Congress Catalog Card Number: 2004048925
ISBN: 1–59158–114–1

First published in 2004

Libraries Unlimited, 88 Post Road West, Westport, CT 06881
A Member of the Greenwood Publishing Group, Inc.
www.lu.com

Printed in the United States of America

∞™

The paper used in this book complies with the
Permanent Paper Standard issued by the National
Information Standards Organization (Z39.48–1984).

10   9   8   7   6   5   4   3   2   1

To my mother,
Martha Anne Shackelford,
a dedicated public servant
at whose knee I learned the value of
promoting self-worth within organizations

Contents

Illustrations

Figures

Tables

Acknowledgments

All that I present on these pages I could not have learned without the invaluable professional relationships I have developed over the years. I would like to thank the faculty of the University of Texas GSLIS who gave me a firm foundation for a career of professional learning. I particularly thank Francis Miksa for introducing postmodernism into my professional consciousness. All the trouble I got into afterward is my fault alone. I would like to thank the dedicated colleagues in Texas, Minnesota, California, Georgia and elsewhere with whom I have had the pleasure to work and learn. This book benefited from the readership and commentary of Beth Bernhardt, Bill Brinegar, Tim Daniels, Beth Jedlicka Thorton, and Erin Smith; from information contributed by the fine members of the ERIL-L listserv; and from my leadership workshop attendees from whom I'm sure I have learned more than they say they have from me. A special thanks goes to Dana Walker. These people meet the highest standards of professional integrity, and any errors within this book are my own. My gratitude goes to Joan B., Wendy G., David B., Renee D. and the warm community of Our Hope MCC for their moral support during the final days. Susan Y. was my rock. Nicole C. will be my anchor. Bonnie Brinegar is an excellent copy editor who kept my grammar and punctuation honest. Again, all errors are due to my failings not her valiant efforts. Finally, I thank my editor Martin Dillon, who had the courage to ask that I write this book.

CHAPTER 1

Introduction

Electronic Resource Management as Library Management

Every fiscal term witnesses an increase in the impact *electronic resources* have on library processes, budgets, professionals, and *customers*. For most libraries the time has passed when electronic resources were a footnote to daily activities. In a typical workday almost all library organization members, from shelvers to administrators in some way decide how to respond to a change that an electronic resource has introduced into accepted procedure.

Because one can find electronic resources at the root of many management concerns, a discussion of electronic resource management quickly becomes a discussion of the overall management of a typical library. Library management challenges faced today include:

- Inadequate budgets. Library *funding authorities* argue that budgets cannot keep pace with the inflation of serials prices, and their subset, the price of electronic resources, especially when these funding authorities labor under the assumption that most *information* on the World Wide Web is free.

- Runaway serials costs. Library funding authorities are correct. No reasonable annual budget can keep pace with the costs of serials and electronic resources. *Library professionals* now must both assertively negotiate lower costs with *vendors* and prove the *value* of these resources to an uninformed constituency.

- An unpredictable impact of electronic resources on library processes. Compared with the print resources that rarely change once placed on the shelf, electronic resources can change their character at least once every license cycle, and often more frequently. Changes can range from the alteration of a *URL* to wholesale removal of content from a product, and these changes will ceaselessly affect the daily work processes of a typical library.

- A shrinking pool of trained library professionals. The number of rising library professionals is not matching the increasing retirement rate of experienced professionals. Couple this reduction in population with a dramatic shift in professional skill sets toward technology and one arrives at an alarmingly small number of professionals prepared to manage an electronic library collection.

- Real competition from other information sources. Dot-com information providers are taking on more and more of the library profession's traditional role of amassing, classifying, and delivering information resources to a public thirsty for knowledge and entertainment. Libraries must demonstrate the value of library services to a *community* targeted by these providers.

- Accountability for customer outcomes. Libraries' parent organizations are passing along mounting accountability pressures during budget negotiations. The quality of library services—such as meeting customers' expectations for access to information from their desktops, the support of distance learning and *virtual* work groups, and library responsibility for information literacy—play no small part in these outcome measurements.

Electronic resources bring turbulent, never-ending change into the management of libraries. The kind of traditional library management that has developed around stable print collections benefits from the continuity of standard procedures. Stability lends predictability and allows competent taskmasters to manage the efficient division of tasks. However, the pervasive effects of electronic resources in a typical library require a different kind of management. Turbulent change disrupts stable efficiency, with the insistent voices of new situations and daily requires unprecedented, creative solutions from professionals throughout a library. Competence becomes less about static knowledge and the application of rules and more about daily, adroit innovation and the use of pooled talent through collaboration. Management becomes less about planning and direction and more about *collaborative management* and *adaptive learning.*

Key Themes

This book holds the following central tenets to be true:

- The *purpose* of libraries is to ensure access to information for a community by providing high-quality collections and services.

- The purpose of libraries is to serve the customer, not from our professional vantage within the constellation of library procedures, but from the customer's vantage within the constellation of library service responsibilities.

- A focus away from procedure and toward the customer will necessarily open our libraries to turbulent change, and turbulent change needs adaptive—not control-based—management practices.
- Finding the *leadership* abilities within every library professional is the pathway to adaptive management, and work in collaborative *groups* amplifies the individual leadership abilities within a successful organization.
- When change is turbulent and continuous, we can never control change, nor can we control for change. But we can use the power of collaborative groups to respond successfully, even joyfully, to change as it happens.
- Library professionals can enjoy their work.

The bedrock beneath these tenets is the belief that the customer is the reason libraries exist. The customer's need should be the rationale for any task undertaken by a library professional, because this need creates the meaning of our work. Because allowing the customer into our workday admits the attendant fluctuations in service expectations, the group becomes the unit of strength. The individual is not as well equipped to learn as is a group. The individual cannot access as much context for decision making as the group. In other words, the individual cannot know as much about an environment in flux, or bring as many skills to bear, as can a group. The individual's contextual experience of a changing environment will not be as broad, or as deep, as the collective contextual experiences of a group. The group will have a richer understanding of the purpose of the organization than will any individual within that organization, from administrator to the front line *implementer* of services.

Collaborative decision making within a group harnesses the power of the group to learn, to successfully respond to daily change, and to successfully achieve the purpose of the library within its service community. Management by collaborative groups comes in many guises with many names, and is exercised to many degrees. The overriding requirement for *manager* and non-manager alike, is the relinquishing of individual control so as to take advantage of collective adaptability.

Therefore, my primary intent throughout this book is not to teach the specific technologies of electronic resource management. Although I do introduce select foundational concepts, technology changes too fast within libraries to focus intently on specifics. My intent throughout this book is to share ideas on the collaborative management of electronic resources, favoring the human element of management over the technical as the best way to grow adaptive organizations.

I found in my work as an electronic resources manager that my colleagues and I encountered a new technology about every eighteen months. Success came to us when we figured out how to "learn" our way through each new change and not necessarily plan for it in advance. This collaborative learning is the essence of adaptive management. For that reason, I include this disclaimer. Advice given in this book is from my perspective and my individual set of experiences and should be applied with due consideration of your own circumstances. Application of the technologies and methodologies discussed here will have different results within different environments. However, what I will assert as a universal truth is the idea that success resides not in applying someone else's solutions, but in the collaborative learning that goes into your own.

With this book I wish to encourage readers to embark upon their own pathways of learning. I wish to start a dialog within the reader of new ways to think about managing electronic resources. Library procedures and technical rules produce continuity and data integrity and they should not be ignored, but I would like to prompt the reader to introduce into this accepted structure some new ideas that will open up the closed *system* of procedure to the influences of change. Our profession has inherited a hierarchical, scientific, and efficient, 19th-century management methodology that cannot flexibly respond to 21st-century change cycles that occur every eighteen months. I would like to motivate the reader to begin, or continue, a process of learning how to restructure relationships with colleagues, customers, vendors, and funding authorities away from *hierarchical management* and control, and toward collaborative management and adaptation. To this end I adopt set of key concepts that may represent a paradigm shift for some working in a more traditional library service model.

Key Concepts

The principles that I rely on in this book are based on a specific understanding of six key concepts:

- Electronic resources
- Library
- Library professional
- Leadership
- Customer
- Value

Electronic Resources

A list of electronic resources managed by a typical library quickly turns encyclopedic and, by the time you read this book, will be quaintly out of date. When I use the term *electronic resources* in this book, I refer to that set of electronic products, technological tools, and freely available *online resources* that together contribute to a library's responsibilities in the delivery of information to its community. More narrowly, electronic products are those packages of electronic content that libraries purchase from vendors, such as electronic journals, online article databases, and electronic reference works. Please bear with me as I alternate between these two definitions depending on context. I apologize for any confusion, but the dual definition is an illustration of the fluidity to which we must become accustomed in electronic resource management.

The management of electronic resources encompasses a set of responsibilities much broader than those associated with electronic products alone. These responsibilities include not only the electronic information products that libraries purchase and the universe of information-rich electronic resources that libraries do not purchase but that nevertheless provide valuable content to our customers, but also the electronic services library professionals create, from chat reference to *dynamic Web sites*, and the technology *infrastructure* we use to deliver these products, from URL-enabled *MARC* records to wireless networks. To serve our communities to the best of our abilities, library professionals must successfully weave all these resources together into a *seamless* information-gathering experience for our customers.

Library

I focus most of my attention on the management of electronic resources within libraries. I am less qualified to comment on the management of electronic resources within other organizations that share the ethics and values of librarianship, such as archives, library consortia, and library vendors. However, as a participant in the activities of these other organizations, I see many parallels between their professionals' experiences with electronic resource management issues and the experiences I will discuss in this book from the library context. The concepts of work design, collaboration, and customer service upon which this book is based are universal in nature, and I hope that this book will offer these other organizations some beginning steps toward solutions as well.

My personal experience in electronic resource management has been within corporate, community college, smaller academic, and larger research libraries in the United States. As I researched this book I tried to expand my knowledge about other kinds of libraries in order to incorporate their experiences into my discussions. I also sought to expand my perception of electronic resource management to include the experiences of those outside the United States, and outside the Western world. Though I realize that I will fall short in these pages of a full understanding of others' experiences, I do hope to encourage the exploration of adaptive electronic resource management as it best fits with the reader's personal experience regardless of library type and geographical location.

Library Professional

I found as I wrote this book that I had to use the term *library professional* to refer to those accomplishing the work of the library profession. The term *librarian* most often refers to library professionals who have received a degree in library science, more recently a library and information science degree, and includes those who implement services in the front lines as well as those in management and administrative positions. While the library degree confers a deeper understanding of library ethics and library procedure, I include in the concept of library professional the valuable contribution of library paraprofessionals, also called library support staff, who put library ethics and an understanding of library procedure to work every day.

I also include the vendor representative in the term *library professional.* The purposes of the vendor representatives' commercial organizations may differ in many ways from those of libraries, but many vendor representatives share the same training, professional ethics, and understanding of library procedure with the professionals to whom they sell their companies' products. Librarians, paraprofessionals, and vendor representatives all work together to create the experiences of library customers, and each group of professionals is equally responsible for and deserving of the successes of these services.

Leadership

Leadership has special qualities that supervision cannot achieve. Supervision travels from problem to solution, and leadership leaps from solution to solution. Supervision perceives solution finding as achieving problem absence or cure, and leadership seeks situation improvement by recognizing the successes already in existence. Supervision tries to change the weights of variables within an equation. Leadership changes the equation itself.

Supervision applies procedure, tries to motivate commitment in others where none existed and exerts the will of the *supervisor* on the supervised. Supervision is hard work, and supervision often frustrates.

Leadership understands a procedural problem as an opportunity to learn and a chance to improve the organization. Leadership applies organizational purpose to adapt organizational activities to each new situation because leadership seeks to leap outside the conventional to find the innovative. Leadership recognizes the motivation already present inside each organization member and treats every professional as a part of the learning process. Leadership creates an environment for all colleagues, including the leader's subordinates (if any), fellow colleagues, and supervisors, that elicits and supports the leadership qualities within each of these people.

Changing another person is impossible, but changing one's own part in another person's environment can lead to deep change for everyone. Leadership creates work relationships that support the work of learning and adaptation. Leadership is the quality through which all members of an organization contribute to the success of that organization. Management relies on supervision for daily task coordination, but successful management also calls on the power of leadership found within each and every individual to achieve the goals of the organization.

Customer

The word *customer* seems to not fit easily within the library ethics of open access to information resources. The word *customer* invokes images of selling. I, however, consciously use this word instead of the more common term *patron* because within the idea of sales is the suggestion that a library customer has a choice, and eagerly exercises that choice, between our services and other information services. As a professional, I know these other services are of lesser content value, but I also know that these services appear to the customer to hold greater convenience value.

Therefore, to fulfill my ethical commitment to open access, I must create convenience value to attract the library customer to my higher content value. Because of this ethical commitment, convenience for the customer is my responsibility as a library professional. My customer should not have to solve problems of convenient access within the services I create. A shift in terminology from *patron* to *customer* will be accompanied by a mental shift in the library professional. As a library professional when I use the word *customer*, I can no longer create services and then wait for *patrons* to approach (learn about, fit into) these services. I must now create services that seek out and respond to the needs of customers who can go elsewhere with the click of a mouse. I no longer create services that best fit my job processes. I now create services that best fit a quality customer experience.

Value

The value of a library, a library's collection, a library's services, or a library's use is not measured by number of uses or number of objects contained therein. A library has value when its collections and service have a positive impact on the library's community. A library has value when a customer prefers the library's services to other sources of information. A library has value when a customer willingly and happily returns for a repeat performance. A library has value when a customer recommends the library to a colleague. A library has value when customers defend the value of the library within its community and to its funding authority. My fundamental job as a library professional is not to adhere to procedure and increase size. These results are secondary. My fundamental job as a library professional is to create, market, and nurture the value my library has for the community it serves. Libraries can best address the value of electronic resource management through the professional position of Electronic Resource Manager.

Electronic Resource Manager

Only recently have libraries begun to create and fill a position with a sole responsibility for electronic resource management. This position finds itself variously in reference, *serials*, cataloging, acquisitions, and collection development departments. Frequently in larger libraries the job is split between two full-time positions, with one professional each in public service and technical service. Based on personal experience, I recommend this multiple-responsibility approach when the number of electronic resources reaches a critical level within a library.

More rarely libraries designate the electronic resource manager as a middle management position. Choosing this direction will most benefit larger libraries trying to respond to the changes that accompany electronic resources as they are incorporated into the processes of all library departments. In a flatter organization (with fewer hierarchical supervisory positions), an electronic resources manager with team leadership responsibilities can harness and channel into electronic resource management the knowledge, skills, and creativity of professionals distributed throughout the library.

More frequently libraries define electronic resource management as "other duties as assigned." Over time a library professional within the organization will have developed the acumen and knowledge to handle daily electronic resource issues, and the library continues to rely on this person to resolve daily electronic resource management issues as they arise. I do not recommend this last approach for a library whose electronic resource collection has or will become more than twenty percent of the *materials management* budget. Based on my experience, and conversations with electronic resource managers across the United States, electronic resource management covers too many areas of responsibility, requires knowledge of too much detail, and uses too many skill sets to expect one professional to couple it with other major job responsibilities. Treating electronic resource management as "other duties" is a sure road to organizational mismanagement and personal burnout.

Combining the responsibilities for electronic resources into one position, or two, has the advantage of concentrating responsibility and knowledge into the mind of one, or two, professionals. This professional can buttress the management of electronic resources with a continuity of experience, a breadth of understanding, and a richness of learned detail that stabilizes the process and contributes to continuous improvement. This manager's greatest skill will be promoting collaborative contributions to electronic resources throughout the library's professional *staff*.

The life cycle of electronic resource product management touches almost every area of library responsibility. The successful electronic resource manager juggles countless details in support of purchase, use, and maintenance tasks. The successful electronic resource manager also nurtures close working relationships with library staff members and throughout the vendor community. Many electronic resource managers rely on personal memory and extensive archives of e-mail communications for the retention of most of this data. Support systems that help manage these diverse data elements are not currently sophisticated or integrated enough, except in isolated in-house library systems, to provide turnkey solutions. Table 1.1 describes sample lists of data necessary to complete each step in the purchase and maintenance life cycle of electronic products purchased from vendors. The Digital Library Foundation (Chandler and Jewell 2004) is working to formalize these data elements, and Table 1.1 reflects their efforts and my own personal experience.

How This Book Changed My Life

Ours is not the only profession experiencing turbulent change and subsequent profound shifts in the way our profession must perceive the world. We are lucky, in a sense, that the experience of turbulence is widespread in the work world, from engineers to health care providers and from the shop floor to the boardroom. This phenomenon of turbulent change has produced a field of study called *organization development* (OD). Researchers and practitioners of organization development draw their knowledge from across the spectrum of the behavioral sciences to study how people within organizations work together, perform, improve, and succeed.

Table 1.1 Stages in the Purchase and Maintenance of Electronic Vendor Products

Stage	Sample Data Collected	Sample Data Sources	Sample Support Systems for Data Collection	Possible Library Departments Involved
1. Trial	Title, URLs, description, fit with selection criteria, usability, vendor contact information, preliminary pricing, and license data.	Conversations, e-mails, Web sites, brochures, e-mail and dynamic Web form responses from interested library customers, results of trial use.	E-mail archives, spreadsheets, paper files, personal memory, dynamic ERMS[a] Web forms (not available to many libraries).	Acquisitions, collection development, reference, systems. Vendor sales staff, vendor support staff.
2. Negotiate	Detailed license and pricing information, technical requirements, fit with selection criteria.	Conversations, e-mails, dynamic Web forms, license and contract originals.	E-mail archives, spreadsheets, paper files, personal memory, dynamic ERMS Web forms, financial management system (not available to many libraries).	Acquisitions, collection development, reference, serials, systems. Vendor sales staff.

3. Cancel Print?	Match analysis between journal holdings, written content, or other content and library holdings or content of paper version.	Vendor holdings lists, comparison of search results, manual comparison of content.	Spreadsheets, relational databases (not available to many libraries because of skill needed).	Acquisitions, collection development, reference, serials. Vendor sales staff, vendor support staff.
4. Order	Final price and license parameters, purchase order (PO) numbers, renewal information, preliminary MARC data.	Conversations, e-mails, dynamic Web forms, license and contract originals.	E-mail archives, spreadsheets, paper files, personal memory, dynamic Web forms, financial management system, ILS[b] Acquisitions module.	Acquisitions, administration, collection development, reference, serials. Vendor sales staff.
5. Order Status	Who has completed their part of the purchase process and handed the order to the next person?	Conversations, e-mails, progressively completed expenditure authorization form.	E-mail archives, paper files, personal memory, dynamic ERMS Web forms.	Acquisitions, administration, collection development, reference, serials.

Table 1.1 Stages in the Purchase and Maintenance of Electronic Vendor Products (Continued)

Stage	Sample Data Collected	Sample Data Sources	Sample Support Systems for Data Collection	Possible Library Departments Involved
6. Receipt of product	Validated IP addresses, user name and password, access URL, remote access enabled, access verified.	Conversations, e-mails, vendor announcement, manual data entry, manual verification of working URL/password/IP addresses.	E-mail archives, spreadsheets, paper files, personal memory, dynamic ERMS Web forms.	Acquisitions, Collection development, reference, serials, systems. Vendor sales staff, vendor support staff.
7. Delivery to customer	Full MARC, full description and access information for library Web site portals, such as subject guide and online journal list; *PURL* for all above; *analytics* of content within product.	Conversations, e-mails, vendor announcement, manual data entry, manual verification of working URL/password/IP addresses.	E-mail archives, spreadsheets, paper files, personal memory, dynamic ERMS Web forms, relational database and dynamic support of portals and PURLs for all above, ILS cataloging module (for MARC only, not for other library portals).	Acquisitions, cataloging, collection development, reference, serials, systems. Vendor support staff.

8. Maintenance during use	Difficulties encountered by library customers and library professionals, technical information from vendor.	E-mails, conversations, dynamic Web forms, vendor announcements, manual verification.	E-mail archives, spreadsheets, paper files, personal memory, dynamic ERMS Web forms, vendor customer support.	Acquisitions, cataloging, collection development, reference, serials, systems. Vendor support staff.
9. Evaluation for renewal	Use statistics, budget data, assessment results.	Conversations, e-mails, license and contract originals.	E-mail archives, spreadsheets, paper files, personal memory, dynamic ERMS Web forms.	Acquisitions, cataloging, collection development, reference, serials, systems. Vendor sales staff.
10. Renewal	Renewal date, evaluations, new negotiations, and new authorizations.	Conversations, e-mails, license and contract originals.	E-mail archives, spreadsheets, paper files, personal memory, dynamic ERMS Web forms, ILS serials and/or acquisitions modules.	Acquisitions, cataloging, collection development, reference, serials, systems. Vendor sales staff.
11. Archive content	Download of data, if appropriate. Record of agreement and access methods.	Conversations, e-mails, license and contract originals, ILS cataloging data	Relational database and dynamic support of portals and PURLs for all above.	Acquisitions, collection development, reference, serials, systems. Vendor sales and support staff.

[a]ERMS, electronic records management system.
[b]ILS, Integrated Library System.
[c]PURL, persistent uniform resource locator.

What OD researchers and practitioners have uncovered is the importance of treating organizations as organic systems influenced by and influencing their environments. Organizations are not discrete collections of people and tasks that proper supervision renders efficient through planning and direction. An organization is that combination of relationships between people, inside and outside the organization that produces a desired result for customers. When turbulent change turns planning into an exercise in frustration, these collaborative relationships give participants the capacity to actively solve, create, and learn in response to change. These relationships create a successful organization.

Organization development practitioners seeking to improve organization cultures have found that improvements that "stick," or that succeed in creating a better organization, are improvements everyone, from managers who illuminate the purpose of the organization to the frontline workers who innovate within this purpose, has collaborated in creating (Weisbord 1987). Familiar names from this effort go back to the 1940s: W. Edwards Deming's Systems Thinking (Deming 2000; Scholtes 1998) and its successor Total Quality Management (ASQ 2004), Douglas McGregor's Theory Y (1960), Chris Argyris's Learning Organizations (1999), Tom Peters's Liberation Management (1982, 1988), and Peter Senge's Fifth Discipline (1994). Organization development seeks to understand how decision making distributed throughout the organization leads to a stronger organization more adaptive in the face of constant change.

When I began writing this book, I was not aware of OD as field of study, and only knew of its principles through accidental "quality training" and "team building" exercises. As I wrote this book, I became curious about what it was that made some of my electronic resource management projects work and others fail. I wanted to intelligently explain the phenomenon for my readers, so I began to read authors in what I was to discover is the OD tradition.

I must admit that I cast a jaundiced eye on the blue-sky principles presented in my first brushes with OD, but over time the principles continued to best explain the successes of project after project. The successes, I found, came not from my attention to procedure or from any prescient planning on my part, but from good relationships that allowed continuously adaptive decision making. My successes came from consciously promoting collaborative effort throughout the organization chart. This meant crossing departmental lines, finding those with the skills that I and others in the group did not have, and expanding the information horizon of decisions to include customer input.

Then one day as I passed the library's New Books shelf on the way to my office, I picked up Margaret Wheatley's *Leadership and the New Science*

(1999). Upon reading that book, what I had learned and experienced over the past years about the importance of relationships clicked into a professional imperative. I needed to become an OD practitioner with deeper skills in organizational change and the ability to serve many libraries as they learn the "new" management. During the next year, I quit my job, finished this book, and became a Ph.D. student in organization development.

Writing this book forced me above the waterline of my daily tasks to an understanding of the importance of collaborative work within human accomplishment. Organization development insights can help the library professional learn more about how to nurture success within libraries and within customers' experiences of libraries. The work of libraries in the global community is more important than ever. My hope is that through the adaptive management practices of OD libraries can develop the flexibility to remain at the heart of a strong society.

Organization of the Book

Chapter 2 discusses the kind of management and decision making necessary for a library to be successful in an environment of constant flux. Command, consultation, vote, and consensus decision making each have their place, but the learning that takes place when *decision makers* in collaborative groups work toward consensus keeps organizations learning, adaptive, and strong. Good decision making takes good information, and a network of learning relationships between all members of an organization creates the best information.

Chapter 3 introduces assessment as the best way to keep decision making adequately informed. The four types of assessment are service quality assessment, workflow analysis, output measures, and outcomes assessment. A cycle of assessment begins with the service quality expectations of customers in order to decide which workflow processes to analyze for improvement. Output measures, such as usage statistics or collection size, have relevance only in the context of these workflow improvements. The final test of successful decision making is how positively the library affects customer outcome, or the impact the library has on the customers' life experiences.

Chapter 4 equates budgeting with planning, but asserts that adaptive, value-conscious budget planning is less a linear process of setting and achieving goals and more a cyclical process of improving value for the library's customer in order to demonstrate value to the library's funding authority. Budgeting includes the control of costs to sustainable levels, and the chapter introduces ways of calculating the true costs and benefits of ownership (or licensure) of electronic products in order to better negotiate both price and cost of ownership with vendors.

Chapter 5 begins the first of four chapters on the management of electronic resources infrastructure. In this chapter's discussion of the *collection development* and acquisitions processes, libraries that develop customer-centered policies will give their library professionals a powerful tool with which to manage the multitude of data required for the negotiating and purchasing process. Customer-centered policies provide an understanding of the values held by the library and its customers and ease the negotiation for low-cost, high-quality products and services. These policies are powerful in that they are learning documents created by collaborative groups of professionals who contribute a breadth of experience, from across the spectrum of professional expertise, and are continuously refined in an *iterative* cycle of information gathering. As learning documents the policies remain continuously responsive to changes in the library environment.

Chapter 6 continues with the purchase process to discuss licensing and the importance of negotiating license provisions for use, users, and access that best achieve the library's purpose for its community. Library professionals often find licenses complex to negotiate and manage. Guidelines, prioritized license terms, and continuous learning help non-lawyer professionals navigate the potential pitfalls of license negotiation.

Chapter 7 addresses cataloging within the broader context of the importance of providing attractive, easy-to-use electronic access to library customers. After reviewing the impact that electronic resources have had on cataloging practices, the chapter expands access capabilities into the future worlds of relational databases, dynamic Web-delivery of information, and developments such as metadata and XML.

Chapter 8 turns to the technological infrastructure of electronic resource management. The chapter strongly suggests that all library professionals gain an understanding of all four levels of infrastructure: hardware, connectivity, software, and user interface. Because a deep knowledge of all four levels would be difficult at best, the most effective management of the technology infrastructure happens in collaborative groups that combine expertise and varied experience for stronger decision making. The chapter goes on to assert that of the four levels, the user interface is the most important. The goal of the successful management of every other level of the infrastructure is the creation of a seamless experience for the user of library services.

Chapter 9 concludes with a discussion of customer services, commonly known as *public services* within the library profession. The chapter addresses three orders of contact—direct service, indirect service, and creating a usable environment—and asserts that the customer must be central to decision making about each. Customer services are the responsibility of all departments in a library, and attention to customer services creates a library with demonstrable value for its community. The chapter outlines the multifaceted process of marketing and equates successful marketing with successful library management. If the goal of marketing is improved customer service, or the improved value of a library for its community, then electronic resource management, and by extension library management, must hold as its highest imperative the collaborative relationships that forge the success of an adaptive organization.

References

Argyris, Chris. 1999. *On organizational learning.* 2d ed. Cambridge, MA: Blackwell Business.

American Society for Quality (ASQ). ©2004. ASQ. URL: http://www.asq.org/ (Accessed August 31, 2004).

Chandler, Adam and Tim Jewell. *A Webhub for Developing Administrative Metadata for Electronic Resource Management.* ©2003. Elicensestudy. URL: http://www.library.cornell.edu/cts/elicensestudy/ (Accessed August 31, 2004).

Deming, W. Edwards. 2000. *Out of the crisis.* Cambridge, MA: MIT.

McGregor, Douglas. 1960. *The human side of enterprise.* New York: McGraw-Hill.

Peters, Thomas J. 1982. *In search of excellence.* New York: Harper & Row.

———— . 1988. *Thriving on chaos.* New York: Alfred A Knopf.

Scholtes, Peter. 1998. *The leader's handbook.* New York: McGraw-Hill.

Senge, Peter, Art Kleiner, Charlotte Roberts, Richard Ross, and Bryan Smith. 1994. *The fifth discipline fieldbook.* New York: Currency/Doubleday.

Weisbord, Marvin R. 1987. *Productive workplaces: Organizing and Managing for dignity, meaning, and community.* San Francisco: Jossey-Bass.

Wheatley, Margaret. 1999. *Leadership and the new science.* 2d ed. San Francisco: Berrett-Koehler.

Further Reading

Ariadne Magazine. ©2004. UK Office for Library Networking (UKOLN). URL: http://www.ariadne.ac.uk/ (Accessed August 31, 2004).

ACQNET-L: Acquisitions listserv. ©2004. Infomotions. URL: http://www.acqweb.org/acqnet.html (Accessed September 15, 2004).

ASIS&T. ©2004. American Society for Information Science and Technology (ASIS&T). URL: http://www.asis.org/ (Accessed August 31, 2004).

Charleston Advisor. ©2004. Charleston Advisor. URL: http://www.charlestonco .com/ (Accessed August 31, 2004).

Computers in Libraries. ©2004. Information Today. URL: http://www .infotoday.com/cilmag/default.shtml (Accessed August 31, 2004).

Council on Library and Information Resources (CLIR). ©2004. CLIR. URL: http://www.clir.org/ (Accessed August 31, 2004).

COLLDV-L: Collection Development listserv ©2004. Infomotions. URL: http://www.infomotions.com/serials/colldv-l/ (Accessed March 3, 2004).

D-Lib Magazine. ©2004. Corporation for National Research Initiatives. URL: http://www.dlib.org/ (Accessed August 31, 2004).

ERIL-L: Electronic Resources in Libraries listserv. ©2004. joanconger.net. URL: http://www.joanconger.net/ERIL/ (Accessed August 31, 2004).

IFLANET. ©2004. International Federation of Library Associations and Institutions (IFLA). URL: http://www.ifla.org (Accessed August 31, 2004).

Joint Information Systems Committee (JISC). ©2004. JISC. URL: http://www.jisc.ac.uk/ (Accessed August 31, 2004).

LIBLICENSE-L Mailing List. ©2000. Yale University Library. URL: http://www.library.yale.edu/~llicense/mailing-list.shtml (Accessed August 31, 2004).

Library Hi-Tech. ©2004. Emerald. URL: http://www.emeraldinsight.com/0737-8831.htm (Accessed August 31, 2004).

LIBREF-L: Reference listserv. ©2004. Kent State University. URL: http://www.library.kent.edu/libref-l/ (Accessed August 31, 2004).

NASIGweb: North American Serials Interest Group. ©2004. NASIG. URL: http://www.nasig.org/ (Accessed August 31, 2004).

Perlman, Gary. *HCI bibliography : Human-computer interaction resources.* ©2004 hcibib.org. URL: http://www.hcibib.org/ (Accessed August 31, 2004).

Portal: Libraries and the academy. ©2004. The Johns Hopkins University Press. URL:http://muse.jhu.edu/journals/portal_libraries_and_the_academy/ (Accessed August 31, 2004).

The resource shelf: Resources and news for information professionals. ©2004. Gary Price. URL: http://www.resourceshelf.com/ (Accessed August 31, 2004).

Webopedia: Dictionary of computer and internet technology. ©2004. Jupitermedia. URL: http://www.pcwebopedia.com/ (Accessed August 31, 2004).

World Wide Web Consortium (W3C). ©2004. W3C. URL: http://www.w3.org/ (Accessed August 31, 2004).

CHAPTER 2

Management

Libraries exist at the behest of a community that wants information services and a collection of materials that support their research and entertainment needs. Through funding authorities, these communities provide budgets for their libraries in support of the creation and maintenance of these services and collections. Therefore, each library process should contribute to or result in a service for the community meeting the community's expectation of that service. If not, the library process becomes a candidate for revision or termination. Library management is the sum of all the decision making that every day affects the creation, continuation, revision, or termination of library processes and the services they support.

Change will often cause a disconnect between the product of a current process and the expectations of the consumers of this product. For example, entering freshmen may expect to find most information online compared with the freshmen of a decade ago. When making a decision about the creation, continuation, revision, or termination of a library process affected by change, the governing "truth" is not an objective entity such as an accepted practice or a rule of thumb or what "ought" to be; instead, the truth of a situation is measured through the subjective experience of that situation by each participant.

The providers of a library service (the vendors and the library) and the consumers of that service (the library customer and the library's funding authority) each have an experience of the product of a library process. The customers' experiences will determine whether they return for more service or walk away. The funding authorities' experiences will determine the funding they approve during the next budget cycle. Successful decision making knows how to use collaborative groups to turn the information contained in all of these contextual experiences into successful action in the face of change. The turbulent change brought about by electronic resources within a library's collection makes collaborative decision making all the more important.

Pinning down a definitive, or even a suggested, set of operational procedures for the complex process of managing electronic resources will never meet with success. The new realities of tomorrow will overturn the truth we learn today. Creative library professionals will find new ways to improve internal library processes. Innovative vendors will find new ways to improve revenue. Industrious library customers and funding authorities will set new expectations for service. Each of these forces pushes the other forward into a spiral of expectation and improvement that will simultaneously benefit and challenge each set of actors.

The key to managing this upward spiral of change is information. Seeking information in large, constant, conscious doses, we library professionals gain the ability to learn both from our external environment and our internal processes. The library profession will continue thrive, not solely on our ability to create standard practice and continuity, but more importantly on our ability to absorb new information, to learn and to adapt.

Seeking information through adaptive learning, individuals and organizations gain the adroitness to deal with the next situation as it arises. In an environment of continuous change, reality itself shifts. A "book," for example, can change from being a discrete bound object to a fluid representation of ongoing advances in a field of study. Therefore, each new situation will not rely on the exactly the same information or the same set of results used before, but also will take advantage of the personal knowledge and relationships developed during a similar situation's learning cycle. Professionals cannot treat information as a static object to be collected and distributed because that information slips through our fingers in a world of fluid reality. Instead, if we treat information as fuel for learning, we can grow with the spiral of change.

When library professionals cease to learn, we freeze ourselves into skill sets and modes of thinking that were once relevant but do not follow the spiral of new realities. When library professionals cease to learn, the task of advancing toward a new reality becomes progressively more complex, and the routine becomes more comfortable and more difficult to relinquish. When library professionals cease to learn and begin to protect daily routine, they begin to lose the relationships one creates with other learning professionals in order to protect the comfort of today being like yesterday and a good indicator of tomorrow. Learning professionals realize that individuals manage this spiral of change better in collaborative groups working across functional lines. Groups pool the information available to each member, and groups create an environment that nurtures adaptive learning smoothing the disruption continuous change causes the individual.

Contextual Information and Change

When confronted with change, action not information tempts us as a first step to follow. Taking action gives the sense of moving forward, of solving the problem, of taking control. The element missing from immediate action is complete information. Because complete information takes time to gather, verify, and assimilate into a decision process, action based on the information contained within our personal and professional experience seems more efficient and effective. The information immediately available from experience may be valid from the decision maker's point of view, but will mislead when the decision maker assumes that all affected by the decision share the same experience. When gathered from the experiences of all participants in the situation (for example, library professionals, customers, and vendors) information will be more complete, will more closely reflect reality and will return more effective solutions. The gathering of complete information, therefore, is by definition a collaborative, group process.

After examining how various management styles assemble information to create and implement a solution, this chapter will explore implications of the skill of using collaborative group work to turn information into successful action. This skill in group dynamics is complex and not something we are born knowing; library professionals must work at learning, practicing, and evolving the skill as we combine our efforts to adapt with our environments.

Systems Thinking

The values these experiences have within any given decision making process will depend on the decision maker's understanding of information flow. If the decision maker sees the decision process as linear, then information will filter through the decision maker to a final solution. If the decision maker sees the decision process as circular, or iterative, information will filter through a repeated series of experiences and return each time to inform a better set of decisions during the next decision cycle.

When a linear decision is seen as final, failure gives rise to blame. When a decision is seen as part of an iterative process, failure is welcomed an opportunity to learn. Paradoxically, failure and learning strengthens decisions over time, and over time failure improves the organization's overall pattern of successes. Welcoming and learning from failure reduces the risk of each new decision.

Management theorists use the systems model (first suggested by Ludwig von Bertalanffy in 1950) to explain the effects of the linear and iterative decision making within an organization (for example, Deming 2000; Senge et al. 1994; Scholtes 1998; Wheatley 1999). A closed system contains all its working parts within a defined space, much like a machine.

From this perspective the decision maker as an authoritative individual processes information in order to feed it into a closed system whose working parts include procedure, measurement, past experience (of the decision makers), policies, and hierarchical interactions. The authoritative decision maker puts faith in the proposition that if the mechanism of the closed system is correctly calibrated through accurate strategy, proper procedure, proper supervision, proper behavior, the right equipment, and enough money, then successful solutions will emerge.

An open system, in contrast, is permeable to the information in its environment. The open systems decision maker uses information, or feedback, from the environment to shape decisions inside the system. Decisions are influenced by the purpose established for the system, measured by that which contributes to the survival of the organization. Successful solutions are those that help the decision maker take actions within the system (in this case, the library) to ensure the library's success, or survival, within the larger environment. Since libraries exist to serve the information needs of the communities that formed them, survival constitutes the continued use by the community demonstrated by continued funding and is measured by how well the library meets the information needs of its customers. The open systems decision maker puts faith in the ability of collaborative groups of professionals to work together to continually learn from the library's environment.

The linear decision maker within the closed system must shape the experiences and behaviors of others to fit the solution devised. The decision maker could be the reference librarian designing a Web page or a library director building a new library. The decision maker must convince subordinates and colleagues, create "buy-in", win over other decision makers, cajole suppliers, and teach customers about the advisability of the decision maker's solution.

The iterative, open-system decision maker creates a collaborative solution out of the experiences of subordinates, colleagues, other decision makers, suppliers, and customers. The decision maker combines these experiences with the decision maker's own professional experience to determine the solution that most ensure the survival of the library according to its expressed purpose. Each decision cycle that seeks information on new experiences and creates better solutions adapts the system to change, keeping the system true to its purpose and strong within its environment.

Contextual Experience

Contextual experiences gain importance from the circumstances within which they occur. An effective decision derives its information from its current environment, not from a time, place, or set of actors other than those that the solution will affect. The contextual experiences of those delivering and receiving a service are the primary source of valid information for decision makers. For example, the speed of an electronic resource matters in different ways when measured through the experiences of a vendor, a library professional, and a library customer. The vendor is satisfied if the speed with which the data processing capacity of their servers meets demand. The library professional is satisfied if the product's search screen offers complex Boolean search options for quick, detailed searches. The library customer is relieved if the first set of search results adequately, and therefore quickly, answers the research question. For each of these instances, the information to support the decision making comes less from millisecond measurements, and more from measurement of experience: server performance, accuracy of initial searches, or number of relevant articles found on first try.

Using contextual experience as the basis for the decision process is not an approach to nihilism through relativism. The spiral does not have us chasing around circles always changing but never getting anywhere. All the trial and error; rules and mavericks; learning and unlearning; order, chaos, and back to order again—all of this is staked and tethered to the library's purpose. This chapter discusses purpose further along, but for the present, know that adaptation is governed by purpose and that organization purpose is most effective when used in an open system that supports adaptive change.

Information for adaptive learning must come from contextual experience, that is, experience gathered from the participant and not assumed by an observer. Contextual experience uses the yardstick called "good enough." How fast is "good enough" for the vendor, the library professional, or the library customer? Without learning what the dimensions of this measurement should be, we waste money on products that are "good enough" to the vendor but not to library customers, or we waste time pursuing the library professional's "good enough" when our customer's "good enough" has already been reached.

Contextual experience, or contextual information, is complex to collect, sort through, analyze, and use. Contextual information is not a static entity to be gathered, stacked, and tallied in spreadsheets and pie charts. Static, "snapshot" measures do support the ongoing learning important to decision making, but when we try to fix contextual information into long-term procedure we relinquish its power to assist us with change. For example, one could use contextual information about customer search behavior to develop procedures for the creation of online public access catalog (OPAC) records, but, whereas customer search behaviors adapt to new search technologies, OPAC procedures would remain consistent and the gap between accepted procedure and customer reality would widen over time. In the next chapter we will explore how to measure experience through assessment. For now, we will discuss how contextual experience provides the complete information necessary for successful decision making.

Decision making based on contextual experience means that a library professional's decision in the present will not be the same as the solution accepted eighteen months ago, five years ago, or two decades ago because the information based on contextual experience will change as experience changes. Open systems decision making introduces a fluidity into institutional practices, and these practices must be able to simultaneously provide continuity of a library's purpose and absorb the constant change of contextual information. In a world of permanent change, collaborative learning sustains the flow of contextual information into effective decision making. If this thought makes you glance apprehensively at the manuals and handbooks on your bookshelf, you are not alone. Remember, groups will help you use collaborative learning to adapt procedure and routine to the constant change in our environments.

Information and Effort

Practices that cause no discomfort may safely remain routine. When routine practices no longer reflect reality either the practitioners or the consumers of these practices' products experience discomfort. Once this discomfort arises, professionals have one of two choices. Some practitioners may choose to ease the discomfort with discouragement, blame, cynicism, and withdrawal. From this vantage point they watch the learning required to remove the discomfort grow more and more complex until learning, and change itself, begins to appear unmanageable.

Fortunate professionals choose to respond to discomfort through adaptation. Adapting to change requires effort, and from this effort a second set of choices arises: reaction or learning. Immediate action, or reaction, to change seems to require the least effort. Reaction provides an immediate feeling of progress, but with consequence. If a decision maker jumps to action as a first step, all the work of responsibility, execution, success, and failure is bundled into that one decision. If instead a decision maker seeks information before taking action, the work distributes to all participants and harnesses a great power, the power of information.

If the decision maker chooses learning over reaction, the decision making process will require work of two kinds: the effort to inform a decision and the effort to implement a decision. Different types of decision making distribute effort between collecting contextual experience to inform a decision and rallying the labor required to implement a decision. Effort not applied to informing a decision may seem expedient, but that effort will reappear in increased effort in implementation. Interestingly, when effective decisions properly distribute effort between information gathering (learning) and implementation, pleasantness appears to lighten the load.

For our purposes, I will classify decision making into four methods: command, consult, vote, and consensus. Each are effective within a given set of circumstances. Figure 2.1 demonstrates how each method distributes effort between information (learning) and implementation and shows how information properly gathered works for us to achieve effective change.

Change occurs not as a result of a decision, but as a result of the implementation of a decision. The work required to gather information for a decision from the experiences within a group and the work required to shift the group into implementation after a decision is made combines for the total amount of work required to effect change. I hold that the total amount of work required to create change is the same regardless of the type of decision making used. The differences between the methods of decision making lie in how each type of decision making distributes the work of gathering information and the work of implementation. The success of each type of decision making in reaching effective change is directly related to the fact that the work of gathering information is more pleasant than the work of convincing people to implement change. Gathering information should not become so absorbing as to preclude implementation, but decision makers, particularly if they are not the decision implementers, can use the collaborative gathering of

Figure 2.1
Decision methods. These methods distribute work between information gathering and implementation.

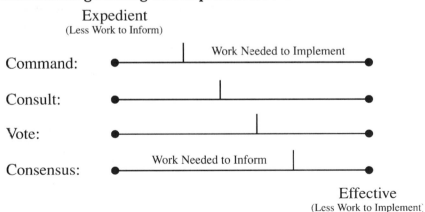

information to give implementers the ownership that makes cooperation more pleasant. Collaborative decision making closes the gap between decision assumptions and implementation reality.

Collaborative decision making is less about changing processes (oiling a cog), and more about changing the experience and commitment of the people involved (allowing people to use the cog where most appropriate). People are not machines. People are driven by the hope for satiation. To cooperate, people must be able to see some benefit before entering into an activity. People must see that the activity fulfills some inner need, and one of the most powerful inner needs, particularly within public service professionals, is the human need to fulfill the needs of another (Argyris 1999; Block 1993; Maslow 1970).

If collaborative information gathering allows decision makers to experience how a change will benefit themselves or others, the decision will garner emotional commitment and reduce the effort of implementation. Decision makers who are told information but do not directly observe it, may intellectually agree but will lack a path of emotional commitment to implementation. If the supervisor who, in order to expedite the gathering of information and the creation of a solution, bypasses direct collaboration with implementers, will find that implementing the solution becomes more effortful and builds a legacy of negative feelings for the next round of decision making.

Command

Under command decision making, one person (or a select group) makes a unilateral decision. This person (or group) then tells others the decision with the expectation that they cooperate in implementation. The decision may include a personal understanding of others' experiences, but it is still formed with only the experience and information available to one person (or small group), and those who must implement a command decision have not themselves experienced the information that supports the decision. The decision makers attempt a myriad ways to create "buy-in" once they decide on a solution, but "selling" a solution is necessary only if the implementers did not collaborate in the information that went into the solution.

Command decisions are effective if time is of the essence. In an emergency the time available is short and one person more efficiently gathers information than a group. However, since command decisions contain only the experience of one person, these decisions have a high risk of failure and responsibility for success or failure is concentrated on the single decision maker. A crucial piece of information not known at the time of decision often proves fatal to implementation.

Command decisions are also effective if the project is small enough for implementation to lie solely in the hands of the decision maker and this person also receives the fruits of the solution. The information available to that one person may be sufficient to ensure a successful result. In most activities, however, the consumer of the results of the decision, whether that person is another library professional or a library customer, as well as the implementer of that decision have a stake in the outcome. An effective decision includes collaborative input from its consumers and implementers to avoid the risk of failure during implementation.

Consult

Under consultative decision making, one person, or a select group, informs a command decision with input from others. This person (or group) then tells others the decision with the expectation that they cooperate in implementation. If the decision maker is the same person who will implement the decision and consume the product of the decision, a consultative decision can be quite effective. But, as discussed above, this insularity is rare and a small project will most often benefit not from the consultative but from the collaborative input from others.

A consultative decision that impacts more than the immediate work of the decision maker treats informants not as participants in the creation of a solution but as (expendable) resources. Implementers will not have had access to the depth of information available to the creator of a solution and useful for committed cooperation. Over time this disconnect between consultative information gathering by decision makers and subsequent implementation may explain an interesting phenomenon in organizations.

Information requested then not used in a solution creates a negative legacy that will impact future participation. Organization members, when asked to share their experiences in aid of a decision, will not do so even when that information would create a better decision. Leaders will rightly assert that they cannot use everyone's ideas when making decisions. In a hierarchy that vests single people with decision-making authority, this is true. However true, this reality does not mend the slight of rejecting another's information. Collaborative management, discussed below, offers a solution.

Vote

When a group decides by vote, it accepts, as the basis of action, the information or experience of the largest contingent within a group. The group then expects everyone to cooperate in implementation. Decision by vote is an expeditious form of group decision making. Voting takes advantage of a larger set of experiences than just one person, but the "losers" of the vote will still not share the internal informative experience required for commitment.

Voting works well if those who lose the vote agree that a quick decision is of more value than the work of implementation. For example, a Web page needs to appear the next day and, to expedite delivery, the minority will accept the parts of the page they personally would not have included. A vote that discounts the information of a minority group is effective if the impact of a possible failure is small. For example, a group chooses between several Web page color schemes that all agree are acceptable. Voting also works if the losers know that future decisions will reflect their experiences, for example, choosing which draft Web page to test first, leaving other tests for a later date.

A voting decision that requires a deeper implementation commitment from those on the losing side of the argument does not benefit from the opportunity to gather information from this minority group's experiences, and this increases the efforts of implementation and the chances of failure.

Consensus

The experience of all who will participate in the implementation informs a consensus decision. In other words, the implementers participate in creating a solution. The amount of contextual information contained in the decision minimizes the risk of failure and maximizes the emotional commitment from implementers. This type of decision making is not expedient, and the large amounts of information gathered can become unwieldy. Collaborative groups are the best tools with which an organization can gather and process this information. Despite this complexity, consensus decisions are excellent for effective change because the organization gains the commitment of a large number of people.

Consensus best serves projects that require the cooperation of more than one implementer and that benefit more than one consumer. For example, the design of even a small Web site benefits from treating such people as the Web editor; programmers; and representatives of reference, cataloging, and the customer base as collective decision makers. With these people present at the creation of the solution, their combined experience creates foresight not available to a single person.

One of the early experts on decision making, Mary Parker Follett (1918), takes the idea of consensus one step further toward the concept of integration. Follett argues that the compromise sometimes present in consensus weakens the effectiveness of the final decision. From her experience serving on citywide civic committees and nationwide association boards of directors, Follett learned that only integration could fully achieve commitment and successful change. Integration brings the unique experience and knowledge of all those present to the task of creating a new idea divergent from and greater than any of the individual ideas and experiences represented in the group. The reconciling of divergent viewpoints into an integrated whole is essential for the creation of resilient solutions. Each individual becomes committed to implementation because each individual is creator of the final decision.

The discussion through which a collaborative group arrives at integration can be difficult as the group weaves together the work of information and implementation. Because the work of integration is as hard as it is rewarding, it is a kind of consensus best reserved for decisions with complex implementation requirements and of great impact to significant numbers of people. Furthermore, managing the dynamics of integration is a skill not often taught and not easy to learn through experience alone. Integrative discussion at times requires the assistance of an expert facilitator, through whom organizations can gradually develop the supportive culture and skill important for integration.

The Effort of Hierarchy and Collaboration

Hierarchical management prefers the command and consultation methods of decision making. These decision making methods reserve agency, or the will to act, for the person "in-charge" and lend a sense of control to this person's activities. This decision maker can be an administrator responsible for an entire unit or a professional responsible for a single task. In cases where the decision affects more than just the implementer, command and consult methods require others to commit to the work of implementation without also asking these others to participate in the information gathering, or learning. When commitment does not appear during implementation, the decision maker can quite rightly point to the people as the problem. For example, the obstructionists raise endless concerns and objections (Evans 2002). The insecure pick apart who has which responsibility. The unwilling passively resist an increase in personal workload, either by not doing the work or not doing it well. I submit that the problem of implementation does not arise from library professionals who are universally indecisive, destructive, and lazy. The problem arises from a decision made without enough information about process, effect, and impact. The command or consult decision maker who assumes that a single individual can sufficiently understand others' experiences of process, effect, and impact plants the seeds for a difficult implementation.

The command or consultative decision can seem to the decision maker to be the most straightforward, but only because the work is shifted from information gathering to removing the psychological barriers to implementation (creating "buy-in"), work that the decision maker may try to avoid by blaming those implementers who will not comply. When those responsible for implementation use consensus (or integration) to inform a decision, implementation no longer needs "selling," because commitment to implementation emerges from an existing sense of solution ownership. Not only are the collaborative decisions saturated with information stronger, but also these decisions create relationships among the participants that reduce the work of the next round of adaptive learning.

The image of a busy library administrator making all decisions by consensus may not make sense. The administrator who must make many decisions on any given day would not have the time to seek consensus on even a small number of these decisions, but this difficulty is a result of the habits of hierarchy and not the consensus process itself. Command and consult environments, by definition, repress information except when solicited. An organization nurtured into a consensus environment would buoy the administrator through these decisions. A consensus organization would have information readily available for the administrator, and it would channel most of the information directly to the decisions. Consensus would integrate the administrator into this decision process as one of the most important sources of information and as the primary source of organizational purpose. Instead of an administrator having to shoulder the success or failure of each new decision that keeps the organization on course, a consensus organization frees an administrator to focus on important work: to set purpose, to create a supportive culture, to strengthen internal and external relationships, and to envision an ideal toward which the organization may grow. Within this culture all other leaders in the organization, from the front line up, become effective decision makers in their own right. The image of the overworked administrator fades into the image of an effective organization managed by a calm, confident leader.

Flip this image over to the frontline professional with defined tasks to complete. In hierarchical structures, employees have individual job descriptions against which they are given individual performance evaluations. Library professionals would often like to gather input from others, but are not permitted by time and personal responsibility (i.e., "if this fails, it's my fault.") In a collaborative work environment, the individual, considered alone, is out of context. Collaborative groups perform series of tasks coordinated to create or contribute to services for the library's community and are evaluated on how well the groups' activities contribute to the purpose of the library within its community. Individuals would be measured on their contribution to information gathering and learning processes of groups and ultimately the organization. In a collaborative environment, individuals tap into a powerful current of information that contributes forward motion to their own work and allows them to contribute to and receive motivation from the organization.

The hierarchical command and consult modes of management are the most familiar to managers and employees of service organizations (Evans et al. 2000; Stueart and Moran 1998). Collaborative consensus can make sense intellectually, but leaving the familiar hierarchy for what may be unfamiliar collaboration will always take effort and courage. A transformation in organizational culture encounters an antipathy between hierarchy and collaboration. The command decision, based as it is on one person's final authority, is unsettled by information that contradicts or reveals unconsidered information. "Open-door" policies in a command culture do not give the authority figure the proper amount of information. Participants who have learned to "get along" in a command culture have learned that sharing risks contradictory information and threatens a command decision with embarrassment or the perception of personal failure. More simply stated, the free flow of information threatens the hegemony of authority. Authority complains of the effort to garner (motivate, coerce) cooperation while ignoring the importance, or impertinence, of information crucial to that cooperation.

Transforming from a hierarchical to a collaborative culture requires first an attention to trust. Participants become more willing to contribute their experience to the pool of contextual information through repeated positive experiences with the integration of information into decision making (Argyris 1999; Evans 2002). The choice by a decision maker to, just once, enjoy the apparent expediency of command decision making undermines all previous attempts to build this trust. The story of the administrator who overturns a committee decision will shadow every future attempt to decide by collaboration.

Leaders can build trust in collaboration when the rewards of a collaborative environment begin to include the following: the resources (time, money, and staff effort) saved from failure, the salaries maximized by implementing the best solution, and the value that the library's community and its funding authorities place on increases in service quality. The decision maker decides whether these rewards outweigh the costs of expediency and perception of control, or whether using a group to manage information for effective change makes everyone's work more effective.

Adaptive Learning

Adaptive learning is the process by which individuals and groups use information to make and implement decisions. If organizations existed in environments that did not change, library professionals would not need to continue to learn or to become skilled decision makers. We library professionals could come in each morning, turn on our computers, and do the same thing we did yesterday, secure in the knowledge that tomorrow would be no different. The moment that our environment (internal or external to our libraries) changes, we must learn and make decisions. In these decisions, we make choices brought about by the new information, which has disrupted the processes we honed through practice and habit. We make choices knowing that more change and new information bears down upon us. One can understand how the option to continue with the established processes seems attractive, but choosing to not learn and adapt creates more work in the long run.

When change occurs, professional habits experience discomfort under the chaos of the new. Established procedure will encounter recalcitrant objects (for example, electronic books whose descriptive information does not fit the fields in a typical MARC record), recalcitrant consumers (who, for example, ask for impossible, *one-click URLs* to a book's content from within the OPAC), or recalcitrant suppliers (who, for example, never provide an *OPAC* record that matches the library's specific access needs). Learning is the effective response to this newness. Learning accepts the chaos into established processes and adapts these processes to the change in the environment.

Each time library professionals avoid the chaos of learning and each time we choose the safety of habits over adaptation, we lose another chance to strengthen our processes and to grow with the change. As these losses accrue, adaptation becomes more and more difficult and professional habits more and more rigid against the encroachment of the chaotic new. If we do not learn, we begin to live in the hope we can keep out the chaos, usually just long enough from some magic date in the future when it will no longer matter. As we rely on old decisions, old versions of a library's purpose, old designs of organization, and old forms of leadership, we watch the spiral of change move further away. The work required for us to catch up spirals out of our control. Our own work becomes progressively unpleasant, and our work becomes a negative force on those whose work we affect.

When library professionals open up to chaos, which is in the form of new information that may threaten established decisions, we accept the challenge to learn and thereby strengthen our organizations with each new change. Every time we take advantage of change through learning, we strengthen professional processes and reduce the work needed to learn and adapt to the next change and the next after that. If learning has accumulated and seems too large to tackle, carve out one small section that will have the most benefit and begin there.

Facing new information, with a willingness to learn, means that we accept the power that the new information has to carry us forward. The next time new information arrives we have only to learn for that new situation. This accumulative, adaptive learning will do work for us if we let it. The information that comes with a change informs us to begin the learning process. A collaborative learning process gathers as much contextual information from the environment as possible—information that comes from the experiences of people internal and external to the organization. This collaborative, adaptive learning changes not just processes, but also the participants and their relationships, and for this reason creates a stronger organization at the encounter of each new round of change, however cataclysmic (Follett 1924; Wenger et al. 2002; Wheatley 1999).

The greater the decision, and the larger the organization that is affected by a change, the more complex the information gathering becomes. Change, to which large groups of people must commit, will require the management of large amounts of information. If we accept the advantage of the collaborative group, over the individual, as effective managers of this information, we are still faced with the practical aspects of capturing and processing this information over time in support of a change. Figure 2.2 diagrams the types of contextual information the decision making process collects and how each type of information impacts other types of information during the learning process.

I present this learning model not so much as a prescribed way to display information during collaborative group decision making but rather as a way to diagram the flow of information. This model is not a step-by-step, linear model as much as it is a suggested container for the iterative, or cyclical, activity of group learning. The group may work on any number of the steps simultaneously, or return to augment the information captured in any one part. The sequential nature of the steps is no accident, however, because *purpose*, for example, is important to know before defining *ideal*, or the ideal before testing the success of trial actions.

The learning model in Figure 2.2 is a tool of use to a consensus or integrative group process. The six parts of the information-gathering process are as follows.

1. The purpose for the organization, the group, and the solution sought
2. The current situation, assumed and measured
3. The ideal situation, assumed and measured

Figure 2.2
**The group learning model. To capture and process complex
information for decision making and change, the group defines
purpose (1); describes the current (2) and ideal (3) situations;
describes the restrictive (4) and assisting (5) forces; and, finally,
suggests and tests actions (6) to move from the current situation
to the ideal.**

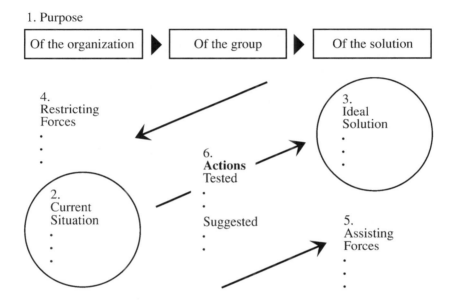

4. Forces holding you back from the ideal, assumed and measured

5. Forces helping you toward the ideal, assumed and measured

6. Actions the group decides to take to move toward the ideal, suggested
   and tested

   This outline is meant to portray the theory of my experiences with
learning processes, and it is best used only after adaptation to unique situations. This diagram is only yours after you have changed it to suit yourself.

   Before I begin, I would like to point out that action is the final step.
Action taken without first gathering information is fraught with risk. The
preliminary work of learning supports the final work of gaining cooperation. The contextual information of Steps 1 through 5 allows decision
makers to launch tested actions that seek to learn from contextual experience of all participants in order to adapt the comfort of the routine to
new circumstances.

A Word on Experimentation

Experimentation and measurement are essential within each of the steps in the learning and decision making process. Assumptions are an important part of professional training and experience, but decisions made through assumption alone will contain error, most particularly the assumption that all present know enough to make a decision without seeking more information from experimentation and assessment. At each point in the diagram, the group has the chance to capture their own assumptions and to paint a picture of reality as seen from the group's experienced point of view. Treat the initial assumptions with the following forms of skepticism:

- Even assumptions based on experience are not factual. Although the professional assumptions made about environmental conditions and the assumptions made about others' experiences (particularly the experiences of customers) will contain important elements of truth gleaned owing to professional experience, be aware that an idea that may *seem* factual is not until tested.

- Experience is not a true test of future behavior. A person's past behavior, for example, may have been based on a skill level, yet some training would have improved the chances of a positive response. Or the past behavior may have been based on desire, and one may find a reason why the person would want to respond positively this time (Carnegie 1998).

- Personal experience is valuable, not as the final word, but as the beginning of an interesting line of questions. If one observes consistent, inappropriate search behavior at the reference desk, for example, the answer is not that students always exhibit inappropriate search behavior, but to question why.

- The three most common reasons to quit finding a solution are lack of money, time, and staff. We should test these reasons for creative solutions more rigorously than any others. Ask other professionals what they did to solve similar problems. Ask customers to describe what their true experiences are and how important to them some perceived obstacle really is. Ask the funding authority what circumstances (matching funds, finding a donor, winning a grant) would free up part of the budget.

In testing assumptions and suggested actions, an important source of data is the pilot test. During the learning process, the group should test crucial pieces of the solution with actual use in a smaller environment. Look forward to the fact that failures will occur. Perform the test in a way that reduces the impact of the outcome. Seek out successes and failures as opportunities to learn and improve parts of the final plan before unveiling the grand Solution. Before one arrives at a solution to test, however, one must first gather information through the discovery of purpose, the current situation, the ideal situation, hindering forces, helping forces, and, finally, possible actions to take toward solution.

Purpose

Most accepted authorities on management theory (Drucker 1954; Deming 2000; Covey 1990) and researchers into organizational success (Peters 1982; Collins 1994) cite purpose as a central component of effective decision making. In the learning model of Figure 2.2, the group first explores the aspects of purpose that will affect their work: organization purpose, group purpose, and solution purpose. Organization purpose is the combination of the intent and values that drive the organization, that influence the decisions of any group within the organization, and that shape the desired result of any activity the organization undertakes. The organization's *purpose* is defined as the lifelong value system that informs every action. The organization's purpose gives direction but does not prescribe the shape of individual actions. Within any organization you will find an expressed, or unexpressed, core value that grounds all actions taken by that organization. This core value helps members of the organization answer the question, "Is this (thought, action, ideal) important for me to pursue on behalf of my organization, or should I direct my energy elsewhere?" The organization's purpose is not found in the mission statement on page two of an organization's website, though elements of the purpose can exist there. The organization's purpose is embodied in the fruits of what members of that organization choose to accomplish over time.

Organization members will have a consistent guide to fall back on at every turn when they receive evidence of a clear purpose from the organization leaders; they perceive that the leaders' purposes are congruent, not conflicting; and they recognize a synchronicity of purpose between the organization and the members' daily learning. If this purpose is inward and self-preserving, decision makers at all levels will react out of fear and uncertainty, not confidence and adaptability. If outwardly serving, the purpose will amplify their efforts and contribute energy to daily work. What are we proud of at the end of a day: the ability to keep our heads down or the ability to produce the next customer service breakthrough?

Purpose is the creative catalyst in collaborative decision making. The learning model in Figure 2.2 starts with purpose because the group will have gathered to resolve an issue, such as to effect some change on organization processes and results. In order to accomplish this, the group must first clarify for itself an understanding of the organization's purpose, the purpose of the group, and from these parameters the purpose of the solution that the group seeks. Group members who experience the act of defining all three aspects of purpose will emotionally commit to the solution's purpose. Defining the organization's purpose may seem redundant, or self-evident, but, by creating a statement within the group, the group benefits from the shadings of understand each individual brings to the purpose statement and benefits from owning the result that everyone had a part in creating.

Keep the following in mind when forming the purpose of groups:

- A group charge dampens creativity. Group members will consciously or unconsciously treat a purpose designed outside the group as a command decision. In some organizations, authority figures form committees, or committees form subcommittees, by first creating a "charge," or a set of instructions, or a description of the solution for that group to follow. Instead, so that the new group can create its own purpose, have the group draw up its own charge at an initial meeting, with its parent committee or authority figure present.

- Group size encourages creativity. A group size of between four and eight people allows for the most productive level of participation. This core group can and should invite numerous special guests to participate in select parts of its learning process. Larger groups of up to twenty are manageable but require a knowledge of group dynamics and group interaction techniques. With trained facilitators, groups into the thousands are also possible. These group skills are easily learned, but are not intuitive and require ongoing training (see, for example, Dyer 1987; Fordyce and Weil 1971; Gottesdiener 2002; Johnson and Johnson 2003; McGregor 1960; Pande et al. 2002; Peters 1988; Scholtes 1998; Senge et al. 1994; Watkins and Mohr 2001; Wenger et al. 2002). The next section on Groups in this chapter briefly discusses group dynamics and interaction strategies.

- Group values drive creativity. Having purpose allows the group to reinforce all future learning with the structure of a central set of values; the purpose of the organization, the purpose of the group, and the purpose of the solution give the group the context to create the product or service that it must produce. A detailed description of the solution will likely go through several permutations as the group gathers and assimilates new information during the learning process, but the group will always have a central set of values on which to stay focused and from which to draw creative energy.

To illustrate the workings of a group, let us take as an example a public library confronted with the issue of a bookmobile that does not have Internet service. (I owe a debt of gratitude to the participants of a workshop I taught in Coral Gables, Florida, for this excellent example, although most of the detail is of my own invention). The library administration forms a committee of the people most affected by or with skills that could contribute to the project. To help shape its purpose, the bookmobile group invites the library director, the public services manager, and anyone else interested to help contribute.

The bookmobile group does not copy its purpose from some preexisting mission statement or charge, but instead defines for itself what purpose the bookmobile should serve. The bookmobile group creates the organization purpose statement, "Access to information and entertainment for all patrons regardless of socioeconomic status." Because of its direct participation in the writing of this purpose, the group now owns this organization purpose statement. From this organization purpose, the bookmobile group creates a group purpose, which turns out to be, "Achieving the highest level of patron access to the Internet while helping the bookmobile librarian, who has many tasks to manage on the road, provide the highest level of service possible." Notice that this is a value statement and does not include hindrances, like references to cost, or actions, like the installation of laptops.

Given the organization and group purposes, the bookmobile group finally defines the solution purpose as living up to the ideal: "Internet access for the bookmobile that is easy on both the patrons and the librarian." If the group had started by first describing only the purpose of the solution it seeks, or had been given a description of the group's purpose by someone outside the group's process, the description may have missed key elements, such as ease of use for the librarian, that would guide all subsequent decisions. Notice also that the purpose statements do not conform to a rigid grammar of action verbs and comprehensive object clauses and therefore do not complicate the simplicity of the statements. Instead the statements are succinct and measurable, as well as memorable.

The Current Situation and the Ideal

Once the bookmobile group establishes three purposes, its members can begin to explore the environment within which the solution will take place. To understand the current situation, they gather data describing all aspects of an issue as it is currently experienced. A quick first step is a poll of the group members present. The group represents a valuable resource of experience and current professional knowledge. Always then support this first pass with measurement and research. Verify statements made in the first pass by asking knowledgeable people from outside the group. Survey customers for their experiences. Find out the current situation and solutions at other libraries. This environmental scan is important because it will uncover the experiences of all affected by the issue both inside and outside the library and because the current situation may contain seeds of a solution within itself. Reserve judgment. Throw away nothing. An uncomfortable piece of information that conflicts with current procedure or culture norms in the library may become the key to the change.

The bookmobile group discovers that the bookmobile has no communication wiring, the systems librarian has previous experience wiring external classrooms at an elementary school, and very little money exists in the current budget to cover a complex networking project. These initial observations raise interesting questions, and, after investigation, the group assembles the following items: other public libraries have completed similar projects with cost-saving innovations that the group can use; the systems librarian knows the owners of several small networking firms in town who may be able to donate time, expertise, or money; and the library director may have a tiny rainy-day budget if matching funds can be found. Over the next few weeks, the group discovers and adds the following to this list: the discovery of five older laptops in storage and known ways to connect a mobile unit to the Internet, along with the cost for each one. For now, cost does not preclude the inclusion of any of the connection methods in the current situation list because the group is reserving judgment until they have all the information they need.Once the bookmobile group describes the current situation, the next step is to begin to design an ideal situation that will give forward momentum to the thoughts and actions of the group. Many organizations become trapped in past experiences, past disappointments. A focus on the current situation, without a balanced focus on the ideal, will bog the group down in the problems without a lifeline to the solutions. A description of the ideal is not complete until all participants can contribute their own ideal experiences. The exercise of unfettered contribution to description of an ideal will give each group member ownership of the ideal and will serve as a motivating focus on a hoped-for future. For more about forward focus, see the work of Ed Oakley and Doug Krug (1991).

The bookmobile group creates a preliminary sketch of their ideal situation: The equipment should not require a high level of technical knowledge from the bookmobile librarian to operate; the mobile network needs a connection that is stable and secure in the far reaches of the county; and the bandwidth should be able to handle a reasonably high level of traffic, but this can be sacrificed for reliable connection if necessary. Over the next few weeks, the group begins to measure the ideals of other participants in the planned change. For example, the bookmobile librarian conducts informal interviews on her rounds and finds that her customers value printing so that they may take what they find with them. In addition, a few minutes of informal discussion with the county commissioners, who are members of the library's funding authority, reveals that the commissioners value the public relations possibilities of an Internet-ready bookmobile.

Forces That Hinder and Help

Once the current and ideal situations start to become clear, the bookmobile group can begin to describe what forces will hinder or help the library move from the current situation to the ideal. Force field analysis was first proposed by a founder of group dynamics research, Kurt Lewin (1947). Naming the negative forces that hinder forward movement reduces the specter of their power and allows the group to test assumptions about the perceived impossibilities. Naming the positive forces that exist in aid of a project increases the group's ability to harness these forces' latent power.

Of these two forces, the positive forces require less work because the energy for forward motion exists already in the force itself. For example, the bookmobile group finds that once several county commissioners learn of the project they move it into a top priority and begin to mobilize community members who may help, quite without the group's asking. Choosing to combat negative forces drains a group's energy and requires more work to achieve the same result. For example, time spent discussing the tightness of the budget takes time away from developing a wish list to hold ready for a windfall from a donor or funds suddenly freed elsewhere in the budget. A profitable exercise is to try to turn a hindrance into an aid. The systems librarian's wiring knowledge is a couple of years old and this may be a training opportunity for the systems librarian's overall contribution to library wiring issues.

As our bookmobile group lists negative forces, they rediscover the three most common hindrances faced by most decision-making groups: lack of money, lack of time, and lack of staff. These three negative forces are listed as soon as possible so that the group may move on toward solutions.

A list of positive forces reveals, among other things, personal support for the project by a commissioner who knows an experienced, recently retired telecommunications engineer from her membership in the Rotary Club. Over the next weeks, the group devotes time to this positive force and finds that the engineer will donate time as consultant in return for public recognition of service to the community. The group looks back on its current situation and finds that the systems librarian can act as liaison with the engineer because of mutual networking experience. Without knowledge of the negative forces and cultivation of the positive forces, the group would have never chosen to devote time to cultivating the assistance of the commissioner or the engineer.

Actions

Learning happens when a group investiga' :s an issue from all angles: purpose, current situation, ideal situation, r :gative forces, and positive forces. During this learning process, the boJkmobile group can begin to outline possible actions toward a solution that are saturated with information. The resources discovered along the way create fertile ground for innovation, and experimentation will be an important component of these innovations. If the group can perform small pilot tests of suggested actions, it can seek points of success and failure from which to learn. Because pilot tests are limited in scope, the group can afford to take the risk of failure in each small test and learning from these small failures bring the final solution closer to success.

The bookmobile group, as a pilot test, decides to accept the offer from the local retired telecommunications expert. The expert and the systems librarian create a pilot mobile network with two laptops and trial accounts with two service providers. The expert and the systems librarian accompany the bookmobile librarian on two trips, one to the urban and one to the rural parts of the county. These tests reveal the following: one *service provider* reaches further into the county than the other; printing is indeed important and a large-capacity printer is needed; and, after a ride on a particularly bumpy dirt road, the expert knows where to obtain inexpensive, possibly free, shock-absorbing cases for the laptops. The systems librarian and the telecommunications expert had privately discounted several of these pieces of information when they heard it from others, but direct experience helped them reshape the network to best fit the unique requirements of the customers and the bookmobile librarian, thus living up to the three purposes first expressed at the beginning of the project.

A Word on Writing

The information learned as a result of many of these steps will seem obvious and not worth the effort of writing down. The act of writing, however, involves more than the immediate capture of ideas. The act of writing down what the group learns makes the idea more tangible.

When written ideas are carried from meeting to meeting on large sheets of butcher paper, flip chart paper, or brown postal wrapping paper, the ideas remain immediate and do not become lost in time or obscured by individual memory. Minutes are less satisfactory than flip charts in that they filter the experience of the group through the experience of one group member. The written thought, particularly thoughts captured in front of the group for all to see, acts as a prompt to remain focused; to cover new ground, not old; and to celebrate just how much the group has learned over time.

Groups

When one person tries to collect, sort through, analyze, and use an appropriate amount of information in order to adapt to change in one function or as a unit or organization leader, the process overwhelms and tempts premature action. A collaborative group, by contrast, has the experiences, perspectives, and energies needed to process the contextual information required for effective decision making. The group can best turn decision making into adaptive learning and continuously informs the next turn of a spiral toward improvement.

The suggested learning model in Figure 2.2 provides a way to collaboratively manage the flow of information in a learning process. Collaboration itself is also a skill and requires the same amount of application and personal growth as learning to be a library professional. Group dynamics and group learning have been studied since the early Twentieth Century (Dewey 1933; Follett 1924; Lewin 1948). Since the last decades of Twentieth Century, the field has exploded, and the student of collaboration may choose from many variations that fit personal preference and organization culture.

The uniform, unchanging principles of collaborative decision making are twofold:

- The free flow of information sustains effective change.
- Through collaboration, everyone shares information with little or no risk.

Many group interaction techniques exist to ensure adherence to these principles, and groups can invent new techniques as they progress toward solutions.

Two elements of group interaction obstruct the free flow of information crucial to effective decisions: the pre-written agenda and the discussion. Pre-written agendas in guide groups through prearranged points of discussion and decision. A pre-written agenda has the capacity to erode into command management because it can become one person's list of topics written before a group convenes, and it therefore directs the actions of the group with little or no input from group members. Agendas are useful within collaborative decision making learning, illustrated in Figure 2.2. Working together the group can form agendas from each step in the learning process, but these groups can at a moment's notice change, add, or delete agenda items or adjust the items' priorities to reflect new information. The flow and pursuit of information takes precedence over, and is the final arbiter of, the meeting agenda.

The second obstacle to information flow is the discussion. Discussions occur among members present physically or virtually who contribute information for the consideration of others present. Consultative management uses discussions as sharing sessions and through them relies on the information shared by those in the organization who choose to speak up. In command and consult organizations, discussions do not elicit valuable information because of the risk associated with divulging embarrassing or contradictory information in a group setting. If past command decisions rejected previous information from discussion participants, the effort of sharing will not seem to participants, and those who, for that reason, choose not to attend the discussion, worth the risk of exposure.

Structured conversation disperses control to all members and reduces risk by pooling interaction and ownership. The creator of an agenda has a stake in the agenda's containing the appropriate issues or the right steps toward a solution. The vocal participants in a discussion have a stake in the acceptance of ideas voiced because the participants are directly associated with these ideas. In structured conversation, the group controls the flow of ideas and ownership of the ideas, and the personal risk of incorrect or rejected ideas ceases to exist. Structured conversation allows ideas to pass from the risk of individual public ownership to a safer group ownership. Through structured conversation, the group can accept or discard information based on measured fact, not on face saving. The group, not the individual, owns the pool of information that results from a structured conversation, and this ownership smoothes the potential embarrassment of an idea that turns out to not be of sterling quality. (The miner pans lots of good dirt before finding a gold nugget.)

The brainstorm is a common technique for group dynamics, and the rules of brainstorming are the same as those of structured conversation. These rules lower the risk associated with sharing information:

- Every idea is a good idea, even (especially) the unconventional.
- One need only clarify an idea, never defend it. Thus, the group should refrain from critique or discussion of the merit of any idea.

- A person can pass, or choose not to contribute, during any one cycle around a group, but the group should attempt to have at least one contribution from each group member by the end of the session.

Underlying these rules is the principle that the group must not discard any idea during the structured conversation. Write out ideas, preferably for all to see, in order to make them less ephemeral.

A natural reaction to some ideas is to point out some impossibility in its execution. Upon hearing an idea, some may say, "We can't do that because of lack of money (or time or staff)." All ideas, however, have the potential, through information gathered later in a learning process, to overturn an earlier improbability. The systems librarian in our bookmobile group example could have said early in the process, "I don't have the time for this project." Little did the group know they would find a helpful volunteer who would donate both time and expertise.

We must also be aware that we are our own worst censors. Make a point of adding all your own ideas, regardless of how outlandish they may sound, to the growing list. Outlandish ideas often contribute to creatively dissolve an impasse.

The best tools of a structured conversation are Post-it note pads, index cards, or slips of paper. When an issue is complex or prone to censure, group members can submit each idea on a slip of paper and not by voice. By piling all the (written) ideas into the middle, the group puts their hands on them to classify and prioritize ideas, thereby participating in tactile group ownership. This method is known by various names, the most common of which is the *normative brainstorm* (de Bono 1970).

You, the Individual

The group is the smallest effective unit of change and solution in an organization, but the individual is the locus of vitality for that change. Within each individual exists the energy required to lift processes up from past practices and adapt them to meet current realities. If, over time, individuals have missed opportunities to adapt to change, the accumulated learning may seem insurmountable. Professional processes begin to seem at odds with the current reality, and no clear way presents itself to bring process and reality back into alignment. This lack of clarity saps the energy necessary to embark on a course of adaptive change. What professionals do have is the energy to show up; we do it every morning. Library professionals can channel that energy into "learning" (as opposed to creating, or forcing) one small change at a time. Choose a small change within your sphere of influence. Learn from the process of creating a solution with a few others; then take that learning to the next small change.

Change can begin with anyone in an organization. All individuals in an organization have, at their fingertips, some piece of the organization, from an entire library to applying the correct labels to book spines. Choose a change that will affect that piece. Just as everyone has a boss and everyone is part of a larger whole, each of us is a leader within a patch of responsibility, and we can treat ourselves as the source of energy for change within that patch. Because we will never change another person, only ourselves, we cannot wait for another person to create a more congenial place to exercise our adaptive learning. We can, however, create and invite others into a small space within our patch that is safe for adaptive learning. Look first to those whose work will affect that patch and to those whose work that patch will affect. These people will have the greatest interest in helping you improve the success of your patch's adaptive learning. Find out what you can do that would improve their lives and get them involved in the learning for that improvement.

Creating learning in your patch requires a bit of bravery because it threatens authoritarianism, and authoritarianism can live as much in the heart of the colleague wanting to follow "what's always been done" as in the heart of an administrator wanting folks to toe the line. If a person seems to perceive such a threat, find out what improvement in your patch would make the threatened person's life better.

The authoritarian in each of us goes through life wondering why life is so hard on us, why success is so difficult to wrest out of a day's work, and why others simply will not cooperate in our efforts. This part of us sees the world for how it can change, rather than how we can change within it. For this reason, a straight question to a person about what you could improve for them may not elicit a direct response because they will not understand your desire to change yourself and your patch. A better way to seek possibilities is simple observation of what troubles the person. Then, with genuine caring, create a way for the adaptive learning in your safe patch to fill that person's need and make that person's life easier (CNVC 2004; Patterson et al. 2002; Peck 1978; Rosenburg 1999; Wheatley 2002).

Always base any changes on the other person's willing and conscious, participation in the learning process. Stay in constant communication; surprise on the part of the other person will undo months of work in an instant. Simple conversations in the break room can reveal the baseline fear driving all other objections. For example, the person may disclose a fear that any change will create more work. From that point on, make sure the top objective for your patch's change is the improvement of the work experience of the other person.

Why, you may ask, should I make life easier for this person who is making mine difficult? Since you cannot change other people, you have a choice. Continue to accept the other's difficulties into your life, or create an improvement that eases the other's difficulties and thereby reduces that person's impact on you. You will make a friend for life, and the best form of bravery is the turning of an adversary into a friend.

Not all attempts at improvement will succeed, nor are some worth starting, but each small change that improves your workday will improve the workday of your customers and may improve the workday of others around you. Either or both of those changes will be well worth the effort. Not only will the improvement make your workday a bit better, but also what you learn will make the next step in your adaptive change a bit easier to make, and you could turn around one day to realize you have created success, measured by pleasant experience, in much more of the world than your small patch.

Conclusion

Decisions are not the reserve of any single stratum of a successful organization. Just as library directors must decide the future course of their libraries, frontline professionals must decide the future course of their tasks at hand. No member of a library is immune from the need to make decisions in the face of some new set of circumstances handed us by our environments. Electronic resource management, in particular, must be able to meet the many changes of the electronic environment with adroitness and flexibility and a weather eye toward a future filled with more change. Since electronic resources will overtake larger and larger portions of library budgets and library staff time, library decision makers need to find a way to make effective decisions in a world of quicksilver change.

Information from the environment, or contextual information, is the crucial element in effective decision making that allows organizations to adapt to changes in the environment, particularly to changes in customer expectation. Information lowers the risk of failure and increases the benefits of a decision, and group learning is the best way to both gather and process contextual information. Collaborative groups help individuals cope with the chaos of learning. Collaborative groups help organizations assimilate the information necessary for adaptive learning.

Command decisions and consultative decisions are made by one person in a hierarchical organization. That person cannot access enough information to protect against failure and ensure cooperation in implementation, especially as the issues of electronic resource management get more complex and affect more people. Consensus through collaboration allows all concerned to participate in the decision, to pool their knowledge for an expanded chance at success, and to experience for themselves the information necessary for change. The shared experience of the decision leads to the ownership necessary for all organization members to willingly join in implementation efforts. Adaptive learning requires bravery, but we each have within us the leadership abilities to direct adaptive learning toward improvement within in our own sphere of influence.

References

Argyris, Chris. 1999. *On organizational learning.* 2d ed. Cambridge, MA: Blackwell Business.

Bertalanffy, Ludwig von. 1950. The theory of open systems in physics and biology. *Science* 111, 23-28.

Block, Peter. 1993. *Stewardship.* San Francisco, CA: Berrett-Koehler.

Carnegie, Dale. 1998. *Dale Carnegie's lifetime plan for success.* New York: Galahad Books.

Center for Nonviolent Communication (CNVC). "Center for Nonviolent Communication home page." ©2004. *Center for Nonviolent Communication.* CNVC.org. URL: http://www.cnvc.org/index.htm (Accessed March 1, 2004).

Collins, James. 1994. *Built to last: Successful habits of visionary companies.* New York: Harper-Collins.

Covey, Stephen. 1990. *Seven habits of highly effective people.* New York: Simon Schuster.

de Bono, Edward. 1970. *Lateral thinking: Creativity step by step.* New York: Harper & Row.

Deming, W. Edwards. 2000. *Out of the crisis.* Cambridge, MA: MIT.

Dewey, John. 1933. *How we think.* New York: Heath.

Drucker, Peter F. 1954. *The practice of management.* New York: Harper Brothers.

Dyer, William G. 1987. *Team building: Issues and alternatives.* 2d ed. Reading, MA: Addison-Wesley.

Evans, G. Edward, Patricia Layzell Ward, and Bendik Rugaas. 2000. *Management basics for information professionals.* New York: Neal-Schuman.

Evans, G. Edward. 2002. Management issues of co-operative ventures and consortia in the USA. Parts 1 and 2. *Library Management* 23 (4/5):213–226; (6/7):275–286.

Follett, Mary Parker. 1918. *The new state: Group organization the solution of popular government.* New York: Longmans, Green and Co.

———. 1924. *Creative experience.* New York: Longmans, Green and Co.

Fordyce, Jack K. and Raymond Weil. 1971. *Managing WITH people: A manager's handbook of organization development methods.* Reading, MA: Addison-Wesley.

Gottesdiener, Ellen. 2002. *Requirements by collaboration: Workshops for defining needs.* Boston, MA: Addison-Wesley.

Johnson, David and Frank Johnson. 2003. *Joining together: Group theory and group skills*. 8th ed. Boston, MA: Pearson Education.

Lewin, Kurt. 1947. Frontiers in group dynamics: Concept, method, and reality in social science, social equilibria and social change. *Human Relations* 1 (June):5–41.

———. 1948. *Resolving social conflicts*. New York: Harper & Row.

Maslow, Abraham. 1970. *Motivation and personality*. New York: Harper & Row.

McGregor, Douglas. 1960. *The human side of enterprise*. New York: McGraw-Hill.

Oakley, Ed and Doug Krug. 1991. *Enlightened leadership*. New York: Simon & Schuster.

Pande, Peter, Robert Neuman, and Roland Cavanagh. 2001. *Six sigma way: Team fieldbook*. New York: McGraw-Hill.

Peters, Thomas J. 1982. *In search of excellence*. New York: Harper & Row.

———. 1988. *Thriving on chaos*. New York: Alfred A Knopf.

Patterson, Kerry, Joseph Grenny, Ron McMillan, and Al Switzler. 2002. *Crucial conversations: Tools for talking when stakes are high*. NY: McGraw-Hill.

Peck, M. Scott. 1978, 2003. *The road less traveled*. CA: Touchstone.

Rosenburg, Marshall. 1999. *Nonviolent communication : A language of compassion*. Encinitas, CA: Puddledancer Press.

Scholtes, Peter. 1998. *The leader's handbook*. New York: McGraw-Hill.

Senge, Peter, Art Kleiner, Charlotte Roberts, Richard Ross, and Bryan Smith. 1994. *The fifth discipline fieldbook*. New York: Currency/Doubleday.

Stueart, Robert D. and Barbara B. Moran. 1998. *Library and information center management*. Englewood, CO: Libraries Unlimited.

Watkins, Jane Magruder, and Bernard J. Mohr. 2001. *Appreciative inquiry: Change at the speed of imagination*. San Francisco: Jossey-Bass/Pfieffer.

Wenger, Etienne, Richard McDermott, and William M. Snyder. 2002. *Cultivating communities of practice*. Boston, MA: Harvard Business School Press.

Wheatley, Margaret. 1999. *Leadership and the new science*. 2d ed. San Francisco: Berrett-Koehler.

———. 2002. *Turning to one another*. San Francisco, CA: Berrett-Koehler.

Further Reading

American Society for Quality (ASQ). ©2004. ASQ. URL: http://www.asq.org/ (Accessed September 1, 2004).

Baldwin, David A. and Robert LaLiberte Migneault. 1996. *Humanistic management by teamwork: An organizational and administrative alternative for Academic Libraries*. Englewood, CO: Libraries Unlimited.

Bridges, Karl. 2004. "Boyd Cycle Theory in the context of non-cooperative games: Implications for libraries." *Library Philosophy and Practice* 6 (2)

URL: http://www.webpages.uidaho.edu/~mbolin/bridges2.htm (Accessed September 1, 2004).

Carson, Kerry David, Paula Phillips Carson, and Joyce Schouest Phillips. 1997. *The ABCs of collaborative change: The manager's guide to library renewal.* Chicago, IL: American Library Association.

Evans, G. Edward and Patricia Layzell Ward. 2003. *Beyond the basics: A management guide for library and information professionals.* New York: Neal-Schuman.

Haricombe, Lorraine J. and T. J. Lusher. 1998. *Creating the agile library: A management guide for librarians.* Westport, CT: Greenwood Press.

St. Clair, Guy. 1999. *Change management in action: The InfoManage interviews, industry leaders describe how they manage change in information services.* Washington, DC: Special Libraries Association.

W. Edwards Deming Institute. ©2004. The W. Edwards Deming Institute. URL: http://www.deming.org/ (Accessed September 1, 2004).

Weingand, Darlene E. 1994. *Managing today's public library: Blueprint for change.* Englewood, CO: Libraries Unlimited.

Weiner, Sharon Gray. 2003. "Resistance to Change in Libraries: Application of Communication Theories." *portal: Libraries and the Academy* 3 (1) URL: http://muse.jhu.edu/journals/portal_libraries_and_the_academy/v003/3.1weiner.pdf (Accessed January 30, 2004).

Wittenborg, Karin, Chris Ferguson, and Michael A. Keller. "Reflecting on Leadership, pub123." ©2003. *CLIR Reports.* CLIR. URL: http://www.clir.org/pubs/reports/pub123/contents.html (Accessed September 1, 2004).

CHAPTER 3

Assessment

The time horizon for change in libraries has shortened from decades to months. Libraries' core responsibilities have always centered on the need to build collections that will support user communities' research, education, and entertainment needs. The advent of electronic resources has not changed these responsibilities; it has simply made them more complex. Into traditional responsibilities for housing and presenting our print collections, library professionals must integrate a complex electronic infrastructure and management system that can support the delivery of print and electronic collections at our communities' times of need and at their points of need. Electronic resources remove us from our own controlled environment and put us on our customers' timetable. The attendant complexity of these responsibilities and the fast pace of change mean that we begin to develop a light-footed and quick-witted response to our environments, both internal and external.

Electronic resource management must, therefore, be agile, and one accomplishes agility most easily when one's eyes are open and all senses are engaged. Agility requires information-rich decision making. To remain agile, libraries integrate many sources of information throughout all levels of professional insight, across functional divisions, and within each library process, and for libraries, as for most organizations, assessment is the most effective method for uncovering this data. Through assessment, libraries absorb the information about their environments, their communities, their vendors, and their infrastructures that contributes to successful decision making. Through effective decision making, libraries create processes of benefit to library staff and services that delight the library's community of users. When the library's community sees service value in its library, the community is more likely to award budgetary value to the library. Assessment creates quality service, which strengthens the budgetary support for further quality service.

Effective decision making requires that assessment activities permeate daily action and become a way of life. Without assessment and without directly gathering data from the library's external and internal environments, all that professionals are left with is assumption, which the opposite of assessment. Of the two, assumption seem provides a more effortless, less stressful route to follow because assumption values internal and immediately available personal experience and standards above external environmental data, which must be captured and analyzed. For trained professionals, personal experience and personal standards constitute our stock-in-trade. All library professionals require some level of training, from librarians with master's degrees in library and information science to specialists with training and experience. Used alone, however, assumption isolates library professionals from the very environment we are trying to impact.

Assessment, on the other hand, looks first to the data in the decision process. Assessment goes out, collects, and analyzes a portrait of the environment that, combined with professional experience and standards, creates value for library customers. When assessment becomes habit, libraries prosper.

This chapter will first explore the impact of decisions founded on assumption, in terms of staff effectiveness and customer experience. The chapter then outlines the benefits of an assessment life cycle and concludes with a discussion of how the four kinds of assessment available to library professionals fit into the learning process of decision making.

Decisions Based on Assumption

In the context of library decision making, professional assumptions are not guesses. Professional assumptions draw on specialized and ongoing training, on a rich daily experience, and on the tallies of output statistics libraries have used for years. All this information still adds up only to assumption, however, because the information is filtered, interpreted, and prioritized within the professional's own experience and values. Excluded from professional assumption is direct feedback both from the customers of the services created—feedback that comes in the form of service quality assessment and outcomes assessment—and from those who receive the results of a work process from within the library, often called *internal customers.*

Output Statistics

Libraries use the valid contributions of experience, training, and output statistics all the time. The numerical solidity of these output statistics seduces professionals into relying on assumption in their decisions. Output statistics are data tabulated to show how many, by how much, how large, how quickly, and at what cost (Hernon and Altman 1998). Not only is output data relatively easy to capture, but also the data becomes the basis for comparison. For example, one may hear the following. "This database is used three times more than that one." "This library has more electronic journals per faculty member than that one." The relative ease with which professionals can collect and present output statistics leads us to feel that the numbers tell us enough to begin to apply professional experience and professional standards to the data for effective decision making. Those who make funding decisions—who sign library budgets into reality—may themselves feel that these output data clearly demonstrate the sum total of the library's place and value within its environment.

However, relying only on output data simply turns the assumption of personal experience and personal standards into assumption based on numbers. The assumptions are still present and unchallenged because the numbers do not communicate value in and of themselves. In order to use output numbers to determine the value of a library's service to its community, or the value of the library collection's impact on the community's research, education, and entertainment needs, then one must make assumptions. For example, if a database's value lies in being used more often, then yes, output data is all that is needed to make decisions. But does a seldom-used database necessarily have less value to the library's community, or does it serve a more specialized need? Is the most-used database achieving its full potential, or is its interface an impediment to better searching that could lead to increased use? Or, in a second example, does a library's value lie in its being larger than another library? Is the library with more electronic journals per faculty member actually serving the research needs of that faculty? Is a library with fewer electronic journals per faculty member finding more innovative ways to serve research needs with a smaller budget? Relying only on tabulated output data to make decisions requires a leap of logic spanned by assumption. Canceling a seldom-used database solely because of its use statistics assumes that these statistics demonstrate its value to the community. Protecting a journal budget solely on the fact that it serves a community with more journals per capita assumes that quantity equals quality.

Politics

Professional assumption verified through output data alone has the unattractive side-effect of creating political pressure. Assumptions lead to *political behavior* characterized either by self-preservation, protection of one's own familiar routine, or protection of one's own division of an organization even if the behavior has a negative impact on other organization members, other divisions of the organization, or the product of the organization as experienced by the customer. Political players value personal desire over assessed fact. Political players make assumptions about the external realities affecting a library that in turn create assumptions about realities internal to the library. For example, an external assumption that researchers use subject headings to find journals supports the internal assumption that devoting time to creating these subject headings is more necessary than devoting time to creating easily-linked URL's. A conflict develops out of the disconnect between assumed realities and the unmeasured reality of the customer experience. This conflict creates fertile ground for cynicism, that most negative of assumptions, which leads to burnout. Figure 3.1 shows the results of a cycle of decision making that relies on assumption.

In the absence of assessment, decision makers at all levels, including the frontline, administration, funding authorities, interpret output data with assumptions about the library's external environment that then impact assumptions about the internal realities of delivering service. For example, an academic library's funding authorities state their belief that

Figure 3.1
Decisions based on assumption. The effects of decisions based on assumption are political pressure and burnout.

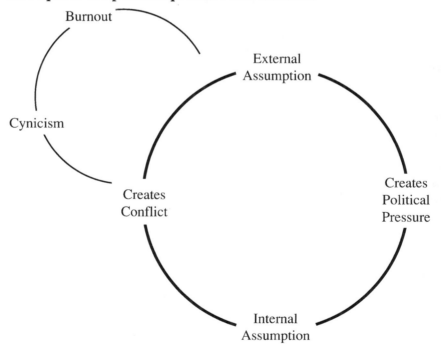

"More electronic journals means faculty will access better research materials." In the absence of assessed proof that quantity equates with quality, the funding authorities identify the more powerful constituencies on campus, and this political pressure then lays claim to larger proportions of the serials budgets. I will use as an example a Chemistry Department on a large university campus. (I respect and admire all chemists, especially their good humor in permitting me to use them as an example.) The Chemistry department is one of these powerful constituencies because faculty members in this department can bring in more grant monies to the parent institution than most other disciplines. The logic of quantity equals quality coupled with political response to this department's self-preservation translates into more chemistry journals per faculty member. Often the faculty members do not themselves express this demand, per se. The decision makers in the library make their selection and budgetary decisions based on the triple assumption that more chemistry journals mean higher quality of service for the Chemistry Department, the Chemistry Department is powerful, therefore Chemistry requests must be unquestionably filled as a general rule.

This unmeasured political pressure gives rise to subsequent internal assumptions about library processes and the relative power of library professionals. For example, because of the assumptions already accumulated, library staff members make a further assumption about a lack of professional power within the collection development process. Collection development decision makers assume they do not have the power to ask Chemistry faculty members to evaluate and reduce the number of journals purchased for the discipline. The pressure that is built up as a result of these internal, unmeasured assumptions comes out as conflict in the form of budgetary cynicism. Because the publishers know that Chemistry attracts proportionately more grant monies to a university budget, the corresponding cost of this discipline's print and electronic journals is far more, on average, than those of other disciplines. Library collection development decision makers come to expect substantial annual subscription cost increases and begin to write them into the budget. Coupled with the assumption about library professionals' lack of power to ask faculty members to reconsider the journal collection that serves them, these assumed realities seal into fact the disproportionate amount of the library budget that goes to Chemistry when compared with other departments.

The library decisions in this example are based on the output measure *number of journals per faculty member.* Chemistry is important on campus and receives a large number of journals per faculty member and, consequently, more than its share of the library serials budget. Librarians live with the unfairness that other disciplines are getting a reduced share of the serials budget and that the library's responsibility to equitably serve its entire community is not being fulfilled, and the honorable chemists never have a chance to contribute their experiences with how well the collection is serving them and how much of the collection could be reduced in order to enhance library services.

Conflict built up over time from a myriad of assumption-based decision cycles turns into the stress that contributes to burnout. Library professionals who repeatedly explain to less-powerful constituencies why no budget is left for their special needs repeatedly lose a small bit of faith in the system. A cynicism can result that contributes to a disintegration of worldview and reinforces assumptions about the external world upon which future decisions are based. A typical response from a librarian to the buildup of assumptions could be, "We don't like the situation but are powerless to reverse it."

University libraries are not alone in these conflicts. All libraries have powerful constituencies, which can create service values based on tallies, and which in turn create conflict that becomes the expected norm, with no way out. Every kind of library can point to major decisions that are affected not by measured fact but by assumptions about the library's external environment that create assumptions about the library's internal realities. One sure sign that decisions are based on assumption is the repeated phrase, "they'll just have to," as in "they [the web user] will just have to enter the password again"; "they [high school students] will just have to come to the library to use that resource"; "they [project engineers at remote locations] will just have to do their research before they leave company headquarters." Note the conflict between process and customer. Conversely, decisions based on assessment create an environment that uses the phrase, "how can we [librarians and customers] find a way to . . . ?"

Decisions Based on Assessment

Assessment breaks the negative cycle that is set up by assumption-based decisions. Tabulated, quantitative output data shows only a small slice of the external and internal environment within which libraries make decisions. To fully realize their responsibilities to library communities, library professionals must incorporate all the data available to them from their internal and external environments, beginning (and ending) with the customer experience.

Customer Experience

Customer experience tells library professionals what and how to improve. By interpreting and applying assessment, data staff become involved, and therefore committed, to the improvement process. The

data from the assessment cycle–from service quality to process improvement, to output, and to outcomes–therefore demonstrates how the
improvements contribute to an improved customer experience. Finally,
this demonstrated improvement translates the potential value that a
library provides its community into an increased library value that the
community can reward. Figure 3.2 shows how the cycle from the assessment of customer experience through improved library value occurs.

The customer's experience is the best way to know what processes are
important enough to improve. A system is a combination of things, people, processes, and resources that an organization brings together in special ways to produce a hoped-for result (Deming 1994; Lazlo 1972;

Figure 3.2
**Decisions based on assessment. Decisions that are based on assess-
ment use customer experience to create library value.**

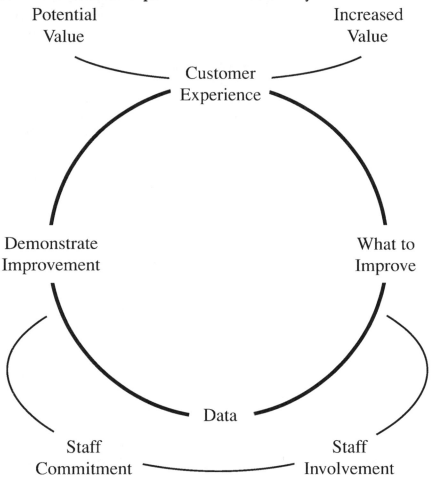

Potential
Value

Increased
Value

Customer
Experience

Demonstrate
Improvement

What to
Improve

Data

Staff
Commitment

Staff
Involvement

Scholtes 1998; Wheatley 1999). An organization expends time and money providing for and maintaining its system of processes. Any system contains within itself a potential value, or ways to improve both efficiency (how successfully time, money, and energy are expended) and effectiveness (how successfully the system's resources are combined to create a desired result). Library professionals discover this potential value when the worldview shifts from serving patrons to serving customers.

In my experience, the library profession sees patrons, customers, and users in different lights. Patrons are supplicants who approach physical or virtual service points to have an information need fulfilled. Patrons come to library on the library's terms. Customers are the people who can choose or choose not to use library services and who can choose or choose not to perceive that libraries have value within their communities. We go out to meet customers on their terms. Users are a subset of customers who actively employ library services, as opposed to customers who are latent (aware of, but do not use, library services), potential (not aware of library services), or lost (once did, but no longer do, use library services).

Decision making that begins with the customer and the customer's experience puts the entire decision making cycle on firm footing. The potential for improvement, or, for increasing the value of the library to its community, is stored in the customer's experience. Assessment shifts the validity of professional assumption toward the experience of the customer.

Learning from the Library's Environment

When evidence from the environment does not conform with assumptions, the observer has a choice: to learn more through assessment or exert force to try to change the environment. Assumption without assessment provides the decision maker with no way forward, and force becomes the easy choice. Assessment, alternatively, allows the professional to learn and adapt through the data available in the environment. In the long run, force takes more work, if it works at all, whereas assessment accomplishes for the professional much of the work of choosing a successful improvement path.

For example, say a Web editor notices that users are not using the proper search field on a web page. Without further information, the easiest assumption to make is that the user does not understand the purpose of the field, so the editor adds instructions to the field in an attempt to change user behavior. (*Force* is a strong word in this case, but the instructions represent effort that is exerted on a foreign object—in this case the user—to change the course of that object.) The field remains underutilized. Futility encroaches on the editor and cynicism sets in: "What am I supposed to do if no one reads instructions?" But what if the Web editor had chosen assessment instead of instructions (force)?

To the unused but important search field in question, the editor now applies data collection activities. The editor solicits the help of several colleagues, and together they watch five novices try to use the page. They record both the novices' reactions to the experience and their own professional reactions to the novices' choices; this is a form of usability testing (Campbell 2001; Covey 2002; Norlin and Winters 2002; Rubin 1994). They study the log of paths selected within the Web site to discover from which originating pages the typical users come, known as *transaction log analysis* (Covey 2002). They survey a small sample of typical users to find out how important to their research the results of the field are, which is one element in the gap analysis of service quality assessment (Hernon and Altman 1998). These and other assessment tools are outlined later this chapter. From all this data, the editor then uses experience and standards to conclude that the search field needs the following changes: a different name; to be placed on a different page; and, based on its proven importance to the users, immediate attention by the programmers in another department. After assessment, the Web editor applies experience and standards not with the force of instructions but with the consideration of good design.

Staff members who can use assessment to choose and plan improvements will become committed to these improvements. Despite the appearance that assessment requires more time and effort than assumption, assessment releases information from the internal and external library environment, which contributes energy, or work, to help professionals create and implement the most successful decision. Assessment, measured by rates of success, requires less work over time than trying to enforce preconceived assumption. Assessment reduces the total workload because professionals use experience and standards to interpret and respond to customer reality. With assessment, decision makers engage the customer's experience with the system, rather than work against this experience. This engagement amplifies, rather than resists, professional commitment and contributions to improvement.

The Assessment Life Cycle

Assessment informs the attention to improvement that lies at the heart of all professional service efforts. Turbulent change in electronic resource management and its effect on overall library management means libraries must engage in constant improvement. Only through constant improvement can we continue to have, and our communities perceive us as having, value for the investments our budgets represent. This value exists in the goodwill that libraries engender naturally, in our long-term professional successes, and in the customer need for high-quality information delivered promptly and with ease. Data that starts with and works toward improving the customer's experience can more easily demonstrate when that experience has improved. Even when we collect data on internal processes seemingly removed from the customer, the customer's experience tells us how important those processes are, whether we should expend effort on their improvement, or cease to work on them at all. By using the cycle of assessment and improvement to factor the customers' experience into decision making, we library professionals are not only making that value tangible to those who sign our paychecks and our budgets, but we also are reducing our own workload and stress levels by choosing the right improvements to make and making them right the first time.

Four kinds of data-gathering methods make up the cycle of assessment and improvement: service quality assessment, process assessment, output measures, and outcomes assessment. Figure 3.3 shows how each method augments the others to strengthen the learning required for successful decisions.

The cycle of assessment begins with customers' service quality expectations. Service quality assessment reveal to decision makers which expectations have been met, so that the library may celebrate, which expectations have not, so that the library may improve, and which expectations the customers consider important, so that the library may prioritize among competing improvement projects. Library professionals may then further narrow this list of improvement priorities to match both their own professional priorities and the declared purpose of the organization. With this list of priorities, library professionals can turn to process analysis to begin improvement efforts. Placed in the context of process analysis, output measures cease to stand alone as tallies to be interpreted politically but as indicators of improvement within a defined improvement process. To round out the assessment cycle, outcomes assessment shows the degree to which the improvements have impacted the lives of library customers. As a result of this cycle of assessment, the value of library services to its community increases and forms a cogent argument for an increase in the value of the community's budgetary investment in the library.

This section on the assessment life cycle will explore how each of these methods of assessment fits into a process of improvement and produces benefits at every turn. The next section providing examples of assessment will outline in more detail the definitions, guiding standards, and examples of each data kind.

Figure 3.3
The assessment life cycle. The assessment life cycle benefits staff member commitment and library value.

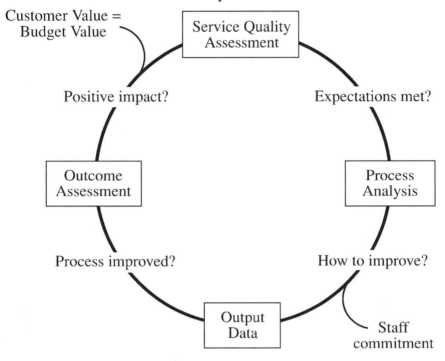

Service Quality Assessment

Service quality assessment (Cook et al. 2000; Hernon and Altman 1998) discovers where gaps lie between the expectations customers hold for a service offered by a library and their overall experience of that service offered by the library in question.

- If the gap exists, then expectations were not met, and the service experience becomes a candidate for improvement.
- If the gap is nonexistent, expectations were met, and the service experience needs no improvement.
- If the gap is positive, expectations were exceeded, and the library can celebrate the service experience as a significant contribution that the library makes to its community.

Service quality assessment provides a way for the library to demonstrate its value to its community. When the library finds that it meets or exceeds customer expectations, it should immediately indulge in public celebration. Success attracts success. Community members like being part of a successful endeavor, and individual community members will begin to think that the library could have value in their own lives. The best marketing is the positive truth that comes directly from the customers themselves.

Service quality gaps show where library professionals can most profitably direct their improvement efforts. When service quality assessment finds that a service has not met expectations, the assessment asks a second question, "How important is that service to the customer?" Thus, only those services both in need of improvement and of high importance to the customers will warrant attention from the library. The work of the library becomes focused on the right things and is expended in appropriate amounts.

Process Analysis

Library professionals do not make the decision to expend improvement efforts in a slavish fit over customer desires but instead filter these decisions through their own experiences and priorities within the context of the organization's purpose. What processes to improve becomes a product of both the customers' needs and the professionals' considered goals for the library. Process analysis, which can range from determining training needs to modeling work flow, tells the library professionals where and how to improve the efficiency and efficacy of a process in order to improve the customer's experience. Customers can be external, or those members of the library community who ultimately benefit from the series of subprocesses that combine to create a service. However, in process analysis, customers can also be internal, or those library professionals who receive the result of a subprocess in order to put the result through their own subprocess or pass the result along to the customer.

Because the impetus toward process improvement comes from the objectivity of customer experience and is filtered through the self-determination of library goals, the process lacks the instability of politically driven priorities. A focus on improvement that rises from customer and professional priorities means that the work of improvement is important enough to blur functional lines and address the librarywide processes. By personally directing the process analysis and improvement efforts, library professionals becomes creators of the change and gain ownership of the change. This ownership means these professionals are no longer reacting to external or top-down pressures; instead, they are guiding their own work based on the hard data of customer expectation and organization purpose.

Process analysis will lead to creative process improvements, but process change cannot be a single-step procedure. When pilot tests lead to redesign that is tested again through more pilot tests, process change becomes saturated with information and comes closer to guaranteeing success. As imperfect beings, library professionals will come closer to significant improvement by learning from several tries, not by stepping back from our first attempt with the observation, "and it was good."

Output Data

Output measures are important data at this point in the improvement process. Output measures tell the creators of an improvement whether the process changes are successful, and an important part of implementing a process change is describing through output goals what success will look like when it arrives. From the library's point of view, success can be decreased time between acquisition and delivery to the customer, reduced interface-related questions at the reference desk, lower negotiated prices, or reduced license-management time and effort. From the library customer's point of view, success can be increased usage opportunities, less time spent searching before achieving desired results, less confusion during the search process, and more relevant results with less search complexity.

The library profession is accustomed to compiling output measures onto blank slates. Few reference desks in the world, I would warrant, go without reference question tally sheets for at least part of any month, and these sheets can become complex devices for tracking content questions (help with a research project) versus directional questions (location of the copy machine). When output measures are folded into an assessment life cycle, they become tools that answer questions relevant to customer service improvement. For example, after installing a new interface for the network printing software, do questions about printing decrease or increase in number? The reference desk tally sheet becomes a *living document* that contributes to the library's ongoing learning cycles.

Outcomes Assessment

Outcomes assessment (Hernon and Dugan 2002) measures the impact the library makes on the life of the customer as a result of the service exchange. Outcome measures show the degree to which the customers' interactions with the library have changed them or their circumstances for the better: anything from learning how to more easily find the text of a cited article, to better discerning between high- and low-quality Web information, to successfully investigating a new life interest. Actually measuring outcomes assessment requires creativity and knowledge of what is important in the goals of an improvement project and to the purpose of the library within its community. For instance, whether the library plays a positive role in improving the research activities of high school students could be measured in a number of ways: Do the faculty members feel that the library has improved the ease with which students conduct their research (survey or interview)? Do the students show an improved grasp of information literacy concepts (pre- and posttests)? Does the research of students show an improved grasp of library resources (comparison of a sample of papers before and after extensive use of a library)?

Outcomes assessment should be a creative response to the questions raised with service quality assessment. But, in addition, outcomes assessment may also need to respond to the standards set by accrediting agencies, or other standards-setting organizations to which the library's parent organization reports. The most profitable outcomes assessment will merge these two assessment demands and in some way fit accountability standards into improvement efforts relevant to the customer. If the library will be held accountable to a set of external outcome standards, turn the "dial" of the diagram in Figure 3.3 to place outcomes assessment at the top. From the outcomes important to library accountability and identified by outcomes assessment as candidates for improvement, use service quality assessment to decide which outcomes should warrant the attention of the library's next improvement efforts.

A funding authority (a school administration, a city council, a university board of regents, a government legislature, a corporate executive board) will more willingly invest in a library's budget if the library can demonstrate a return on this investment in the form of positive community impact. The crucial element in the demonstration of value is a continuing dialog between the funding authority and the library on what constitutes value. Both groups have something to learn from the other. When the library can actively manage this learning relationship, it can begin to show both a continuous improvement and a measurable, positive effect on the community it serves and will thus have more value to trade at the budgeting table.

Examples of Assessment

The assessment cycle in Figure 3.3 shows how each kind of assessment relies on all other kinds of assessment for clarity and applicability to library service improvement. Only when treated together can each kind of assessment gain context and meaning in the decision-making process.

- Service quality assessment is a dead end if library professionals do not use what this assessment tells them to celebrate successes, define needed improvements, and move forward with process analysis.
- Library professionals will not waste effort on process analysis that is of proven importance to the customer and for which output measures can clearly demonstrate improvement.
- Measuring output tallies is a fruitful exercise only for services of importance to the customer as well as the library professionals and for which the library can prove positive outcomes within the community.
- Outcome measures demonstrate the value of the library to its funding authorities.
- Direct customer feedback completes and then begins again the cycle of improved service quality.

Descriptions and examples of each kind of assessment follow below. Please treat this list not as comprehensive but as the beginning of a personal education. Methods of assessment are as varied as the unique situations in which we library professionals find ourselves and are only limited by our imaginations. Treated as a cycle, these assessment tools bring decision making to its ultimate goal, that of an information-rich mixture of forethought and action that energizes and creates momentum to carry libraries forward as indispensable institutions within our communities. The discussion of each assessment tool gives a definition that describes the role each kind of assessment plays in the learning process of adaptive decision making, lists efforts to standardize measurements across and within organizations, and provides example implementations with citations to further reading.

Service Quality Assessment

Definition
Service quality assessment (Hernon and Altman 1998; Zeithaml et al. 1990; Hernon and Whitman 2001) measures the customers' perceptions of how well a selected library's services meet their overall expectations of those services. A further comparison ranks the services by how important the customers think the services are in their overall experience of the library. This kind of assessment does not measure satisfaction with a single transaction but instead the customers' overall experiences with content fulfillment (they usually got what they came to the library for) and context

fulfillment (they would willingly go through the interactions again). The principle central to this form of assessment is that the customer provides the data directly. This principle assumes that customers themselves are the only legitimate source of a measure of the customers' experience.

Standards

Service quality assessment uses the goals and techniques of quantitative (Huck 2003; Thompson 2004), qualitative research (Lincoln and Denzin 2000), and qualitative market research (Mariampolski 2001; Zeithaml et al. 1990) to discover the expectations and experiences of a product's customers. Quantitative research strives to uncover the representation of a physical reality (in this case, survey responses) in numerical form. Qualitative research strives to uncover personal experience and is verbal, contextual, and subjective. Qualitative market research seeks to uncover the customer experience of an organization's products and services.

Examples

Service quality assessment frequently seeks to give the qualitative customer experience a quantitative, numerical measurement through the instrument of the survey. The most widely known service quality survey is LibQual+™ (ARL 2004), which uses a tested survey instrument to capture the service quality experience within a library's entire community, but some libraries also use their own surveys (UW 2001). Learning the principles of LibQual+ creates a firm foundation for the invention of smaller-scale, more project-specific service quality surveys.

Qualitative assessment includes content or text analysis, such as citation analysis (Bakker 2002; Davis 2002), in research produced by members of the library community. A form of citation analysis compares the citations in the output of library users, for example, dissertations or faculty papers, to library holdings to discover how well the library collection supports the research conducted. More qualitative tools include (Fern 2001; Mariampolski 2001) interviews, focus groups, and creativity sessions (in which activities augment interviews or focus group discussions). Qualitative assessment tools can range from short entry or exit questionnaires to life stories unstructured by interview questions or time limit, and either elicit from subjects their cultural experiences of a service or gather new ideas for service improvements.

Process Analysis

Definition

Process analysis, or task-flow analysis, provides data for changes in the experience of either library customers (Norlin and Winters 2002; Rubin

1994; Whitlach 2000) or library staff members (Holman 2003; Hupp 1995; Niebel and Freivalds 1999). Process analysis discovers the most efficient, cost-saving way to complete a task and considers what is best for both the person completing the task and the end user of the task's product.

Standards

Work flow process analysis may focus on the work processes of library staff or library customers. Often this analysis uses a set of principles and practices called *quality*, or *total quality management* (TQM; Gryna 2001; ISO 2003c; Jurow and Barnard 1993; Scholtes 1998). The methodology of TQM is complex but well worth learning. Its practices encompass goal design, technical process analysis, and human systems analysis. Goal design matches the influence on a process of organizational goals, or purpose, and environmental demands. Technical process design studies the group and seeks to understand how group members work together toward a goal or finished product while building speed, focus, and integration into the flow of work. Human systems design analyzes individuals and their jobs and how these are organized and supported, including the integration of initiative and teamwork into the individual's tasks. Libraries, in addition, are also concerned about usability and accessibility for both staff and customer. Usability standards seek to ensure accepted norms for human–computer interaction (see, for example, Nielsen 2003). Accessibility standards seek to ensure ease of use by people with differing abilities, including color recognition, motor control, or sightedness (see, for example, W3C 2003).

Examples

The impetus for staff work flow improvement can come from an internal staff survey and produces deeper resonance when combined with service quality assessment to also identify processes important to the customer. Most often a library targets a specific library service, such as digital reference (McClure et al. 2003), but Total Quality continuous improvement efforts have focused on the library as a whole for more than a decade (Jurow and Barnard 1993; Laughlin et al. 2003). Measurements of process improvement can rely on observation, secret shopper, critical incident analysis, timeline diagrams, throughput statistics, and personal portfolios.

Assessment of a customer's work flow most often takes the form of usability testing (Campbell 2001; Covey 2002; Ruben 1994). The thinking aloud protocol is an example of usability testing in which library professionals observe or videotape several typical users completing an assigned task while the users verbalize their thought processes.

Input and Output Data

Definition

Tallying inputs and outputs is the kind of assessment most familiar to library professionals. Inputs are those resources that are fed into a system to produce a product, including money, time, labor, and materials. Input measure examples include cost of subscriptions, wages, time required to complete a task, or supplies required to create the finished product. Outputs are the tangible results of putting these resources into the production system, and examples include service transactions, transaction accuracy and success, web resources used, full-text articles downloaded, or frequency of printing failures.

Inputs can be measured by spreadsheet tabulation, user demographic studies, market research, collection analysis, or economic (cost-based) analysis. Outputs can be measured with spreadsheet tabulation, benchmarking, and use statistics. Frequently these measures are presented as ratios to other measures: number of searches per dollar cost of online resource, amount spent on electronic journals per number of full-time faculty member, number of instructional reference desk transactions per hours of reference desk operation. Improvement efforts can use these measures to demonstrate process improvement success, but the measures need to be used in conjunction with other assessment tools to show improved customer service quality or outcomes achievement.

Standards and Examples

Input and output measures have been used the longest of the four assessment methods and benefit from a plentitude of standards. The Association of Research Libraries Statistics (ARL 2003a); the U.K. Department of Culture, Media, and Sport standard for public libraries (DCMS 2000); ISO standards 2789:2003, 11620:1998, and 11620:1998/ Amd 1:2003 (ISO 1998, 2003a, 2003b); Equinox (EC 2002); and NISO standard Z39.7 (NISO 2003) are a few prominent examples. Of particular interest for electronic resource management is the concept of usage statistics, the amount of times an electronic resource is used within a certain interval, for example, number of keyword searches, full-text downloads, or user logins (ARL 2003b). Two organizations have developed electronic resource use statistics: ICOLC (2001) and COUNTER (2003).

Outcomes Assessment

Definition

Outcomes are the impact a library's activities have on library customers' current and future life successes, including how the library's community members use lifelong learning skills to replace obsolete information and to explore new fields of knowledge (Baker 2002; Hernon and Dugan 2002; Fraser and McClure 2002; NIST 2003; UVA 2003). Outcomes assessment is most frequently discussed in the context of educational institutions but the concept of accountability has also reached public libraries and corporate information services. Through accountability standards, funding authorities and other influential organizations, such as accrediting agencies, set expectations for how well a library fulfills its role in the community it serves.

Standards

Higher education libraries must meet the increasingly stringent accreditation requirements of their parent institutions (Baker, 2002), including learning, research, and institutional outcomes, and personal control or electronic service quality (ARL 2003c, 2003d; NIST 2003). The primary contribution libraries make to lifelong learning, beyond providing the information resources, is the instruction of customers in information literacy, and this standard is often a key part of outcomes assessment (ACRL 2003).

Examples

Outcomes assessment can range from transaction specific to organizationwide. Assessment of the impact of transactions on the customer includes focus groups (Fern 2001), interviews (Mariampolski 2001), and pre- and posttests, quizzes, and student portfolios (Lener 2003a, 2003b). An example of organizationwide outcomes assessment is the balanced scorecard approach (UVA 2003), in which an organization measures performance from the customer, process, staff development, and financial perspective to get an overall view of the organization's effectiveness within its expressed mission, or purpose.

Conclusion

When library professionals use only professional opinions and experiences to make decisions, we are making professional assumptions. The most experienced professional lacks current information from internal and external environments until assessing this information, and can always benefit from a broad enough perspective of process and customer experience. Decisions should benefit from a purposefulness that comes from the customer. Decision makers should accept into their deliberations the fresh air of real data and direct customer experience.

Assessment provides the primary source of information from the environment and takes four forms: assessment of customer experiences, analysis of work flow, measurement of outputs, and assessment of customer outcomes. Each of these kinds of assessment has little meaning as separate entities. Treated as a cycle, these four forms of assessment infuse meaning into agile, effective decision making.

Through a cycle of assessment and improvement, decision makers both improve customer service, which is a library's primary reason for being, and demonstrate the library's value to the community, which, through community funding authorities, is the library's primary source of revenue. Electronic resource management in particular suffers from ongoing turbulence in technology, customer expectation, and internal process. Through information-rich decision making based on a habit of assessment, decision making gains a sense of stability and continuity responsive to a world of constant change. In the next chapter we will explore how collaborative groups turn information-rich decision making into value-conscious planning.

References

Association of College and Research Libraries (ACRL). "Information Literacy Competency Standards for Higher Education." ©2003. *Standards & Guidelines*. American Libraries Association. Association of College and Research Libraries. URL: http://www.ala.org/ala/acrl/acrlstandards/informationliteracycompetency.htm (Accessed March 1, 2004).

Association of Research Libraries (ARL). "ARL statistics homepage." ©2003a. *ARL Statistics and Measurement Program*. Association of Research Libraries. URL: http://www.arl.org/stats/arlstat/ (Accessed September 3, 2004).

———. "E-metrics: Measures for electronic resources." ©2003b. *ARL Statistics and Measurement Program*. Association of Research Libraries. URL: http://www.arl.org/stats/newmeas/emetrics/ (Accessed September 3, 2004).

———. "Higher Education Outcomes (HEO) Research Review." ©2003c. *ARL Statistics and Measurement Program*. Association of Research Libraries. URL: http://www.arl.org/stats/newmeas/outcomes/heo.html (Accessed September 3, 2004).

———. "Learning Outcomes Working Group." ©2003d. *ARL Statistics and Measurement Program*. Association of Research Libraries. URL: http://www.arl.org/stats/newmeas/outcomes/workgroup.html (Accessed September 3, 2004).

———. "LIBQUAL™: Charting library quality." ©2004. *LIBQUAL+™*. Association of Research Libraries. URL: http://www.libqual.org/ (Accessed September 3, 2004).

Bakker, Suzanne. 2002. Citation analysis and collection management. *Medizin Bibliothek Information* 2 (1):39-40.

Baker, Ronald. 2002. Evaluating quality and effectiveness: Regional accreditation principles and practices. *The Journal of Academic Librarianship* 28 (1):3–7.

Campbell, Nicole, ed. 2001. *Usability assessment of library-related web sites: Methods & case studies.* Chicago: American Library Association.

Cook, Colleen, Fred M. Heath, Bruce Thompson. 2000. The Search for New Measures: The ARL LibQUAL+ Project--A Preliminary Report. *portal: Libraries and the Academy* 1 (1) URL: http://muse.jhu.edu/journals/portal_libraries_and_the_academy/v001/1.1cook.pdf (Accessed January 30, 2004).

Counting Online Usage of Networked Electronic Resources (COUNTER). "COUNTER: Counting Online Usage of Networked Electronic Resources." ©2003. COUNTER. URL: http://www.projectcounter.org/about.html (Accessed September 3, 2004).

Covey, Denise Troll. 2002. *Usage and usability assessment: Library practices and concerns.* Washington, DC: Council on Library and Information Resources.

Davis, Philip. 2002. Where to spend our e-journal money? Defining a university library's core collection through citation analysis." *portal: Libraries and the Academy* 2 (1) URL: http://muse.jhu.edu/journals/portal_libraries_and_the_academy/v002/2.1davis.pdf (Accessed January 30, 2004).

Deming, W. Edwards. 1994. *The new economics for industry/government/education.* Cambridge, MA: MIT CAES.

Department for Culture, Media and Sport (DCMS). "Comprehensive, efficient and modern public libraries." ©2000. *Department for Culture, Media and Sport.* Libraries, Information and Archives Division. URL: http://www.culture.gov.uk/PDF/libraries_pls_assess.pdf (Accessed September 3, 2004).

European Commission (EC). "Equinox: Library Performance Measurement and Quality Management System." ©2002. *Telematics for Libraries Programme.* European Commission. URL: http://equinox.dcu.ie/ (Accessed September 3, 2004).

Fern, Edward. 2001. *Advanced focus group research.* Thousand Oaks, CA: Sage.

Fraser, Bruce and Charles McClure. "Toward a framework of library and institutional outcomes." ©2002. *ARL Statistics and Measurement Program.* Information and Use Management Institute. URL: http://www.arl.org/stats/newmeas/emetrics/phase3/ARL.Emetrics.Outcomes.Paper.Final.Jan.8.02.pdf (Accessed September 3, 2004).

Gryna, Frank. 2001. *Quality planning and analysis: From product development through use.* 4th ed. Milwaukee, WI: American Society for Quality.

Hernon, Peter and Ellen Altman. 1998. *Assessing service quality: Satisfying the expectations of library customers.* Chicago: American Library Association.

Hernon, Peter and Robert Dugan. 2002. *Outcomes assessment in your library.* Chicago: American Library Association.

Hernon, Peter and John Whitman. 2001. *Delivering satisfaction and service quality: A customer-based approach for libraries.* Chicago: American Library Association.

Holman, David. 2003. *The new workplace: A guide to the human impact of modern working practices.* Hoboken, NJ: Wiley.

Huck, Schuyler W. 2003. *Reading Statistics and Research.* 4th ed. New York: Pearson Allyn & Bacon.

Hupp, Toni. 1995. *Designing work groups, jobs, and work flow.* San Francisco: Jossey-Bass.

International Coalition of Library Consortia (ICOLC). "Guidelines for statistical measures of usage of web-based information resources." ©2001 *Statements and Documents of the International Coalition of Library Consortia.* ICOLC. URL: http://www.library.yale.edu/consortia/2001webstats.htm (Accessed September 3, 2004).

International Organization for Standardization (ISO). 1998. *Information and documentation: Library performance indicators.* ISO 11620:1998.

———. 2003a. *Additional performance indicators for libraries.* ISO 11620:1998/ Amd 1:2003.

———. 2003b. *Information and documentation: International library statistics.* ISO 2789:2003.

———. "ISO 9000." ©2003c. *ISOOnline.* ISO. URL: http://www.iso.ch/iso/ en/iso9000-14000/iso9000/iso9000index.html (Accessed September 3, 2004).

Jurow, Susan and Susan B. Barnard, eds. 1993. *Integrating Total Quality Management in a library setting.* Binghamton, NY: Haworth.

Laughlin, Sara, Denise Sisco Shockley, Ray Wilson. 2003. *The library's continuous improvement fieldbook: 29 ready-to-use tools.* Chicago: American Library Association.

Lazlo, Ervin. 1972. *The systems view of the world.* NewYork: George Braziller.

Lener, Ed. "Student-centered assessment tools." ©2003a. *Instruction Initiative Clearinghouse & Resource Pages.* Virginia Tech University Libraries. Instruction and Outreach Department. URL: http://www.lib.vt.edu/services/ clearinghouse/studentcentered.html(Accessed March 1, 2004).

———. "Teacher-centered assessment tools." ©2003b. *Instruction Initiative Clearinghouse & Resource Pages.* Virginia Tech. University Libraries. Instruction and Outreach Department. URL: http://www.lib.vt.edu/services/ clearinghouse/teachercentered.html(Accessed March 1, 2004).

Lincoln, Yvonna and Norman K. Denzin, eds. 2000. *Handbook of qualitative research.* 2d ed. Thousand Oaks, CA: Sage.

Mariampolski, Hy. 2001. *Qualitative market research: A comprehensive guide.* Thousand Oaks, CA: Sage.

McClure, Charles, R. David Lankes, Melissa Gross, and Beverly Choltco-Devlin. 2002. "Statistics, measures and quality standards for assessing digital reference library services: Guidelines and procedures." ©2002. *Assessing Quality in Digital Reference.* Information Use Management and Policy

Institute. URL: http://quartz.syr.edu/quality/quality.pdf (Accessed September 3, 2004).

National Information Standards Organization (NISO). "NISO Z39.7-2002 Information Services and Use: Metrics & statistics for libraries and information providers--Data Dictionary." ©2003. NISO Standards Committee AY: Library Statistics. URL: http://www.niso.org/emetrics/ (Accessed September 3, 2004).

National Institute of Standards and Technology (NIST). "Education Criteria for Performance Excellence." ©2003. *Baldridge National Quality Program.* NIST. URL: http://www.quality.nist.gov/Education_Criteria.htm (Accessed September 3, 2004).

Niebel, Benjamin and Andris Freivalds. 1999. *Methods, standards, and work design.* Boston, MA: WCB/McGraw-Hill.

Nielsen, Jacob. *useit.com: Jakob Nielsen's Website.* ©2003. Nielsen Norman Group. URL: http://www.useit.com/ (Accessed September 3, 2004).

Norlin, Eliana and CM! Winters. 2002. *Usability testing for library web sites.* Chicago: American Library Association.

Rubin, Jeffrey. 1994. *Handbook of usability testing: How to plan, design and conduct effective tests.* New York: Wiley.

Scholtes, Peter. 1998. *The leader's handbook.* New York: McGraw-Hill.

Thompson, Bruce. 2004. *Exploratory and confirmatory factor analysis: Understanding concepts and applications.* Washington, DC: American Psychological Association.

University of Virginia Library (UVA). *Balanced scorecard at the University of Virginia Library.* ©2003. University of Virginia Library. Management Information Services. URL: http://www.lib.virginia.edu/bsc/ (Accessed September 3, 2004).

University of Washington Libraries (UW). "UW Libraries Triennial Surveys." © 2001. *UW Libraries Assessment.* University of Washington. URL: http://www.lib.washington.edu/assessment/surveys.htm (Accessed September 3, 2004).

Wheatley, Margaret J. 1999. *Leadership and the new science.* San Francisco: Berrett-Koehler.

Whitlatch, Jo Bell. 2000. *Evaluating reference services: A practical guide.* Chicago: American Library Association.

World Wide Web Consortium (W3C). "Web Accessibility Initiative (WAI)." ©2003. W3C. URL: http://www.w3.org/WAI/ (Accessed September 3, 2004).

Zeithaml, Valarie, A. Parasuraman and Leonard Berry. 1990. *Delivering Quality Services.* New York: The Free Press.

Further Reading

Against the Grain. 2004. 15 (6). [Special issue: Electronic resource statistics.]

Association of Research Libraries (ARL). *Service Quality Evaluation Academy.* ©2004. *LibQUAL+TM Events.* Association of Research Libraries. URL: http://www.libqual.org/Events/index.cfm (Accessed January 30, 2004.)

Bertot, John Carlo and Charles R. McClure, eds. 2001. *Evaluating networked information services: Techniques, policies, and issues.* Medford, NJ: Information Today.

Bertot, John Carlo, Charles McClure and Joe Ryan. 2001. *Statistics and performance measures for public library networked services.* Chicago: American Library Association.

Heath, Fred M., Martha Kyrillidou, and Consuella A. Askew. 2004. *Libraries Act on Their LibQUAL+™ Finding: From Data to Action.* Binghamton, NY: Haworth Press.

Lakos, Amos and Shelley E. Phipps. 2004. "Creating a culture of assessment: a catalyst for organizational change." *portal: Libraries and the Academy* 4 (3) URL: http://muse.jhu.edu/journals/portal_libraries_and_the_academy/v004/4.3lakos.pdf (Accessed September 3, 2004).

Westbrook, Lynn. 2000. *Identifying and Analyzing User Needs: A Complete Handbook and Ready-To-Use Assessment Workbook with Disk.* New York: Neal-Schuman.

CHAPTER 4

Budgeting and Planning

The operational responsibility of a library is to serve the information, learning, and recreation needs of a service community. By extension, the financial responsibility of a library is not, usually, to maximize profit but to marshal and deliver resources and services that will benefit this community. Within these responsibilities, electronic resource management has gradually become a central component of libraries' financial stewardship, but so gradually, in fact, that budgeting for electronic resources risks falling outside the usual budgetary controls. For example, a normal budgetary cycle could not support an 8 to 25% annual inflation of library employee wages, nor would a library expect to hire the very best with last decade's salaries. However, electronic resource vendors often expect 8 to 25% price hikes, which libraries are expected to pay from annual budgets reflecting decades-old financial models that do not match this rate of inflation.

The new financial model will start with the library's funding authority. A funding authority is a group of community leaders who act as stewards of a community's pooled funds. Examples of funding authorities include city councils acting for taxpayers, corporate executives acting for corporate boards and corporate employees, state legislatures acting for state taxpayers, higher education administrators acting for boards of regents and the institution's students and faculty, and boards of education acting for local governments and parents of school children. Libraries, as organizations designed to serve a community, receive income not from revenue-generated profit but from a budget paid out of community funds and awarded based on a funding authority's perceptions of that library's value to the community. This holds true as much for public libraries receiving funds from a pool of public taxes as for corporate libraries receiving funds from the corporate operating budget. (In some cases libraries are self-supporting profit centers, charging organizational customers for services rendered. However, the following arguments still hold as the library attempts to create and demonstrate value for its customer base.) The budget awarded by a funding authority demonstrates the value that such a group of community leaders places on the library as a community service. The budget allocation, therefore, reflects the funding authority's perception of the value that the library's customers they represent place on the library's services. The library's customers in turn develop a perception of the library's value based on the way the library meets customer needs with the funds they receive from the funding authority.

When library professionals view the process of library budget planning as an adaptive cycle of demonstrating value, they gain the power to improve a library's success within the budget cycle. For example, value-conscious budget planning can improve the library's response to rising costs by expecting vendors' products to show value proportionate to the bite they take from the budget. Value-conscious budget planning can improve the library's ability to demonstrate for a funding authority the library's value to the community. Value-conscious budget planning acts as an engine for the improvement of the library's service quality for its customers. Unfortunately, electronic resources introduce into this planning cycle a level of complexity and continuous change that library professionals cannot support unless the planning process becomes a collaborative group learning process throughout the organization and out into the community the library serves.

This chapter will first place budget planning into the context of the collaborative group learning that effectively manages high levels of complexity and turbulent change. Following this overview of management practices is a discussion of how this planning must include knowledge of the costs and benefits of products purchased because such knowledge assists in the negotiation of sustainable purchase prices, simplifies the choice of pricing models, and lowers the impact of product cost on the budget. Finally, the chapter returns to the idea of demonstrated value, discussing the kinds of demonstrated value a library can measure and showing how the library can help its funding authority apply the demonstrated service value the library holds for its community as a rationale for a new, sustainable financial model in budget allocation.

Planning for Value

Current library budgeting handbooks (Farmer 1993; Prentice 1996; Smith 2002) also describe budgeting as a planning process. For these authors, the planning process begins when planners establish, or review, the library's purpose, usually expressed as a statement of vision, mission, and goals. All the authors assert that without a clear set of values, politics and self-interest can dilute budgetary decisions. Within this structure of a clear purpose, the budget becomes an annual proposed estimate of future financial needs based not just on the past but also on projected demands. To create this estimate, the library must predict what internal or external pressures it will experience as it pursues the realization of its purpose. However, library planning in general and electronic resource planning in particular relies heavily on the projection of frequently unknowable variables. Even within a purpose, a budget is a plan for the unknowable. Although I agree that the budget planning process must begin with organizational purpose and I believe that the result must be the demonstration of a library's value to its community, I also believe that budgeting is not a linear process, with a beginning and an end, but an iterative process of continuous learning that must collaboratively include all library professionals.

Planning as Learning

At the end of the movie *Butch Cassidy and the Sundance Kid* (1969), Robert Redford and Paul Newman stand in an protected arcade staring into what everyone (audience, main characters, and killers) knows will be certain death, and one of them asks, "What's the plan?" After a pause, the other replies, "A plan is a list of things you'll never do."

Linear planning is a frustrating exercise in expecting a future fraught with surprise. With linear plans we assume that we first work out a sequence of actions leading to expected results and then we follow steps to what is hoped will be a successful conclusion. Budget planning in libraries often follows this procedure, predicting in advance how much budget the library needs to cover expected expenditures and, after receiving the budget, adjusting these expenditures to fit the amount awarded by the funding authority. In traditional budgets, expenditure for print resources can be reasonably predicted both because expenditure leads to ownership, for which the library does not have to pay again, and because the prices for print resources remain at a reasonable rate of inflation. The difference between the asked-for and received budgets does not require large adjustments because projected and actual expenditure remain stable. The unsustainable increase in print serials subscriptions are the exception, and the economics of serials act as a precursor to the economics of electronic resources (ALA et al. 2004; Schonfeld et al. 2004).

Electronic resources do not have either the advantage of ownership or an expectation of sustainable price increases. In most electronic resource purchases, the library does not obtain ownership but instead gains permission through a license to access an electronic resource for an established amount of time and must repurchase that permission at regular intervals. Simultaneously, inflation has had great impact on library relationships with commercial partners. Since the late eighties, most libraries have habituated themselves to an 8 to 25% annual increase in serials and electronic resource prices, and they are not unduly surprised to see annual price hikes of up to 35%, especially when the library switches from print to electronic format or after the latest round of vendor mergers and acquisitions (ARL, ACRL, and SPARC 2003; Guedon 2001; McCabe 1999; ELSSS 2001). In budgets that include electronic resource expenditure, prediction becomes guesswork in the fast pace of technology change, and adjustments are nothing but a painful reminder of the inequality between inflation in the information market and the restricted availability of awarded community funds.

Adaptive planning through learning breaks the library out of the confines of guesswork and acceptance of one's plight. Planning as learning grounds itself with the purpose of the library and actively applies this purpose to collaborative decision making, while relying on continuous assessment for data about the situation as it is currently experienced. Collaborative decision making does not sound like planning because actions are not worked out in advance. Instead planning through learning allows the library to work out in advance the purpose of the library, what its customers expect of it, what the library subsequently expects from the products it purchases, and what the funding authority expects as a return for the investment of community funds it has made in the library's budget. Within the framework of these expectations, the decisions to expend money from a budget come to reflect the value the library expects of itself, instead of an externally conceived amount the library must squeeze its value into. The budgetary question becomes not, "How can we make do?" but, "How can we provide and show value to the community we serve?"

A planning-through-learning process looks something like the following.

- Library professionals at all levels collaboratively reconfirm the library's purpose within the community served.
- The library establishes, through purpose and assessment, the value the library has within the community.
- The library establishes, through purpose and assessment, the set of expectations that will guide it through decisions made in the near future.

- Library professionals make each expenditure decision with the goal of living up to expectations and demonstrating its current value.

- Library professionals make each expenditure decision by calculating the balance between a current understanding of the cost-benefit ratio of a purchase and a current knowledge of purpose and expectation. With this calculation, the library negotiates a fair price, including the cost to the library of providing access, and ensures that the purchase fits within the expectations of the library and contributes to the library's value.

- New assessment shows that, as a result of purchase decisions, the library has lived up to expectations and can demonstrate discrete value for the community. Some libraries will go so far as to only claim success when the library surpasses expectations and increases value.

- The new demonstrated value forms the basis for the new budget awarded by the funding authority, a budget that reflects the value the library contributes to the community that the funding authority serves.

Treating planning as a learning process is much like planning a bicycle ride. The cyclist does not plan in advance all the moves necessary to respond to changes in the environment as the ride progresses. The cyclist neither plans the myriad muscular adjustments needed to avoid an unexpected small rock, nor does she plan for the attractive setting that draws the cyclist down the road heretofore untaken. To plan for a ride, the cyclist learns and practices in advance the complex musculoskeletal adjustments required to keep the bicycle upright, decides that today the purpose of the ride is to enjoy the scenery (not win a race or arrive at a specific destination), and, before she leaves, asks when she is expected home for dinner. This type of adaptive planning allows the rider to choose the road less traveled with little worry.

In an environment as turbulent as that of electronic resource management, and increasingly library management as a whole, success takes the form of collaborative learning-based planning that nurtures fluid adaptation. Successful planning is not isolated into a separate planning team, a day-long seminar, or the last weeks before the end of the fiscal year. In a learning organization, planning (and learning) is so inextricably bound to everyone's daily activity that it forms the matrix for that activity and even the measurement of the success of a day's productivity. Value-conscious budget planning daily negotiates sustainable prices, daily works to improve and demonstrate the library's value to its customers, and daily influences the funding authority's perception of the library's value within the community.

My Funding Authority Does Not Ask for Value

Demonstrating value turns a typical budgetary process on its head. The library is no longer in receipt of paternalistic support from its community. The library now demonstrates its value in order to receive value from the community. Conversely, and this is important, the funding authority no longer makes budget decisions from a separate position of authority. Its members now respond to demonstrated value with funds that reflect that value and reflect the future value that the community desires of its library. Members of a funding authority, as stewards of the community's purse, should be able to point to demonstrated value as the basis for funding decisions. Members of the funding authority can defend decisions neither with assumptions about value nor with the perceived *political* strengths of the budget recipient relative to other recipients. The funding authority becomes as much a part of the library's purpose-setting, expectation-defining, and value-assessment process as are library professionals and customers. In other words, any library professional charged with assessing library value should know all the leaders of the library's funding authority well enough to say hello. The library professional knows the funding authorities because dialog with each leader is open and active.

The members of the funding authority will expect to see value in the library, but their definition of value and the library's definition may not look the same. I argue that libraries should define demonstrated value as the assessed level of service quality the library provides its customers and the assessed outcome, or impact, the library has within these customers' lives. Value is not, as some funding authorities may perceive, a data count of the size of a journal collection, number of book volumes, frequency of database searches, or the level of traffic through the front door. This output data is important only when we use it to show progression toward a targeted improvement in service quality and customer outcome. In addition, value is not the political importance, prestige, or clout of the library or its director, although by marketing achieved customer value the library does gain stature in the community. Because a focus on service and outcome value may diverge from values prized by some funding authorities, an open and continuous dialog with these leaders is crucial for the demonstration of the library's true value.

I will be the first to admit that a library director who walks into a budget meeting prepared with evidence of the library's value to the community may receive blank stares from members of the funding authority not expecting such information. At first, demonstrated value will be a colorful, seemingly superfluous, addendum to the traditional data the funding authority expects. However, over time, the self-imposed discipline of demonstrating value will positively influence the library's value as the library becomes sensitive to customer expectations. This sensitivity will touch off internal cycles of assessment and improvement that can only contribute to further increases in library value. Increases in library value will not go unnoticed by the customers, especially if the library markets this value to attract customers. Strong support from the community will be heard by the funding authority. (Think of the powerful voices of a university faculty senate in support of a university library, the top income-producing corporate researchers of a corporate library, city business leaders of a public library, or the interested parents of school children who use a school media center.) When the library consciously pursues a dialog of defining value with the funding authority, the funding authority can come to see the library's real value measured by its impact on the community. Over time, the funding authority will not be able to avoid the consistent value the library contributes to the community and will have a hard time not recognizing that value when signing a budget.

Political reality can make this causal link between customer support and funding decisions seem like a pie in the sky. Maybe in particular instances the funding authority is so disconnected from the community it represents that it does not react to the values of that community, but I argue that a funding authority this removed from the community is not long in power. Willful neglect of community values in funding decisions may be possible from one year to the next, but a history of demonstrable library value that builds year after year is hard to ignore. If the library chooses to demonstrate value for the positive reasons of library improvement toward quality customer service, the difficulties of gaining funding authority recognition will resolve in time. Five years from now the library can point back to the intervening years of recorded customer service improvement and success.

Many will recognize elements of the accountability movement within the principles of a budget that reflects demonstrated value, and they will not be far wrong. Accrediting agencies for colleges and universities are beginning to require evidence of a cycle of service improvement and demonstrated value. In the United States, accountability for primary and secondary schools is widely debated as children are tested for achievement and schools are graded for success (and funding) based on these test scores. Just as accountability holds an organization to a standard in order to receive community support, accountability must also hold funding authorities to the responsibility of awarding funding commensurate with demonstrated value. Libraries, from their side of the dialog partnership, can develop early the habits of demonstrating value. Through these habits, libraries can not only gain the experience and the data history necessary for smooth entrance into any future formalized accountability requirements, but can also prepare the expectations of the funding authority with regard to what exactly demonstrated value means for the library serving its community.

Collaborative Groups

The complexity of the electronic resource budgetary process includes planning, determining true costs and benefits, negotiation, designing pricing models, and demonstrating value. This process requires large amounts of constant information input. As discussed in Chapter 2, Management, this flow of information is best managed through group effort. Collaborative groups apportion tasks over many contributors and combine the expertise and creativity of many participants. One of the few exceptions to the benefits of group work is license negotiation. A single staff member who acts as negotiator with vendors simplifies that negotiation relationship and ensures clear communication. However, a collaborative group then supports this negotiator with decisions relating to the calibration of negotiations to library purpose, customer assessment results, computing infrastructure costs, maintenance costs, and funding authority expectations. A collaborative group creates a stable learning environment from which library professionals can confront the ever-shifting tides of electronic resource markets and customer expectations.

Negotiation Through Cost and Benefit

With a purpose, or a clear vision for the importance of its service to its community, the library can use a budget to plan expenditure with the goal of fulfilling that vision. The library assesses its customers' service experiences in order to both improve service quality and to demonstrate its value in terms of its positive impact on the community. In a user-centered library, the costs of electronic resources are a combination of the price of the resource plus the costs and benefits of ownership. The costs of ownership are the effort and resources that the library needs to provide the resource, and the benefits of ownership are reflected in how well the resources serve the needs of the community. Ownership, in the case of electronic resources, most often means licensure, not outright purchase.

Negotiation uses knowledge of cost and benefit of ownership to bring the price of an electronic resource within a range the library's budget can support, given the expectations and value the library would like to achieve. Libraries rarely have difficulty demonstrating the overall benefit of electronic resources for their customers. Electronic resources bring the library to the customer's desktop, and most customers consider this convenience a boon to their research efforts. Electronic resources have introduced new ways of calculating the cost of ownership.

Negotiation Through Costs

Invoiced price is the direct cost of the electronic resource. Inflation rates of 8 to 25% in prices for electronic resources create exceptional cost burdens for budget planning. This level of inflation is not sustainable over time, as library budgets will never increase by the same rate. For libraries charged with creating collections useful to their communities, the issue becomes how to best balance expenditure for electronic resources with expenditure on the total collection of print and electronic information resources. Libraries best achieve this balance through open and knowledgeable negotiation with vendors for pricing advantageous to both parties, capturing the library and customer needs through group-based decision making and sharing the value of the library with library customers and funding authorities.

Electronic resources also incur the indirect costs of ongoing financial commitments to licensed and obsolescence-prone electronic content and technical infrastructure. Robert E. Dugan (2002) lists the indirect ownership costs of electronic resources as time spent investigating, negotiating, and acquiring licenses; time and resources required to build the library's technical delivery infrastructure; time and resources devoted to train for and maintain such an infrastructure; and the time required to evaluate products' performance histories to decide to "upgrade, migrate, replace, or abandon." Time should always be stated in the monetary terms of salary cost per hour. Planning for electronic resource expenditure must continuously work to accurately describe these costs of ownership.

Negotiation is a meeting of the minds in which both sides of an agreement realize gains to offset any incurred costs or terms given up. In any negotiation the final price invoiced can accurately reflect the balance of a product's costs and benefits to its producer and to its buyer. The more a library negotiator and the negotiator's supporting group of professionals (both inside the library and externally from peer professionals, cooperatives, and statewide consortial networks) know about the costs of ownership balanced by the potential benefits of a product, the more creatively they can meet the needs of both the library and the vendor. This knowledge will also allow the group more control over the final impact of electronic resource prices on the library budget.

The planning of an electronic resources budget is not simply a projection of inflation on current prices. Indeed, price is only the beginning. The well-informed planning group will also investigate costs incurred by the vendor in producing the product, by the library's staff and infrastructure in maintaining and delivering the product, and by the end users as they incorporate the product into a research workflow. Coupled with the ability to state in real terms the benefits a product brings to the library and the library's customers, knowledge of the total cost of a product allows the library negotiator to achieve the terms most advantageous for the library and for the vendor.

Vendor Profit

Many, though not all, vendors of electronic products hold as their primary objective the maximization of profit. Profit keeps the vendor in business. For profit to occur, the price charged libraries must contain some margin of revenue above the cost to the vendor of producing and delivering the product. Depending on the type of electronic resource sold, vendors experience different pressures on their margin of profit. For example, publishers of journals in the last quarter of the twentieth century experienced reductions in the number of personal subscriptions and an increase in the number of competing journals published. This reduction in demand lowers total revenue and when the cost of production remains the same or increases the product price must increase to maintain a healthy profit margin. Innovations in online publishing adds the cost of creating online technology to the cost of maintaining a parallel print publishing process (Bot et al. 1998). A greater pressure on commercial publishers, however, is the investor expectation of profit margins of 35% or higher. These expectations have prompted many of the publishing industry mergers and acquisitions over the past two decades and put greater pressure on a higher product price to fulfill this profit margin expectation (Information Access Alliance 2003).

Some electronic journals, online databases, and electronic data products are produced by nonprofit organizations, such as associations, societies, and government agencies. These producers are not subject to profit expectations, but many do still have the cost of dual print and online production responsibilities. Price is therefore much lower and much less prone to inflationary pressure.. However, some nonprofit organizations use net income from their publications (income left after covering the cost of production) to support other organizational efforts and this pushes the publication arm of the organization into the realm of meeting profit expectations.

Because vendor profit is income minus cost of production, library negotiators can educate themselves on whether the proposed price appropriately reflects vendor claims of costs. For example, must the library accept the full brunt of a delayed awareness by the vendor of online technology innovation? The library can accept a new interface but at a lower price. Or when price increases by 35% from one year to the next, the library can have prepared a way to communicate to the community why it must say no to the vendor.

Moreover, library negotiators must be aware that as with any trade, smart sellers initially ask the very highest price they think they can get. Acknowledging the need for vendor profit, the library negotiator can still try to judge by how much the seller can lower the initial asking price and, short of a lower price, what other non-monetary concessions the negotiator could seek from the vendor that would make the price more attractive. By unquestioningly accepting the initial asking price, the library is likely shouldering as a cost to the budget the widest possible profit margin for the vendor rather than a more reasonable margin that benefits both the library and the vendor.

Publisher embargo is a special cost consideration. Aggregating vendors enter into agreements with third-party publishers to collect, or aggregate, publishers' content for resale. Despite the fact that only the largest libraries subscribe to as wide an array of journals as are represented in an aggregated database, as publishers' online delivery of content matures, publishers begin to see the aggregators as competitors selling the same content to the same customers (Brooks 2001). The publishers will use aggregators to generate secondary income from published material but will "embargo" the aggregated display of recently published content. Under embargo, for example, all but the most recent six months of a journal's content is represented in an aggregator's database. To obtain the most recent six months for its customers, the library must have a separate subscription to the journal, which is not a tenable choice for most mid- to small-sized libraries. From the librarian's point of view—access for their community—embargo has the effect of dramatically reducing the quality of an aggregated product. Embargo, therefore, can have two costs. The library must carefully consider the impact of embargo on the content of a particular aggregated product. The library can also consider entering into pay-per-view relationships with publishers or publisher agents, in which the library pays by the article and not by the subscription (Brandsma et al. 2003).

Cost to the Library

The second important element of a product's price is the cost to the library of delivering the electronic resource to the customer. The two major delivery costs are staff time and computing infrastructure. Staff time, or labor cost per hour, is the single greatest expense of any organization. When negotiating a product's contract, formal evaluations of the product's possible drain on staff resources and evidence of past experience with a product's technical difficulties and negative impact on an infrastructure can be powerful leverage. For example, how much time was spent last year with the product's technical service representatives because customers had difficulty accessing the web site? How much time was spent installing, or updating, on local computers the client software required by the product to operate? Does the product not live up to usability standards, thereby increasing the time that library professionals will spend on instruction because the interface is not intuitive?

The costs of purchasing and maintaining infrastructure, such as computers, networking, servers, and printers, are easy to ignore as part of the cost of each electronic resource. These infrastructure resources are frequently viewed as overhead, already expensed, and not worth refiguring into the cost of individual products. However, knowing an average cost of providing past access can make a product's delivery costs stand in stark relief to its benefit for the price. For example, when a product's Web site is image-intensive, its drain on network bandwidth may be unsupportable. Full-text PDF images require high-capacity printers, print networking, and print servers. The true price of a product must include cost of ownership or the product's impact on the library's staff time and infrastructure.

Cost to the Customer

Given that the objective of libraries is to provide the service of access to its community, the cost of a product is not complete until one tallies the cost to library customers of incorporating the product into their own workflow. These costs are similar in many ways to those of the library. What bandwidth, computing power, and printing capacity are required for the user not in the library? What is the "learning curve," or time for self-instruction, necessary for the interface, for downloading required software, and for authenticating oneself as a remote user? And what about the cost of what I began to call "*walk-away*," in which the user decides not to benefit from the product's content because using it is "too hard"? If product evaluation shows that these costs are high, a negotiator should use this information to reach mutually beneficial terms that reflect these costs. The library's counteroffer will be discussed below.

Negotiation Through Benefits

When planning for electronic resource expenditure, library professionals must also calculate the benefit received as a result of purchasing the product and the balance of that benefit against the costs. Benefits accrue for the vendor, the library, and the customer alike.

Vendor Benefits

In addition to the benefit of income, a vendor can benefit from a sale in ways that are not immediately financial but are tangible nonetheless.

First, if the library has stature locally, regionally, or nationally, a contract with that library becomes a selling point when that vendor approaches other potential customers. If the vendor wishes to use the library's name, this can be reflected in the change to a better price model for the library. Second, if the library's community members will become future purchasers of a product, a lower price that prompts a sale now can create a cadre of future clients. A form of this price consideration is "academic" pricing. For example, an academic library serving a business school that grants diplomas to future corporate CEOs can convince a producer of business information that alumni familiar with the product will likely choose to license the product at higher corporate prices once in the business world.

Libraries do not have to be renowned or have powerful community members to imaginatively find benefits to offer a vendor. Have the negotiating group investigate the vendor perspective, imagine what vendors perceive as benefits, and incorporate this into the negotiation. These non-monetary benefits for the vendor can translate into a monetary benefit for the library in the form of a more advantageous pricing structure.

Library and Customer Benefits

Benefits such as ease of use and low maintenance costs can have a positive impact on a decision to choose one product over another, even if the chosen product is more expensive. The negotiation group should be able to show the dollar amount of the indirect cost savings of a low-maintenance product and add this to the benefits balance when determining the product's overall cost to the library. If the product is unknown to the library, develop an estimate by asking other libraries for their experiences with the product.

If the vendor promises benefits not yet in evidence, the library could negotiate a graduated price structure, starting low and progressively increasing as technical quality increases. This trade-off of higher price for higher quality is only beneficial to the library if it can actively demonstrate a balance between an increased invoice cost and a cost-savings benefit of reduced labor, improved customer experience, or reduced demand on infrastructure.

The effort that goes into discovering the true costs and benefits for all participants in electronic resources budgeting—the vendor, the library, and the library customers—allows the negotiating librarian and the vendor the creative freedom to design an agreement advantageous to all three participants. The vendor may be open to a lower price if other associated costs would cause a library to not license the product at all. The library may be able to afford a higher cost if other concessions from the vendor lower the overall cost of a product for the library or for the library customer.

A meeting of the minds occurs when the negotiators on both sides agree to the lowest cost and the highest benefit for the library, vendor, and library customer. Once the library's negotiating group gives monetary value to the array of product costs and benefits, the group not only has the necessary information to help the negotiator arrive at prices beneficial to both the library and the vendors, but also can plan the electronic resource budget with more confidence.

The Library's Counteroffer

When negotiating a counteroffer, the library negotiator grounds the new price in reality with an estimation of the impact of cost of production on the vendor's negotiable profit margin, a calculation of the product's cost of ownership, including staff time and infrastructure, and an awareness of the costs to the customer. When the library negotiator makes this knowledge clear in the counteroffer, the vendor can understand the rationale behind a recalculated price and thereby gains a direct monetary incentive to solve these issues for all its clients. Know, however, that hardship external to the library's relationship with the vendor or the product is not a cost within the library-vendor relationship. The complaint, for instance, that "we will have to cancel another publisher's journals to buy your product," will not in most cases move a vendor to action. The library is in the business of serving a community with a comprehensive, useable collection of resources. The vendor is in the business of generating the widest income margin, whether for profit or for nonprofit administrative costs. Community service may be a heartfelt ethic to these vendors but it is still secondary to income. The negotiator can only communicate library costs and benefits of ownership to the vendor through product price or other beneficial license provisions. For example, if a cost of ownership includes the labor cost of installing client software on 500 library computers (such as if library technical staff members do not have centralized software installation through special-purpose server software), can the license reflect a price break to cover the calculated hourly wage cost of the installation?

A library is never forced to take the offering price of an electronic resource. If the price plus other costs is more than the projected benefit, communicate this information with the vendor. Provide documentation of your calculations of other costs and benefits. The vendor who is in touch with the customer will appreciate the feedback. The vendor cannot immediately remedy some costs, such as a new interface that is difficult to use, but a reduction in price this year in expectation of a higher price for an improved interface next year, or an increase in some other licensed benefit, can bring more balance to the equation. The negotiating group helps the negotiating professional answer the question, "Is what we are giving up (in terms of both price and cost) worth what we are getting (in terms of all cumulative benefits)?"

If the vendor cannot reduce the price plus cost of ownership to below the benefit, the library negotiator must be willing to walk away without making a purchase. If the negotiator does not walk away, the library is then choosing to accept a product at a higher cost than benefit received. The negotiating group can support a negotiating professional through collaborative group determination of whether the decision helps the library fulfill its purpose within the community.

Negotiation

Successful negotiators live by two basic rules. First, one should never surprise, or be surprised. Second, to get what you really want, always be willing to walk away.

Rule 1: Surprise is the enemy to you both.

- Know what you want before entering into discussions.
  - *Why* do you want what you want? for what ultimate purpose?
  - What can you give up? to get exactly what?
  - It's not just price. Think of other benefits you could give or receive.
  - Make sure the other party knows what you want before entering into discussions.
  - Published policies and requirements are more difficult to dispute, especially if they were developed before the current negotiation.
- Do your homework.
  - Know your customers' needs, the vendor's needs, the product's needs, etc.
  - Know all the negative and positive impacts of this product on other products you license, on your infrastructure, on staff time, etc.
  - Investigate other libraries' creative solutions.
- Know what the other party wants.
  - Ask why? why not?
  - If you must give up something, know how they can "sweeten the deal."
  - It's not about you; it's about you both.
- Know basic negotiating ploys and pitfalls.

- Time pressure: "We must know by Friday." Last-minute decisions usually end badly for the pressured party. Don't succumb. If the vendor wants the sale, they will make the sale.
- "I've got to talk to my manager." Citing the negative decision of a third-party decision-maker is the best way to avoid taking a loss. (The library negotiator may also use this tactic.)
- "We can't go *any* lower" is put into perspective by whether they want to make the sale at all.

Rule 2: Be willing to walk away.

- Prepare (in advance) your own customers for no sale. Use open discussions with your customers of how the product, or product category, like serials, impacts the library's ability to serve them overall.
- Soften the decision with the vocalized intention to revisit the sale next year to see whether the sustainable price or provisions have materialized over time.

If you have not educated yourself before negotiations begin, and if you are not willing to walk away, you will give up more than the other party—guaranteed. Consider how not walking away hurts the library's ability to serve its customers overall. Compare the cost of taking an undesired outcome, for example, higher price, with the benefit of using that money in other collection purchases. Walking away takes courage, practice, and a lot of communication—with library customers, library colleagues, and the vendor.

Pricing Models

Methods of structuring the price of a product, also called *pricing models*, or *business models*, come in many forms, and both libraries and vendors are free to invent new models with each new contract. Pricing models are any combination of pricing, beneficial license terms, and license restrictions upon which the library and vendor agree. Basic pricing models include price per unit, price per user, price per use, and consortial purchasing.

The first model, price per unit, most frequently occurs when a vendor or publisher sells what in the print world were discrete packages, for example: journals, reference works, or books. The vendor can allow the library to choose the titles to which it would like to subscribe. The vendor can also offer all titles as a package and, at times, make individual title purchases more expensive or impossible. Kenneth Frazier calls this the "big deal," in which libraries are forced to buy into a complete package of journals from a publisher including titles not normally used by their community base (2001). Studies show more use than expected of titles not previously thought of enough value to license separately (Nicholas et al. 2003; Sanville 2001).

With effective cost–benefit analysis, a library can determine which scenario works best. For example, is the library's clientele so specialized that negotiating higher per-title costs is cheaper than paying for a complete package? A cost–benefit analysis applies equally well to decisions between print-plus-online and online-only packages. Is the potential loss of a permanent print archive worth the price and convenience of an electronic-only subscription? For libraries of record, on which a region depends for permanent access, maybe not; but for a library that can rely on interlibrary loan services to fill gaps, maybe so.

The second basic business model is the price per number of potential users. The traditional basis for this business model has been size of population served. In academic and school library settings, this is full-time equivalent (FTE) enrollment; for public libraries, the population of the geographic region served; and for special, corporate and nonprofit libraries, the FTE employees served by the library. A variation on this model is the charge per additional branch, or satellite, of the main library. Charging per potential user can be a logical pricing structure for general-interest products, but when the price for special-subject products is calculated by population size, the specialized content will never interest a large portion of that population. A solution is to pay for "simultaneous user logins or sessions," usually set at some number less than twenty, in which a product will be available only to a certain number of users at a time. The negotiator is always advised to factor in the cost of "turn-away," or those library customers denied access when all simultaneous user slots are in use.

With the advent of more sophisticated Web technology, a third business model—paying per use—has begun to grow in acceptance. The most common form of this business model, "pay per view," is not a new concept, but some libraries are beginning to revisit it as an alternative if other pricing models become unsustainable. Library professionals at the University of North Carolina at Greensboro have begun to use prepaid accounts that fully subsidize document delivery. The Greensboro creators of the regional Journal Finder interface have their software display the pay-per-view option only when no other option is available. In 2002, for a cost of $80,000, the library tapped 2,300 journals (Brandsmaet al. 2003). If one accepts an average cost of $3,000 per journal subscription, this equals a single annual subscription savings of $6,900,000 worth of journals. Bernhardt doubts that her library would have subscribed to any of the journals tapped for the per-use service, and believes that the journals' publishers benefit from a previously unavailable income (Bernhardt 2003).

A fourth business model that has reached almost global acceptance is consortial purchasing. Consortia range from informal buyers' clubs, in which a few libraries band together to pay for an occasional contract, to national (JISC 2004) and even international (eIFL 2004) efforts to provide central purchasing power for a group of service communities. The primary contribution of consortia is lowered prices for libraries through collective bargaining and lowered administrative costs to vendors able to negotiate a single contract with multiple libraries. Larger consortia with permanent staff can provide a central infrastructure and Web site for electronic product access, as well as central fund collection and distribution services. Finally, consortia can assist libraries subject to adverse financial constraints. In this case the consortium acts as a third party in financial and legal transactions not subject to national laws, currencies not shared by the vendor, or a financial limitation as simple as a different fiscal year. If a library that must spend money before the end of a fiscal year or lose it in next year's budget, the consortium can "bank" the money, or hold the funds in reserve, for a contract payment due after the fiscal year turns.

Participation in a consortium can have associated costs as well. As consortia grow and become formal organizations, the overhead costs of staff and infrastructure increase the price libraries pay for contracts signed through consortial deals. At times, larger consortial members will even pay more than they would have as independent purchasers to make the contract attractive to their smaller consortial partners. If this fits with the purpose of the library for its community, it can be justified as a reasonable cost; however, this is not sustainable in long-term budget planning, and savvy consortial negotiators use the participation of larger client libraries to reduce rather than increase these clients' costs.

Conclusion

Individual faculty members and students, individual townspeople, and individual company or organization employees cannot afford a collection of electronic information resources, the expertise to maintain them, and a fully operational computing infrastructure through which to access the products. The community, therefore, creates a collective library for itself and allows a funding authority to act as steward. The library's primary purpose is to provide the service of a useful library collection to its community. The library's second most important job is showing the community leaders in a funding authority the value that these library services have for the community.

The funding authority is the library's link between its demonstrated value in the community and its income, and the library is responsible for keeping that link open. The library demonstrates to its funding authority the value it has for the customer by discovering through assessment the impact of a library's services on its customers. Service quality and outcomes assessment is a recent and complex development in library management. Because of this, traditional input data, such as the number of volumes, number of uses, and the amount purchased, may seem more straightforward for funding authorities and libraries when negotiating a budget. However, by not knowing the value of the library within its community, both parties make budgetary decisions that are not sustainable over time.

Electronic resources, in all their diversity, create a kaleidoscope of competing demands on a library budget. A collaborative group of professionals can help a library negotiator manage the inflationary pressures of vendor pricing. This group can develop a thorough description of the costs and benefits of ownership and help the negotiator determine what will be important to vendor, library, and the library customer in an acceptable contract.

Without attention to value, the budget will not reflect the real costs and benefits the library incurs as it fulfills its purpose for the community. A disconnect between awarded budget and real value does not allow the library to adapt to market forces or customer expectations. Demonstrating the library's true value within its purpose builds a solid foundation for adaptive, value-conscious budget planning, justification, and allocation.

References

American Library Association (ALA) and Association for Library Collections and Technical Services (ALCTS). 2004. *2004 U.S. Periodicals Price Index*. Chicago: American Library Association.

Association of Research Libraries (ARL), Association of College and Research Libraries (ACRL), and SPARC. "Create change: A resource for faculty and librarian action to reclaim scholarly communication." ©2003. Association of Research Libraries. URL: http://www.arl.org/create/home.html (Accessed September 3, 2004).

Bernhardt, Elizabeth. 2003. Conversation with author, Washington, DC. March 12, 2003.

Bot, Margolein, Johan Burgemeester and Hans Roes. 1998. "The cost of publishing an electronic journal: A general model and a case study." *D-Lib Magazine* (November). URL: http://www.dlib.org/dlib/november98/11roes.html (Accessed September 3, 2004).

Butch Cassidy and the Sundance Kid. 1969. Produced by John Foreman. Directed by George Roy Hill. 110 min. 20th Century Fox. Videocassette.

Brandsma, Terry W., Elizabeth R. Bernhardt and Dana M. Sally. 2003. Journal Finder, a second look: Implications for serials access in today's library. *Serials Review* 29 (4):287–294

Brooks, Sam. 2001. Integration of Information Resources and Collection Development Strategy. *Journal of Academic Librarianship* 27 (4):316–319.

Dugan, Robert E. 2002. Information technology budgets and costs: Do you know what your information technology costs each year? *The Journal of Academic Librarianship* 28 (4):238–243.

Electronic Information for Libraries (eIFL). *eIFL.net: Electronic information for libraries.* ©2004. eIFL Foundation and Open Society Institute (OSI). URL: http://www.eifl.net/ (Accessed September 3, 2004).

Electronic Society for Social Scientists (ELSSS). "A selection of the press coverage of the ELSSS project" ©2001 *What is ELSSS.* ELSSS. URL: http://www.elsss.org.uk/?current=Press+coverage (Accessed March 3, 2004).

Farmer, Lesley. 1993. *When your library budget is almost zero.* Englewood, CO: Libraries Unlimited.

Frazier, Kenneth. 2001. The Librarians' Dilemma: Contemplating the Costs of the 'Big Deal.' *D-Lib Magazine* 7(March) URL: http://www.dlib.org/dlib/march01/frazier/03frazier.html (Accessed September 3, 2004).

Guedon, Jean-Claude. 2001. In Oldenburg's Long Shadow: Librarians, Research Scientists, Publishers, and the Control of Scientific Publishing. Paper read at the 138th Annual Membership Meeting of the Association of Research Libraries: Creating the Digital Future, 23-25 May, in Toronto, Ontario. URL: http://www.arl.org/arl/proceedings/138/guedon.html (Accessed September 3, 2004).

Information Access Alliance. "Libraries urge Justice Department to block CINVEN and Candover purchase of Bertelsmannspringer." ©2003. *Supporting Documents.* Information Access Alliance. URL: http://www.informationaccess.org/MergerRelease-530.pdf (Accessed September 3, 2004).

Joint Information Systems Committee (JISC). *JISC The Joint Information Systems Committee.* ©2004. JISC. URL: http://www.jisc.ac.uk/ (Accessed September 3, 2004).

McCabe, Mark J. 1999. The Impact of Publisher Mergers on Journal Prices: An Update. *ARL Bimonthly Report,* no. 207. URL: http://www.arl.org/newsltr/207/jrnlprices.html (Accessed September 3, 2004).

Nicholas, David, Paul Huntington, Anthony Watkinson. 2003. Digital Journals, Big Deals and Online Searching Behaviour: A Pilot Study. *Aslib Proceedings* 55 (1/2):84–109.

Prentice, Ann E. 1996. *Financial planning for libraries.* 2d ed. London: Scarecrow Press.

Sanville T. J. 2001. A method out of the madness: OhioLINK's collaborative response to the serials crisis. *Serials: The Journal for the Serials Community* 14 (2):163–177.

Schonfeld, Roger C., Donald W. King, Ann Okerson, and Eileen Gifford Fenton. "The nonsubscription side of periodicals: Changes in library operations and costs between print and electronic formats." ©2004. *CLIR Reports.* CLIR. URL: http://www.clir.org/pubs/reports/pub127/contents .html (Accessed September 17, 2004).

Smith, G. Stevenson. 2002. *Managerial accounting for libraries and other not-for-profit organizations.* Chicago, IL: American Library Association.

Further Reading

Abel, Richard and Lyman W. Newlin. 2002. *Scholarly publishing: Books, journals, publishers, and libraries in the twentieth century.* New York: Wiley.

Bailey, Charles W., Jr. *Scholarly Electronic Publishing Bibliography.* © 2003. University of Houston Libraries. URL: http://info.lib.uh.edu/sepb/ sepb.html (Accessed September 3, 2004).

Bluh, Pamela M. 2001. *Managing electronic serials.* Chicago, IL: American Library Association.

Cox, John. 2002. Pricing Electronic Information: A Snapshot of New Serials Pricing Models. *Serials Review* 28 (3):171–175.

Cox, John and Laura Cox. "Scholarly publishing practice: The ALPSP report on academic journal publishers' policies and practices in online publishing." ©2003 *ALPSP: Association of Learned and Professional Society Publishers.* ALPSP. URL: http://www.alpsp.org/news/sppsummary0603.pdf (Accessed September 3, 2004).

German, Lisa. 2001. *Guide to the management of the information resources budget.* Lanham, MD: Scarecrow Press.

Litman, Jessica. 2001. *Digital copyright: Protecting intellectual property on the Internet.* Amherst, NY: Prometheus Books.

Liu, Lewis G. and Bryce Allen. 2003. *Economics of Libraries.* Library Trends vol. 51, no. 3 (Urbana Champaign: University of Illinois).

Matthews, Joseph R. 2002. *The bottom line: Determining and communicating the value of the special library.* Westport, CT: Libraries Unlimited.

——— 2004. *Measuring for results: The dimensions of public library effectiveness.* Westport, CT: Libraries Unlimited.

Siess, Judith. 2003. *The visible librarian: Asserting your value with marketing and advocacy.* Chicago, IL: American Library Association.

CHAPTER 5

Collection Development and Acquisitions

Libraries have long held as their central purpose the provision of access to data, information, knowledge, and entertainment for the express benefit of a defined service community. Collection development as a function within this central purpose goes beyond the aggregating and warehousing of information. In collection development, library professionals consciously select information resources that are of most use to the library's community. The acquisitions process completes collection development when library professionals negotiate the expenditure and resource delivery that best meet the library's larger purpose. Only after the decision to add an object or service to a collection can the other traditional library functions follow, such as classification, delivery, and instruction. As a result, all other processes within a library must inform a well-managed collection development and acquisitions process. Therefore, a well-managed collection development and acquisitions process cannot exist as a separate microcosm of decision making within a library, but instead actively learns the needs of the customer and the needs of the library through adaptive policies and selection criteria.

Electronic resources have irrevocably changed the process of collection development and acquisitions for every type of library. Library professionals have had to revisit not only at how they select and add resources to their collections, but also their relationships with the communities they serve and even their awareness of other libraries' collection efforts. In traditional collection building, the largely print materials added to library collections have been finite packages, owned in reasonable perpetuity, unchanging over time, and with a physical mass that library professionals can mark, catalog, and shelve. In traditional customer relations, the library's community members make a trip to the library for these materials. Our patrons walk through our doors, wend their way through our classification system, pick up the resources they want, and approach a service desk to borrow these materials or make photocopies.

Electronic resources, when introduced into this working-well-enough-for-decades-thank-you process for print collections, cause disturbances and frustration for library staff and customers. We library professionals have come to realize that we cannot expect virtual products to behave like the print resources around which our procedures have evolved, or we will be continuously disappointed by these electronic resources' inability to sit still and behave. We have also come to realize that if we expect the communities we serve to approach electronic resources in the same way they have our print, we will be continually surprised by our customers' infinite ability to change their expectations in response to the latest technological developments in information delivery.

Library professionals, as quick thinkers and astute observers, have a long history of grafting new processes onto standard procedure in order to innovate ways to serve their communities. Despite the fluidity of change inherent in electronic resource management, most libraries continue to have library customers enter through the "doorways" of Web interfaces and authentication protocols; we offer electronic resources on the virtual "shelving" of Web-delivered lists; and we provide physical and virtual service "desks" that library customers may approach for assistance. Electronic resources have expanded library professionals' daily work from the building and maintenance of a physical collection to choreographing the delivery of suites of electronic resources through a virtual infrastructure of delivery mechanisms, that bring the resources to library customers' computers.

Therefore, the majority of any discussion of the collection development and acquisitions process for electronic resources will not deviate in substance from those discussions that have gone before. Indeed, other collection development textbooks should be considered complementary with this work (Chapman 2001; Clayton and Gorman 2001; Evans 2000; Gardner 1981; Lukenbill 2002; Spiller 2000). The process of adaptive collection development and acquisitions of electronic resources continues to include the following phases:

- Use assessment to determine the information needs of a library's community.
- Use a policy or a set of written or unwritten agreed practices to decide among available electronic resources, given the library's environment and mission.
- During selection, decide among available electronic resources using selection criteria that reflect the library's budget and purpose.
- During evaluation, review electronic resources to determine the feasibility and acceptability of purchase, renewal, or cancellation.
- During acquisition, manage relationships with vendors, including licensing, payment, receiving delivery, and verifying access.

Other chapters discuss important elements of collection development and acquisitions, including: assessment, budgeting, licensing, and preparing electronic resources for access through cataloging and a delivery infrastructure. This chapter will focus on the three pillars of collection development and acquisitions—customer needs, library policies, and selection criteria—in the context of the turbulent change inherent in electronic resource management.

Customer Needs

Jennifer Younger (2002) writes of the frequent divergence between collection developers' need to collect for all possible future needs and the requirement by customers that libraries distribute information on demand, at the time and place of demand. Dennis Dillon (2002) paints a picture of libraries moving from a world of information scarcity, in which libraries could conceive of adequately representing within their walls the universe of knowledge for one or many disciplines, to a world of information flood, in which libraries increasingly work to stem the tide, make sense of the overflow, and siphon off for use that of the highest quality. Charlie Robinson and Joey Rodger (1998) have debated whether library professionals develop collections from a position of determinism or responsiveness. In other words, are library professionals in the business of deciding what is best for library customers or the business of learning from the customers what they want in order to fulfill that demand?

Peter Drucker (2001) writes in the *Economist* that service institutions may act locally, for a clearly defined community, but that they compete globally, against Web-delivered sources of information and services available on the user's desktop "because the Internet will keep customers everywhere informed on what is available anywhere in the world."

While libraries devote considerable resources to the selection and delivery of high-quality collections, library customers are attracted by the ease of use and ubiquity of, at times, the lesser-quality resources not purchased or managed by the library (ARL and TAM 2002; DLF and CLIR 2002; Baruchson-Arbib and Shor 2002; Ileperuma 2002; Lee and Sinn 2002; Monopoli et al 2002; OCLC 2002; Pew Internet & American Life Project 2002; Quigley et al 2002). Through electronic resources, libraries are beginning to profoundly impact their communities' research habits by pulling their resources together into streamlined interfaces similar to those of the search engines and Web sites that users find attractive.

Although collection development and acquisitions processes remain concerned about meeting projected long-term information needs, the processes must also become responsive, agile creators of collections that support on-demand services and be the innovative contributor of new services that meet customer needs. Library professionals in collection development, or selectors, are expanding their roles as generalists or subject specialists building a collection to assess and meet future demand with the additional abilities to assess and respond to shifts in the immediate information needs of library customers (Christie and Kristick 2001; Gooden 2001; Hiller 2002). Preparation for collection development and acquisitions begins with the customer. Continually renewed knowledge of customer needs supports the building and review of the policies that are so important to successfully managing electronic resources collection development and acquisitions.

Underlying the purpose of meeting the information needs of the community is the necessity that the community continues to consider, and fund, the library as a valuable, even irreplaceable, resource to that community. Applying diligence in discovering what the community values will allow the collection development and acquisitions efforts to contribute to keeping the library relevant and valuable to its service community.

Policies

A collection development and acquisitions policy outlines how the values and purpose of a library will influence the collection development decisions and acquisitions processes that add, or remove, resources from the library's offerings to its community. Tim Jewell (2001) drafted a map of the collection development and acquisitions work flow and discovered a conservative list of almost 150 data elements that these professionals must keep track of to complete a purchase of an electronic resource. A policy, treated as a learning document, helps these professionals manage this level of detail while living up to the library's core purpose.

I use the word *document* not in the sense of a single printed statement, but more as an adaptive dossier recording the learning of collaborative groups of library professionals. As the collection development process increases in complexity, the attendant learning will increase. The policy will become a collection of observations, agreed responses to certain situations, exceptions, and other sources of collected experience. See Yale University Library (2004) for an example of such a collection.

Libraries, large and small, public, school, special, academic, and consortial can usually find a copy of their policies in a drawer largely unused. Other libraries have put off writing a policy because they dread spending the time on something that will go in a drawer. Some collection development teachers (Spiller 2000; Evans 2000) begin a discussion of policy development with discussions on how these policies are either absent in many libraries or are rarely applied to daily decisions. Policy statements can, however, become relevant, useful documents that help selectors strengthen collections and manage their daily workload.

Policy statements have the following advantages; they:

• Provide a coherent, long-term direction for the overall collection
• Describe the value of a collection to those who are making funding decisions
• Provide guidance to selectors in their daily decisions to purchase or pass
• Standardize acquisitions, particularly for review, negotiation, and licensing
• Communicate selection priorities and values to the library's customers

Drawbacks to policy statements are, however, real. Policies can be:

• Too static and inflexible to help with the fast changes in collection choices
• Too densely written to actually be read
• Too prescriptive to be a learning document capable of guiding selectors in times of change
• Not easily used in the daily routine of selectors or acquisitions professionals

When the disadvantages of policy statements mean that policies that are not written, or are written and not read, then "adhocracy" develops. Adhocracy is the exercise of personal judgment to make decisions without reference to accepted standards to guide those decisions, which leads decision makers to respond more to immediate needs and less to universal needs, which take the entire organization purpose into account. Adhocracy weakens the selection process and the collection itself. Selectors are often overwhelmed with the complex data required to make a purchase decision. Out of expediency, selectors make decisions in what seems like a vacuum, accompanied by an uncertainty about fully supporting the needs of the organization as a whole. To make matters worse, without an objective strategy to back up selectors' decisions, politically powerful parts of the library's community can, case-by-case, encroach on more than their share of the library's budget. An adaptive policy allows selectors to swiftly compare selection intent and outcome across the breadth of the library's responsibilities to its community. An adaptive policy allows those making funding decisions to determine the overall value of a collection to the community by placing into context the ongoing importance of each investment within the library's budget strategy.

A successful collection policy is a policy formed around customers' needs for the information that a resource provides, not necessarily its format. Print and electronic resources together form a vibrant collection for the library's customers, and both of these formats need the selector's subject expertise and understanding of customer need to inform purchasing decisions. If a collection and acquisition policy exists for the print resources in a library, electronic resource collection policies are best used to strengthen, not replace, these existing principles. Treating both the core and electronic resource policies as learning documents responsive to the library's internal and external environment strengthens the activities of collection development and acquisitions and strengthens the resulting collections.

Policies as Learning Documents

A policy that continually strengthens itself with new information from its environment is a learning document. The concept of treating a policy as an adaptive learning document brings into relief the idea that an organization is in constant communication with its environment. A well-managed collection development and acquisitions policy becomes a learning document when it:

- Starts with the discovery of customers' needs and ends with analyzing the impact of policy-guided purchase decisions on customer needs
- Acts as a catalyst for selectors and other library staff members to learn from each other and from the environment of publishing, technology, and customer expectations that surround electronic resource management

- Acts as a guiding tool and not as an exact regulatory instrument because the final decision remains in the selectors' hands. Instead of restrictive selection and funding formulas, checklists of ideal characteristics support decisions
- Clarifies, based on the data of customer expectation and internal process improvement, how the library professional can prioritize difficult budgeting and licensing decisions and evaluate complex selection criteria
- Remains relevant to the peculiarities of each resource, electronic or print, by providing guidelines, best practices, and ideal scenarios that assist the selectors in applying professional expertise that remains the last and best deciding factor
- Provides a clear sense of direction to the collection development and acquisitions process, and allows print and electronic formats to complement each other and strengthen the library's offerings to its community

Customers, vendors, those who authorize the library's budget, and library professionals all make up this environment, and all possess information crucial to creating responsive policy documents and strong collections. Without this information, the policy might calcify and inhibit quality collection building and acquisitions. Learning documents allow information from the environment to penetrate and improve policy, and, through this policy selection, decisions benefit from rich information environments. Policies become the springboard for a continuous collaborative dialog within the library's group of selectors and acquisitions staff, between diverse library processes, and between the library and the community it serves.

A policy is a learning document when the policy is periodically renewed with continuous discussion and revision. The library professionals involved reconfirm the core values of a collection and adjust selection to new products and innovative services as they arise. The continued review inherent in learning documents also means that a diverse cross-section of the library regularly discusses what is working in a policy and what could be made better. In this way, all the documents that make up a policy dossier become learning documents. For an example of a collection development policy treated as a living, learning document, see Yale University Library (2004).

Regular discussion allows participants to learn from each other, and the documents themselves benefit from continuous improvement. Selectors, acquisitions staff, public service staff, technical experts, library and community leaders, and even customers can share new ideas, new technologies, and new skills learned during the daily management and use of electronic products. This regular learning produces innovations in budgeting, technology, and purchase negotiation that can be lost because they go unshared without regular face-to-face meetings. The collaborative contribution to a policy life cycle best facilitates this kind of communication.

Policy Life Cycle

The existence of a collection development and acquisitions policy that guides library professionals toward a collection of continuing relevance to the library's community is not a linear, one-time project but instead is a cycle of learning and review. The life cycle outlined below allows input of information into the collection development and acquisitions processes guided by the experience and priorities of professionals with the purpose of the entire organization as a guiding principle.

The life cycle of a policy that is a learning document relevant to the daily activities of collection development and acquisitions has the following characteristics.

- Begin with a learning meeting. Hold a learning meeting open to all concerned, from selectors to administrators to customers. Discover what is successful about policies you have now, written or unwritten. What would make a policy better? What would an ideal policy look like? How can you get from the policy you have to this ideal?

- Promote stewardship. To collect and draft the innumerable details, designate a group of stewards to lead the new policy through a collaborative group learning process. These stewards should use the assessment cycle to gather information from a wide range of people affected by the policy. Include selectors, acquisitions professionals, catalogers, systems professionals, public service professionals, administrators, members of the funding authority, and customers, and investigate the innovations of other libraries.

- Use frequent data collection. The assessment cycle creates a policy relevant to the current environments inside and outside a library. What are library customer expectations for the collection? What are library professionals' expectations for vendors and their products? How can library professionals improve the efficiency (for example, deciding to purchase quickly but with all the facts) and effectiveness (for example, spending money "wisely") of our purchasing process? What data should we collect to show us how our purchase process is improving (for example, time required to make a purchase or more customers served for the money spent)? How can we measure the outcomes on our customers of the products we decide to purchase (for example, do products for which we request improvements of the vendors indeed change or what is the impact of the products on our customers' research habits)?

- Draft a policy. Write a draft policy, or set of policy documents. The stewards can be responsible for this first version, or they can solicit assistance from others.
- Review the draft. The stewards seek discussion, revision, and final approval by each of the groups interviewed above. Open and public contribution to and endorsement of the new policy helps everyone accept it as the way forward because they have been a part of its creation and have ownership.
- Pilot sections of the draft. At times, suggested parts of the new policy may be controversial. Consider adding them on a trial basis, as pilots. Actively collect feedback on the pilot points' daily effectiveness. After three to six months, use this feedback to decide whether to keep, improve, or jettison the trial point.
- Use periodic review. Review the new policy's success with regular learning meetings, convened monthly, quarterly, or semiannually, to incorporate new information learned from the environment and update the policy accordingly. The more who are involved, the more relevant the policy will continue to be.
- Use periodic revision. At a certain point, members of these ongoing review meetings will conclude that the environment inside and outside the library has changed enough to warrant a revision of the policy as a whole, and the process starts again from the top.

This policy life cycle is flexible enough to contain infinite variations that fit the library's needs. At any point of this cycle, the stewards can recruit others for a steering committee, or panel of experts, to provide guidance or help with the data gathering. The size of the library will influence the number of professionals managing each phase. The phases may be changed to best fit the complexity of the library's collection development and acquisitions efforts. However, the most important aspect of the life cycle is the collaborative participation of as many different sources of information as can be included.

Some would argue that this process, particularly the gathering of input and approval of the draft from so many people is too time-consuming. They would rightly assert that a policy written in an appointed committee and approved by one or more administrators would be more efficient. However, the recipients of this policy, those who will have to put it to use, would not have directly participated in the development process—in the discussion, revision, and approval. "Buy-in" (characterized by a daily use of the policy) will be a difficult sell and will likely not occur because these people do not have ownership through participation. Without ownership, and without personal participation in a regular review of the policy, a person could find it easier to put the policy in a drawer and forget it in daily decision making.

Additionally, some would question the wisdom of having a policy that changes over time. If one of the main advantages of a policy is the lending of consistency to decision making, a policy that rarely changes would seem more logical. This makes sense if the policy is the final arbiter in the decision process. However, I would argue that, with or without a collection development and acquisitions policy, selectors and acquisitions professionals are the final arbiters of every decision, not a document. A competent professional making intelligent and conscientious decisions within the influence of the organization purpose lends consistency to collection development and acquisitions. A document will only ever be one of several tools within this decision making. Treating the policy as a living, learning document (or dossier) makes it a powerful instrument that enables these professionals to manage the complex selection and acquisitions processes they face daily. Above all, a policy continuously updated as a learning document contributes vitality and relevant information to the intellectual activity of creating a collection valued by the community that the library serves.

A Word on Short Documents, Bullets, and Prioritization

Matching the benefits of an electronic resource to the existing content and desired direction of a library's largely print collection can be daunting, because licensing, budgeting, and delivery to the library customer overwhelm us in detail and complexity. In order for the policy to assist in the selection process, it is best divided into a series of short documents, and rendered usable with bulleted lists and prioritization.

Examples of shorter documents that can make up a larger policy are:

- A strategic statement that describes the ideal collection in two, five, ten years. For examples, see JISC (2000) and Cornell University Library (2000).
- A *genre statement* attached to the main collection development and acquisitions policy, or to each of the subject-specific policies, that states special considerations for electronic resources that would affect the main policy's selection criteria. For examples, see Weintraub and McKinney (1999) and Faulkner and Hahn (2001).
- Selection criteria checklists and tip sheets for details, such as license and price negotiation, technical considerations, use statistics, budget details, and user interface requirements. For examples, see University of Texas General Libraries (2003).

A way to manage large lists within a policy statement is to prioritize their contents by what is most important to the selection goals and process. You can divide these lists according to three levels of importance, for example:

- *Need* means that the library must have this element (of, for example, an interface, license terms, or pricing structure), or we don't buy the product.
- *Want* means that this element is important to the library, but other considerations (for example, lower price or more simultaneous users at no cost) could make not having this element palatable.
- *Plus* means that this element is nice to have, and, if it exists, it could either make us choose favorably between two otherwise similar products, or it could make the loss of a "Want" more palatable.

The prioritization will reflect the library's unique situation. The advantage of this prioritization is that the library as a whole measures importance and supports cool objectivity during what can be pressured moments with a salesperson.

Paragraphs in a collection development and acquisitions policy will rarely, if ever, be read. Write paragraphs initially, because for most of us that is a more natural way to write. Then prepare the final draft by tightening and clarifying the language into single-line, active-verb statements. Organize these statements into a progression that is easy to follow when scanning a page. For example:

- Paragraphs are not read.
- Bulleted statements are.
- To create bulleted statements,
  - write paragraphs initially,
  - then convert the paragraphs into:
    - concise active statements
    - with a natural progression.
- Most reader's eyes will alight on this list,
  - before reading the paragraphs surrounding it.

Because the frustrations of daily tasks at times makes efficacy more attractive than serving the best interests of the customer, these documents can help ensure that the customer takes highest priority, not adhocracy. Multiple documents break the monolithic "policy" down into manageable portions. Continued review of all aspects of the policy, involving many people inside and outside the library, provides fertile ground for imaginative solutions in the best interest of customer service.

Selection Criteria

Of the learning documents created, the selection criteria for electronic resources will be among the most important for collection development and acquisitions. Purchase of print resources means that the library can build a physical collection that is permanent (not geologically so, just beyond our lifetimes) and useful to both current and future library customers. The advent of electronic resources shifts the expectations of collection development and acquisitions.

As an electronic resources manager of over 350 databases and other online products, I spent more than half of every day responding to access problems. When customers could not open and use an electronic product, a small minority contacted the library with a description of the problem. Note that by then the customers already considered themselves behind schedule. They had expected to access the resource and be on their way, but they found themselves shuffled into my e-mail inbox. The clock of my responsibility to get them back to the business of creating knowledge had begun ticking before they contacted me, and the ball of yarn that I had to unravel before their patience ran out was often tangled and confusing. I first pulled a likely set of five or ten "strings," or potential problems, that may have existed in the vast network of virtual connections between a customer's mouse and the denial of service. Once I saw one or more promising directions, I traded e-mails with whoever managed that portion of the vast network to find out whether the problem was on "my" side, somewhere within my library's network (over which I personally had no control), on "their" side somewhere in the network of library consortia, vendors, or the amalgam of service providers that make up the Internet.

Usually no single direction clearly presented itself, and I would begin the task of unraveling several balls of yarn at one time. Five to fifty e-mails later (I kept a time-study log during a two-week period and discovered that number), I would get that customer (and every other customer who experienced the same problem, I hoped) back on their researcherly way. One customer e-mail would start all that activity, and, during the middle of a semester, I would average five to six access problem emails per day. Meanwhile, I had to contribute to improving the electronic resource acquisitions processes and the delivery infrastructure that the library used to manage these resources; then our major journal subscriptions became electronic-only, and all these responsibilities increased exponentially.

Although print collections still make up a major proportion of the library's collection, the library customer benefits from a diminishing reliance on physical location and on an expanded access to formerly obscure resources via his or her computer desktop. Licensure (rather than purchase) of electronic resources means that the library has the opportunity to regularly review and improve what the library's collection means to the customer. Even when balancing the complexity and intransigence of many of these licensed resources against the advantages, few would dispute the enormous worth of electronic resources.

Effective management of the difficulties inherent in the turbulence of electronic resource management begins during the selection process. When successful, this process relies on both traditional and electronic-resource-specific criteria to identify and reduce product difficulties at time of purchase. The collection development and acquisitions professionals have the responsibility to not only create collections useful to the needs of the library community, but also to contribute to the customers' experiences of these products by establishing through clear and firm selection criteria that the resources fit smoothly into the library's electronic delivery infrastructure.

Traditional Selection Criteria

Because the desired result, meeting the library customers' needs, is the same for print and electronic, most selection criteria for electronic resources will be natural extensions of established collection development and acquisitions practices. Before the advent of computers in libraries, S. R. Ranganathan (1966) suggested a list of selection criteria that seem as if written to apply to the world of electronic information delivery:

- Books are for use.
- Every reader his book.
- Every book its reader.
- Save the reader's time.
- A library is a growing organism.

When included as part of the policy review process, these statements, like no others, prompt discussions that will prove valuable in the creation of a learning document.

Most collection development texts (Clayton and Gorman 2001; Gardner 1981), measure a product for selection by the following traditional criteria.

- The resource is relevant to library customers' interests, reading levels, need for timeliness, and appropriate depth of content–ranging from recreational to scholarly.
- The resource is packaged with acceptable aesthetic appeal, navigability, and physical quality, including longevity.
- The resource is suitable for the collection, given current library holdings, the need to increase holdings in a subject area, and customer demand.
- The resource's price fits within the library's overall budget and takes a reasonable proportion of that budget, given the product's usefulness to library customers.

Core selection criteria will already exist whether written or understood as part of a library's general practice. All traditional criteria are easily applied to electronic resources.

- For example, in one library, selectors may feel it necessary to consider the following. Does the content of the electronic resource meet customer needs for *full text* and does it augment or replace current print holdings?
- Does the interface design meet legally required and locally important standards of usability and accessibility?
- Does the pricing model establish a recurring subscription expense that the budget can support over time?

Established professional practice provides a firm foundation for well-crafted electronic resource selection criteria.

Criteria Unique to Electronic Resources

Electronic resources will also come with a set of special considerations. These special criteria can get quite specific given the technical and service needs of a particular library. During the review and learning process, library professionals can develop criteria by analyzing typical purchases recently concluded or currently underway, by interviewing vendors to discover what the library could best contribute early in a typical transaction, and finally by finding policy documents of other libraries (UT General Libraries 2003; Yale 2004) and consortia (CSU SEIR 2003; JISC 2001).

Our example library, introduced in the preceding subsection, developed a list, and the first items listed were as follows:

- If moving from print to electronic access, was the print used often enough to change from ownership to subscription? How complete is the electronic version compared with the print?

- Will archiving, back-file coverage, and update frequency be adequate for the future needs of the library's customers?
- Do technical advantages, such as improved accessibility, currency, searching, indexing, limiting, and *linking* to other content outweigh technical concerns, such as hardware and software requirements, Web *browser* compatibility, infrastructure required for storage (if necessary), delivery, authentication and printing, or other output?
- How restrictive or advantageous is the license? (This question will be developed into a separate document listing desired license parameters. See Chapter 6, Licensing.)
- How robust is the vendor's technical support, user support, and training?

The technology, licensing and pricing models, and customer expectations can change fundamentally every eighteen months not once a decade. These criteria specific to electronic resource management need review more frequently than most other parts of the collection development and acquisitions policy.

The advice to create bulleted checklists is worth repeating. These lists, especially if they are published on easily accessed Web pages, help selectors when they are on the phone with salespeople, when they are fielding requests for products from library customers, and when they are choosing between competing products with complex offerings. Publishing these lists as Web documents also helps clearly inform vendors of the library's expectations for a product. The collection development and acquisitions policy is a tool for, not a mandate for, the selectors' decisions, and selection criteria should always be helpful, not restrictive. The review and learning process will ensure that selection criteria remain a relevant partner for selectors in their daily tasks.

Conclusion

Collection development and acquisitions of electronic resources are complex and data-intensive processes. Successful libraries manage these processes with attention to user needs and with the support of regular, collaborative review. Customer needs assessment always keeps the library customers' needs at the forefront of decision processes. Library professionals create relevant and effective policies and selection criteria through regular review and learning processes. Library professionals ensure the success of this review and learning process with the input of all library professionals affected by the policy and learning from instances when the policy is successful as well as the need for future improvements.

Successful library professionals implement policies not as a dictating authority but as an adaptive tool to maintain the core purpose of the library and to remain current with changes in the environment of electronic resource management. A library's collection is only as strong as its selection and acquisitions processes. When selectors and acquisitions professionals are supported by a collaboratively updated learning document that reflects the needs of the library customers and other library staff, the professionals have a document with the objective strength and comprehensive criteria upon which to build a collection of value to the community it serves.

References

Association of Research Libraries (ARL) and Texas A&M University (TAM). 2002. *LibQUAL+TM Spring 2002 survey results: Aggregate survey results, volume 1.* Washington, DC: Association of Research Libraries.

Baruchson-Arbib, Shifra and Frida Shor. 2002. The use of electronic information sources by Israeli college students. *The Journal of Academic Librarianship* 28 (4):255–257.

California State University (CSU). Systemwide Electronic Information Resources (SEIR). "EAR Documents." ©2003. *Electronic Access to Information Resources (EAR) Committee.* CSU SEIR. URL: http://seir.calstate.edu/acom/ear/docs/index.shtml (Accessed September 14, 2004).

Chapman, Liz. 2001. *Managing acquisitions in library and information services.* London: Library Association Publishing.

Christie, Anne and Laurel Kristick. 2001. Developing an Online Science Journal Collection: A Quick Tool For Assigning Priorities. *Issues in Science and Technology Librarianship* 30 (Spring) URL: http://www.library.ucsb.edu/istl/01-spring/article2.html (Accessed September 14, 2004).

Clayton, Peter and G. E. Gorman. 2001. *Managing information resources in libraries: Collection management in theory and practice.* London: Library Association Publishing.

Cornell University Library. "Cornell University Library Digital Futures Plan July 2000 to June 2002." ©2000. *StaffWeb.* Cornell University Library. URL: http://www.library.cornell.edu/staffweb/CULDigitalFuturesPlan/ (Accessed September 14, 2004).

Digital Library Federation (DLF) and Council on Library and Information Resources (CLIR). "Dimensions and use of the scholarly information environment: Introduction to a data set assembled by the Digital Library Federation and Outsell, Inc." ©2002. *CLIR Publications and Resources.* CLIR. URL: http://www.clir.org/pubs/reports/pub110/contents.html (Accessed September 14, 2004).

Dillon, Dennis. 2002. Fishing the electronic river: Disruptive technologies, the Unlibrary, and the ecology of information. *Journal of Library Administration* 36 (3):45–58.

Drucker, Peter F. 2001. The next society. *The Economist* 361 (November 3):3–5.

Evans, G. Edward. 2000. *Developing library and information center collections.* 4th ed. Englewood, CO: Libraries Unlimited.

Faulkner, Lila and Karla Hahn. 2001. Selecting electronic publications: The development of a genre statement. *Issues in Science and Technology Librarianship* 30 (Spring). URL: http://www.istl.org/istl/01-spring/article1.html (Accessed September 14, 2004).

Gardner, Richard K. 1981. *Library collections, their origin, selection, and development.* New York: McGraw-Hill.

Gooden, Angela. 2001. Citation analysis of chemistry doctoral dissertations: An Ohio State University case study. *Issues in Science and Technology Librarianship* 32 (Fall). URL: http://www.istl.org/01-fall/refereed.html (Accessed September 14, 2004).

Hiller, Steve. 2002. How different are they? A comparison by academic area of library use, priorities, and information needs at the University of Washington. *Issues in Science and Technology Librarianship* 33 (Winter). URL http://www.istl.org/istl/02-winter/article1.html (Accessed September 14, 2004).

Jewell, Tim. "Elicense survey data: Appendix from a forthcoming Digital Library Federation report." ©2001. *A Webhub for Developing Administrative Metadata for Electronic Resource Management.* Elicensestudy. URL: http://www.library.cornell.edu/cts/elicensestudy/u-washington/FinalAppendixB.xls (Accessed September 14, 2004).

Joint Information Systems Committee (JISC). "3-Year Collection Strategy" ©2000. *Collections.* JISC. URL: http://www.jisc.ac.uk/index.cfm?name=collections_coll_strat (Accessed September 14, 2004).

———. "JISC Collections Development Policy." ©2001. *Collections.* JISC. URL: http://www.jisc.ac.uk/index.cfm?name=collections_dev_pol (Accessed September 14, 2004).

Ileperuma, Sriyani. 2002. Information gathering behaviour of arts scholars in Sri Lankan universities: A critical evaluation. *Collection Building* 21 (1):22–31.

Lee, Wade M. and Robin N. Sinn. 2002. Scientists and the journal article: Choices for access. *Journal of Interlibrary Loan, Document Delivery & Information Supply* 12 (3):37–56.

Lukenbill, W. Bernard. 2002. *Collection development for a new century in the school library media center.* Westport, CT: Greenwood Press.

Monopoli, Maria, David Nicholas, Panagiotis Georgiou, and Mariana Korfiati. 2002. A user-oriented evaluation of digital libraries: Case study the "electronic journals" service of the library and information service of the University of Patras, Greece. *ASLIB Proceedings* 54 (2):103–117.

OCLC (Online Computer Library Center). "OCLC white paper on the information habits of college students: How academic librarian can influence students' web-based information choices." ©2002. *OCLC: A worldwide library cooperative.* OCLC. URL: http://www5.oclc.org/downloads/community/informationhabits.pdf (Accessed September 14, 2004).

Pew Internet & American Life Project. "The internet goes to college: How students are living in the future with today's technology." ©2002. *Pew Internet & American Life Project.* Pew Research Center. URL: http://www.pewinternet.org/reports/toc.asp?Report=71 (Accessed September 14, 2004).

Quigley, Jane, David Peck, Sara Rutter, and Elizabeth McKee Williams. 2002. Making choices: Factors in the selection of information resources among science faculty at the University of Michigan, results of a survey conducted July–September, 2000. *Issues in Science and Technology Librarianship* 34 (Spring). URL: http://www.istl.org/02-spring/refereed.html (Accessed September 14, 2004).

Ranganathan, S. R. 1966. *Library book selection.* New York: Asia Publishing House.

Rodger, Joey and Charlie Robinson. 1998. Conference Call: Purveyors or Prescribers? Joey Rodger and Charlie Robinson debate wants versus needs. *American Libraries* 29(5):66–71.

Spiller, David. 2000. *Providing materials for library users.* London: Library Association Publishing.

University of Texas at Austin (UT). General Libraries. "Collection development policies." ©2003. *Collection Development Policies, Principles & Guidelines.* University of Texas at Austin. General Libraries. Collections & Information Resources Division. URL: http://www.lib.utexas.edu/admin/cird/cird.html (Accessed September 14, 2004).

Weintraub, Jennifer and McKinney, Janet. 1999. The development and use of a genre statement for electronic journals. *Serials Librarian* 36 (3/4):429–434.

Yale University Library. "Managing electronic resources at Yale University Library." ©2004. Yale University Library. URL: http://www.library.yale.edu/ecollections/eresmanage.html (Accessed September 14, 2004).

Younger, Jennifer. 2002. From the inside out: An organizational view of electronic resources and collection development. *Journal of Library Administration* 36 (3):19–38.

Further Reading

Baker, Sharon L. and Karen L. Wallace. 2002. *The responsive public library.* Englewood, CO: Libraries Unlimited.

Billings, Harold. 2002. *Magic and hypersystems: Constructing the information-sharing library.* Chicago, IL: American Library Association.

Brooks, Sam. 2001. Integration of information resources and collection development strategy. *Journal of Academic Librarianship* 27 (4):316–319.

Case, Beau David. 2000. Love's labour's lost: The failure of traditional selection practice in the acquisition of Humanities electronic texts. *Library Trends* 48 (4):729–747.

Dilevko, Juris and Lisa Gottlieb. 2002. Print sources in an electronic age: A vital part of the research process for undergraduate students. *The Journal of Academic Librarianship* 28 (6):381–392.

International Coalition of Library Consortia (ICOLC). "Statement of current perspective and preferred practices for the selection and purchase of electronic information: Update No. 1, new developments in e-journal licensing" ©2001. *Statements and Documents.* ICOLC. URL: http://www.library.yale.edu/consortia/2001currentpractices.htm (Accessed September 14, 2004).

Jordon, Jay. 2002. New directions in electronic collection development. *Journal of Library Administration* 36 (3):5–17.

Kovacs, Diane K. and Robinson, Kara L. 2004. *The Kovacs guide to electronic library collection development: Essential core subject collections, selection criteria, and guidelines.* New York: Neal-Schuman Publishers.

Lee, Stuart D. 2002. *Electronic collection development: A practical guide.* New York: Neal-Schuman and London: Library Association Publishing.

Lee, Sul H. 2002. *Electronic resources and collection development.* Binghamton, New York: Haworth Press.

Mack, Daniel C. ed. 2003. *Collection development policies: New directions for changing collections.* Binghamton, NY: Haworth Press.

Maxwell, Kim and Bob Biossy. 2002. The art of claiming. *The Serials Librarian* 42 (3/4):229–233.

Metz, Paul. 2000. Principles of selection for electronic resources. *Library Trends* 48 (4):711–738.

Neelankavil, John. 2003. Indian innovative ways are more than digitization: *Bhodhivanam,* the library's forest environment. *Library Philosophy and Practice* 5 (2). URL: http://www.webpages.uidaho.edu/~mbolin/neelankavil.pdf (Accessed September 14, 2004).

Thomas, Sarah E. 2002. Think globally, act locally: Electronic resources and collection development. *Journal of Library Administration* 36 (3):93–107.

CHAPTER 6

Licensing

The impact of the relationships of libraries to content aggregators and publishers (hereafter combined under the term "vendors"), vendors to authors, and authors to libraries on the economics of electronic publishing, are under an intense discussion called the *scholarly communication debate* (Bailey 2004). This chapter will not enter into this debate; instead, it will focus more narrowly on how the licensing of electronic resources by libraries contributes to and is influenced by the relationships between vendors, libraries, and authors. Since, in its simplest conceptualization, licensure seeks to alleviate the difficulties that arise from the ease of transferability of electronic content from one possessor to another, licensure does not allow libraries to take ownership of most electronically published content, as they can with the purchase of a print resource. Instead, with a *license*, the library gains for its service community, including the authors of published content, rights to access content in an electronic resource, in return for which the library agrees to terms of access that protect the vendors' revenue streams.

More broadly defined, licenses are agreements between two parties concerning what will be given up and gained by both parties. When library professionals understand copyright and other granted rights and understand what service needs the license must protect for the library they can enter into licenses with a clear sense of the following:

- Rights already protected by law that library professionals may inadvertently sign away
- Rights library professionals are entitled to ask for in any license
- Rights library professionals need to ask for to protect the research experience of the library customer

This chapter will provide an overview of the complex activity of electronic resource licensing by libraries and how library professionals can manage this new relationship with old and new partners in the publishing world. This chapter discusses what to expect of the license as a contract, how to set beneficial license provisions in advance, how to negotiate license terms, and how to manage vendor relationships. The unique circumstances of each library and its relationships with vendors and customers, coupled with the fast pace of change within the economics of electronic resources, mean that this topic will become a source of constant, collaborative learning for all library professionals involved in the purchase process.

The Economics of Publishing and Open Access

Library service communities that are as diverse from each other as municipalities are from corporations choose, through their libraries, to pool their resources for a collection accessible for all members of a particular community. Libraries provide their service communities access to one or a few copies of high quality, desirable content that many can use. Through the library, community members are able to access far greater print and electronic collections than would be available to them in a world of one copy per reader. Viewed through this lens of responsibility, licensing becomes for library professionals the central activity through which they may protect their customers' rights to freely access published content. With an understanding of the economics of publishing and open access, library professionals can negotiate the licenses both acceptable to vendors and beneficial to library customers.

Bookstores, and through them publishers, seek profit from a one-copy-per-user model, and thus a dialectical tension arises. On the one hand, libraries pool information resources and reduce the cost of (i.e., the expenditure on) these resources. On the other hand, the production of these information resources is costly for three types of producers. Publishers of content, aggregators of published content repackaged into new products, and authors of content all seek a profitable return on investment of capital and labor for producing salable content. Nonprofit publishers may seem an exception to this drive for revenue, but these organizations seek revenues to support the cost of their publishing efforts and at times seek an income higher than production cost to cover other, non-publishing organizational costs. To maximize revenue, vendors (publishers and aggregators) would prefer a one-copy-per-user model of information access. Content authors—including researchers, writers, and artists—bridge the dialectic between the libraries' open-access pooling of resources and the producers' seeking of revenue through restricted access.

Content authors are the key to this tension between access and revenue. Content authors invest part of their creative effort into understanding other's published knowledge and often rely on libraries to provide access to a large portion of this knowledge. Many library customers never reach the level of effort that results in publication. These library customers use library collections solely to create personal understanding. Select library customers, however, use library collections to create knowledge that is published and consumed by other authors, creating a rich system of *scholarly communication*. In the scholarly communication economy, authors are often not paid outright for publication; instead, they gain the research grant monies, tenure, pay, job security, and prestige that result from publication. The irony within this economy lies in the fact that whereas vendors rely on the revenue generated by sales of these authors' efforts, most authors rely on libraries to amass few-copies-per-community collections that the authors could never afford for themselves. Thus, the library creates a few-copies-per-community collection for the benefit of authors who in turn rely on vendors to publish the authors' works. Vendors rely on the revenue of a one-copy-per-user system to stay in business and seek to bring the copy-to-user ratio the closest possible to one-to-one. In the print world, this balance is preserved with special copyright and other intellectual property exclusions that the library has from the vendors' one-copy-per-user ideal, exclusions that protect these authors' access to knowledge by protecting libraries' right to build few-copies-per-community collections. Electronic resources have upset this balance of the three-cornered relationship between vendors, authors, and libraries.

Copyright law expressly states the belief that protecting open access to published content is an engine for human learning and innovation and at the same time recognizes that revenue from content is the engine of further publication. Copyright law has balanced the tension between the open-access intent of libraries and the revenue generation pursued by producers. United States copyright law (U.S. GPO 2003) relies on the following: Section 107: Fair Use Doctrine; Section 108: Rules for Copying by Libraries and Archives; Section 109: the First Sale Doctrine; the concept defined by copyright law as "public domain"; and the 1998 Digital Millennium Copyright Act (LC Copyright Office 1998). Under the Section 107: Fair Use Doctrine, copyrighted material may be used for "criticism, comment, news reporting, teaching, scholarship, or research" without the user paying the producer or asking for permission. Under Section 108: Copying by Libraries and Archives, library professionals may make a single copy of an item at the request of a patron, or for archival purposes in case of loss, theft, deterioration, or technical obsolescence. Under Section 109: the First Sale Doctrine, the purchaser of copyrighted work (a library, in this case) has the right to resell, rent, lease, or lend the work without paying or asking permission of the copyright holder. The public domain portion of copyright law relaxes copyright restrictions on the reproducing of works after a certain passage of time, thus allowing unfettered reproduction for generations that follow that of the author. What electronic resources means for this publication revenue and open access balance was legislatively explored in 1998 when the copyright law was amended by the Digital Millennium Copyright Act, which seeks to control the use of a copyrighted work based on its format, software, or electronic, instead of content.

Library professionals are stewards of the collections that communities have shaped for themselves, and vendors are interested in the solvency of their respective organizations. In the realm of print publication, copyright has been an accepted arbiter of transfer of ownership and revenue protection. Print objects are tangible and thus controllable because ownership of print is difficult to transfer. Photocopies are not perfect replications and are not likely to replace originals in the marketplace. When I loan you my copy of a book, I no longer have it for my own use.

Content in electronic form, however, opens new vistas for ease of transfer and subsequent loss of revenue. When a book is in electronic form, I can use a computer to make an exact electronic copy to give to you and retain a pristine copy for my own use. Because of this ability, libraries have a more difficult time maintaining trust for their side of the copyright bargain on behalf of the revenue-seeking producers. The vendors' worldview—ownership as revenue-generating property—shows revenue slipping away into the streams of too-open access. Libraries agree to protect the revenue for the vendors in exchange for being able to provide open access by patrons to a communitywide collection.

Library professionals and vendors have more of an interest in maintaining the access-revenue tension than ever before. Vendors do not make money if authors cannot access an open library collection, and open collections would not exist if vendors could not make money from publishing. At issue is the quality of the content available to all three groups: libraries, vendors, and authors (along with the majority readers who consume but do not create). Whereas vendors rely on the revenue generated from publication to create, aggregate, and provide quality information, library professionals, as stewards of library collections, rely on vendors to provide to library customers content of a consistent and dependable quality. Authors, the libraries' constituents and vendors' suppliers, rely on this quality content to support the efforts they put into consistent, dependable output. In the world of electronic publication, libraries and vendors enter into license agreements to protect this three-part balance, and these license agreements define users, uses, and access in order to both protect vendor revenue and help libraries protect their community members' rights to open access.

License as Contract

Copyright has allowed library customers to enjoy access to print and vendors to enjoy revenue generation from their works within a set of rules that maintained the balance. Electronic resources throw that relationship out of equilibrium, and licenses are the new way in which library professionals and vendors renegotiate the economics of publication. Unfortunately for both parties, the number of relationships library professionals have with vendors and vendors have with libraries multiplies the number of licenses for which each must maintain records. Intellectual property law, rights management, and access management become the daily work of library professionals and vendor professionals alike. The expense of time and labor required to manage these licenses becomes a real cost for any licensed product.

Contracts can look intimidating to the most courageous among us, yet with the right set of tools anyone who is not a lawyer can feel competent to read, edit, and sign a contract that reflects the best interests of their library and the library's constituency. One should take advantage of the expertise of a lawyer when available. Know, however, that library professionals also bring expertise that lawyers, unless they are also library professionals, do not bring to the reading of a contract. Library professionals, as stewards of the library the community has created for itself, are the most aware of the issues of access that the license contract is attempting to control. When they read contracts, library professionals are guardians of three entities: users, uses, and access. Vendors, on the other hand, are guardians of their organizations' revenue and are interested in controlling the users, uses, and access that a licensed payment covers in order to increase the margin of return on their investment. License contracts allow both parties to protect their interests as much as is possible and still come to an agreement.

I am not a lawyer. I offer the following thoughts only as a starting place for the reader's further learning. The Association of Research Libraries (2003) offers an online lyceum that teaches license review and negotiation, and Lesley Ellen Harris has recently published the book *Licensing Digital Content: A Practical Guide for Librarians* (2002). These are both designed and written by lawyers and are excellent introductions.

What I will do is offer a window on the detail that a manager of the electronic resource purchase process must keep track of, and I will offer ways to not have that detail overwhelm the effectiveness of the process. I will begin with the basic fact that a license does not confer ownership, and agreeing to a license does not bring the same protections to the recipient of the content as a purchaser of that content had in the past. A license is a set of rights granted, usually for a stated amount of time, in exchange for cash payment or other consideration. Both the rights granted or taken away and the consideration that is exchanged result from a mutual agreement by both parties, called a *meeting of minds*. The agreement process consists of the following steps (ARL 2003):

- An offer is an initial written license given by one party to the other.
- Under mutuality, both parties have a "meeting of minds" over terms and conditions.
- Upon acceptance, both parties agree to the terms, usually, but not always, with a signature affixed to a final version of the contract.
- Consideration, usually in the form of payment, is tendered and accepted in exchange for the agreed rights and restrictions.
- During enforcement, penalties expressed in a license can be exacted for failure to live up to the terms of the contract.

When a license agreement is offered, it becomes the basis for negotiation. Both parties have the right to change any and all terms of a license during the mutuality stage, and changing any part of a license is a refusal of the first offer and creates a new offer, which is, in essence, a new license. After acceptance is reached, consideration (payment) turns the offer into a transaction and seals the contract. After consideration, the license enters the period of enforcement, and the tenets of contract law assume that the terms represent a meeting of minds and that no party was coerced by the superior bargaining power of the other, so ignorance of the terms of an agreement is not a valid argument against enforcement.

Table 6.1 describes a few of the licensing essentials that I learned by talking with others and by attending classes on licensing. The best way to learn to read a license for the best interests of use, users, and access is to continually discuss the process with others.

Use the facts presented in this subsection and in Table 6.1 as the beginning of your education, and avidly read other library professionals' experiences with licenses. Learning what terms in a contract may negatively impact the library and what terms your library wants to see included is a complex process and takes time and experience. Learn from others and collaborate on expanding the knowledge of all concerned library professionals in your library. The resource list at the end of this chapter points to recent additions to the knowledge of license terms from librarians around the world. The section below on license management will outline

Table 6.1 Selected Essentials for Each Stage of the Licensing Process	
Stage	**Essential**
Offer	• You may strike through the text in an offer (a copy of a license) from a vendor, insert your own text, add your own text in an addendum, or send an entirely new contract to the vendor. • Know the rights you have already so as to not lose them in the license, for example: fair use rights for library patrons and libraries' rights to copy for non-commercial purposes.
Mutuality	• Mutuality occurs most easily when the parties understand each other's needs. Communicate the library's needs, and work to elicit the needs of the vendor. • When you do not like something in a contract, find out from the vendor why it is there and use that information to work toward a mutually agreeable solution. • Know in advance why you need certain license provisions to exist, or not exist, so that you can be clear with the vendor and work toward a mutually agreeable solution.
Acceptance	• At acceptance, the last version of a license that both parties know the other has seen is the version in effect after payment has been made and accepted. • Make sure (through written documentation) that both parties have seen a copy of the license version you are comfortable with before you send payment.
Consideration	• If you make changes to the license, clearly number and date the versions. • If the first offer, or version of the license, was changed in any way, clarify in writing which version of the license you are agreeing to when you send payment. • When consideration (payment or other in-kind trade) exchanges hands, mutuality has occurred and the license is enforceable. • Payment, even without signature on a physical copy of the license, is acceptance. This is equally true for the library's mailing of the check as for the vendor's cashing of the check.

(Continued)

Enforcement	• Just like libraries, vendors can be held to rights and responsibilities within terms of a contract. For example: Vendors can have responsibilities to collect usage data, to not violate user privacy, or to not create unreasonable barriers to access.
	• If the contract has no stated time of cancellation, or if consideration is again exchanged at time of renewal without change to the original contract, the original contract terms remain enforceable. Because of this, library professionals are advised to know such dates as the date the terms go into effect, the date a renewal decision is needed by the vendor, and the date the license lapses due to nonpayment.
	• Clearly know cancellation policies and rights of termination, for example, appeals processes, length of notice before termination of access, and recourse for wrongful termination.
	• Vendors can be responsible for a clearly stated guarantee of content and notification if content changes substantially within the time covered by the license. "Clearly" means in writing, not verbally.
	• The library has the right to ensure reasonably low liability on its part, and should not accept responsibility for the actions of users that the library cannot control.
	• Be clear about "controlling law," or the state or country within which disputes are settled. Prefer the library's own state or country.

how library professional can take their learning one step further and collaboratively document the terms beneficial for the library and its customers in order to streamline the licensing process. First, we will discuss the primary goal of licensing for the library professional, that of protecting users, uses, and access for the library's customers.

Protecting Users, Uses, and Access

Because libraries are stewards of a collection for a community, library professionals are charged with providing access to those collections that is of the highest possible quality. Unlike print resources owned by the library, products licensed from vendors can come with access restrictions unique to each product. As the number of electronic resources grows, the complexity of managing the details of each contract grows as well. The best way to manage this complexity is with foreknowledge. In order to simplify the licensing process for you and the vendor, know what you want of every license before entering into individual agreements.

License provisions can be classified into users, uses, and access; the library–vendor relationship given the three provisions; and the impact of a contract's definition of these provisions on the customers' experiences with the licensed electronic resource. First, define the users the library serves, both in broad terms and by special populations. Second, define uses of electronic resources important to the library and its community, which can range from the article printouts, course packs, and interlibrary loan to the download of large data sets. Third, access is an important component of a product's service, but what a library assumes is self-evident and not necessary to clarify can be a point of contention for a vendor if not written into the contract. For example, access can be restricted by overly complex *authentication* protocols insisted on by the vendor, but not acceptable to the library. Fourth, in the vendor relationship, the library has the right to expect certain actions from the vendor (for example, to not substantially change the content of a product without notice and remedy if the change is negative), and the library must know what responsibilities the vendor expects of the library (for example, to properly authenticate users of the product).

Finally, license management also includes attention to the impact of each license on a library's technical and staff infrastructure. The library must be able to support license terms, not just monetarily, but also in the time and labor necessary to implement parts of a license. For example, authenticating remote users requires software, equipment, and expertise; difficult-to-use interfaces require instruction efforts and may hinder services to the disabled; and very short renewal notification periods require more effort to keep track of than library professionals may have time for.

Uncovering past experience and current knowledge from a wide range of people will help the library build documentation of what is important in a license before license negotiation starts. The larger the pool of informants within and outside the library and the clearer the library's definition of what users, uses, and access mean to the library's unique situation, the more manageable the vendor relationships and the impact on infrastructure. Ask library professionals with responsibilities in collection development, serials, systems, acquisitions, reference, instruction, and administration. Ask customers. Ask the legal counsel for the library's parent organization. Discover what license requirements other libraries seek for their constituencies. Ask vendors for their impressions of the licensing process and what they would like out of the libraries they serve. With this breadth of input, all involved in purchase and license negotiations will understand the library's needs and licenses will truly reflect what is best for the library and its community.

Become comfortable reading contracts. Practice. Take out old contracts and make copies to examine. Highlight and comment on all language you cannot clearly picture as benefiting your library or your library's community members. Highlight everything that does not make sense to you. What do the circled license clauses mean for your library's definitions of users, uses, access, vendor relationships, and impact on the library? From these circled clauses, what lists could you make in advance that would help you read contracts in the future? In a collaborative group, these exercises allow library professionals to compare comments, discuss reactions, and learn from each other. The Liblicense-L listserv (Yale University Library and CLIR 2000b) is a worldwide community dedicated to helping library professionals learn more about licensing. The Liblicense Web site, for example, offers lists of sample provisions (Yale University Library and CLIR 2000c) and vocabulary (Yale University Library and CLIR 2000a).

Table 6.2 gives examples of license provisions that library professionals do well to define in advance of any license negotiations.

Documentation of learning is crucial. Whether one person manages the entire purchasing and licensing process or subject specialists and serials professionals collectively make licensing decisions, documentation will provide guidance when the pressure to sign a license arises. Copy licenses and write comments about the lessons learned in the margins. Keep notes during negotiations and use them to host a learning session with colleagues. Treat license guidelines as a living document that benefits from regular review and discussion with colleagues inside and outside the library. Documented guidelines that describe what is important to a library can mean the difference between signing on to a good deal and signing away needed rights and privileges.

License Management

When library professionals learn before a purchase event how the library wants to respond to elements in a license, these professionals harness the knowledge of many in the library and manage change with less effort. Whereas reactive management, or waiting until an event occurs to decide how to handle it, seems to take less work, it results in ad hoc decisions that are more chaotic, stressful, effortful, and, in the long run, less successful. Solutions that worked when the library was encountering two or three licenses per year are not sustainable as licenses multiply and more of a library budget is spent on electronic resources.

Table 6.2 Sample License Provisions Best Defined in Advance of Negotiations	
	License Provision
Users	• Describe all affiliated library community members, with attendant IP addresses (explained in Chapter 8, Technology Infrastructure).
	• How does the library support "walk-in users" who are not formally a part of the library's community?
	• What priority within the library's constellation of services are services to remote users?
	• What are the parameters, geographical and technical, of your library's service area, for example, satellite campuses, or a complete list of IP address ranges served by the library?
Uses	• Will the library's users fall under educational use protections, for example, fair use? Is commercial use of product content likely?
	• In what ways is copying important for library service to its community? For example: digitized and paper options for document delivery, reserves, course packs, and online course Web sites.
	• Would a hard copy–only requirement in a license create undue burden on the library's ability to offer services to customers?
Access	• How important is access to your customers? 24 hours a day? 7 days a week? 365 days a year? What remedies can the vendor provide in case of long-term failure to deliver access? (What is "long term?") For example, if engineers in the field cannot access geophysical data for more than two weeks, will the library receive a reduced fee for next year's contract?
	• How important is it to the library to arrange for perpetual access to the content, for example, through archiving?

(Continued)

	• What remedies will result from substantial adverse changes to content? Right to cancel with no penalty? What is "substantial," more than 25%? What is "adverse," loss of content, degradation of quality, content not in keeping with what existed at time of purchase?
Relationship	• How much advance notice from the vendor is necessary for the library to make a renewal decision?
	• With how much advance notice and under what circumstances can a vendor cancel in response to a breach on the library's part? What allowance exists for continued service during appeals?
	• How and when should a vendor notify the library of substantial content changes?
	• What kind, how frequently, and by what standard (ICOLC 2001; COUNTER 2003) should the vendor send usage statistics?
Infrastructure	• How will this product impact the library's support of remote users?
	• By what methods can the library reasonably authenticate users? For example, can the library support unique user name and password authentication for a multitude of products?
	• By what measurement will a product meet usability and *accessibility* standards? How are requests for improvement communicated to the vendor?
	• Does the library want to support products that require the installation of special client software?

A license manager who begins each new negotiation as a blank slate, relying on personal experience and instinct to spot the unwelcome parts of every new contract, will quickly become overwhelmed. More reasonably the library professional will succumb to logical reasons, such as lack of time, lack of contract expertise, or trust in the vendor's ethics to assume that there is no need to read each and every contract. The professional can justify the decision with, "How bad could it be? I'll just send payment and trust that the contract will have no repercussions on my service to my customers."

As library professionals, we protect community-level open access, a universal good to all except to vendors. Vendors are protecting revenue, a goal that, if left unchecked during the purchase and license negotiations, may result in unbearable restrictions on user access. Learning-supported license management provides a set of license provisions that are unique to a library's special needs yet responsive to ongoing changes in the electronic resource marketplace. Library professionals can most easily manage licenses when provisions are widely understood, prioritized from essential to sacrificial, and subject to regular review.

Learning-supported license management is not the setting of hard and fast rules before you know the particulars of each purchase. Flexible yet clear guidelines, collaboratively established outside the immediacy of a negotiation, prepare all professionals in the library for license management by creating a set of provisions expected in all contracts signed. These guidelines give library professionals confidence over a myriad of elements repeatable from one contract to the next and provide a framework for the special considerations of each case.

Establish Guidelines

To establish guidelines, begin with a review of the work of others in the library field, and from that review begin to gather expertise from those within the library who know the library's local situation. Within a group of library professionals knowledgeable about a diverse range of library responsibilities from selection to delivery, develop standard contract language (see Figure 2.2) and checklists of important points that support your library's unique situation. Manage the collaborative input through checklists and standard provisions. This collaborative insight refines and streamlines how licenses ultimately serve the access needs of the library's community. The collaborative work invested in this review may seem to be extraneous to a library professional's central duties, but it reduces the time required for each contract and saves time and personal stress over the long run.

The guidelines allow the clear communication and understanding that are the cornerstones of mutuality and acceptance between the library and vendor. With this understanding, library professionals will not have to treat the review of every contract's language as a new endeavor; instead, the collaboratively developed checklists will provide guidance and insight into what to look for and what to add. A standard set of expectations will also make all library professionals who speak with vendors more comfortable. Library professionals will know what they should ask for in a product and will be clearer with the vendor on what your library needs. A Web site displaying the lists of licensing provisions and standards will help librarians on the phone with a vendor be clearer about library expectations, especially if the vendor can see the same site.

Prioritize License Provisions

Prioritize license provisions into "needs, wants, and plusses." "Needed" provisions are crucial for the library to meet its purpose and are nonnegotiable. Needed provisions should be few and communicated to a vendor at the beginning of the negotiation process. If a library is willing to walk away from a contract because a provision is needed, a vendor may find a way to meet the needed provisions. "Wanted" provisions are important but can be given up for some balancing consideration from a vendor. "Plus" provisions make a deal sweeter if the library must give up a wanted provision or must pay a higher fee than expected. In negotiation, this prioritization allows trade-offs. If the vendor cannot give on an aspect of the license, this may be another wanted provision or plus provision they would be willing to provide the library.

Because the library publishes all these guidelines in advance, on the Web, the library negotiator can be clear during the mutuality phase and the vendor is not surprised by an expectation. When uses a collaborative group to develop and publish a set of expectations in advance, the negotiating librarian and the vendor save time and effort, which are expensive commodities for both organizations. The library's negotiating position is strengthened by a foundation of collaboratively developed standard license provisions—provisions with which both libraries and vendors are familiar—Reducing the uncertainty of unfamiliar contract language on both sides leads to quicker mutuality and acceptance during the negotiating process, saving money in the library budget and avoiding the wear of lost time and stress on the library professional.

Review and Training

Review and training are essential for learning-based license management. The market for electronic resources, from databases to electronic journals, is in a constant state of change. The expectations and standard provisions that library professionals may have developed two years ago will need thorough collaborative review in light of advances in the market and in delivery options. At regular intervals of eighteen months to two years, library professionals from selection to delivery should review the guidelines against advances in the licensing environment and contribute valuable improvements to the standard provisions and priorities. Ongoing collaborative review and training are crucial to contributing valuable new information to the license management in a library.

Both the details and assertiveness needed to negotiate license terms in the best interests of uses, users, and access can be overwhelming. Building a firm foundation into the library's license management process liberates all library professionals involved from reinventing the process

Table 6.3 The Foundation of Successful License Management	
Establish	**In the Form**
Clear Expectations	• Web-based checklists • Vocabulary sheets • Standard licenses • A single negotiator
Clear priorities	• Provisions needed or the library does not sign • Provisions wanted for the license to attract • Provisions that would be plusses to outweigh negatives
Review and training	• Best practices of other libraries • Input from across the library's spectrum of professionals • Input from external professionals, including vendors • Workshops that include open discussion to share learning

with every new license. Table 6.3 outlines the foundational concepts crucial for successful license management.

Third-Party License Management

Libraries of all types see benefit in third party management of license agreements. While subscription agents and license management consultants provide this service, the consortium is the most common third-party license manager. Learning-based management, including group involvement, checklists, and documentation review, still hold true for the consortium. Although consortia managers are best served by discovering and reviewing consortium members' priorities concerning license provisions, consortia members not only have the responsibility to communicate these with consortia manager, but also they must help this manager develop a set of standards that will serve all members of the consortium. This holds true especially if the manager is not a consortium staff member, but is instead a library professional volunteer working from within another member library. Vendors themselves state a preference for the cost savings of one license and one voice for all members brought to the table by consortia (Elsevier Science 1998).

Some licensing consultants and to a lesser degree subscription agents offer to outsource license management (NESLI2 2002). These third-party vendors can provide management of the burden of detail, but the burden of communication is rarely reduced for library professionals.

Automating License Management

The process of license management quickly becomes complex and data intensive. Whether one person or a group revises and signs licenses, and whether the license benefits one library or *consortial partnerships* between libraries, the work can only be enhanced by automating data tracking and data sharing. An electronic resource management system much like the relational databases discussed in Chapter 7, Cataloging and Access, can include both the provisions expected by a library or consortia and the provisions negotiated into the final version of each product's license. A relational database available from a central location would allow a collection development librarian to discuss renewal provisions for a resource with vendor sales professionals while an interlibrary loan librarian finds out whether the resource allows paper or electronic copies and a reference librarian shows a customer the resource's journal holdings. The construction of such relational databases is under discussion at the WebHub for Developing Administrative Metadata for Electronic Resource Management (Jewell 2001).

Conclusion

More often, libraries license electronic content than purchase ownership. Even though copyright law helps balance the relationship between the content vendor's desire for revenue and the library professional's desire for open library customer access, the protections it provides cannot sufficiently govern the potential for loss of revenue that highly transferable electronic copies allow. To maintain the balance in the relationship between the vendors' need for publishing revenue and libraries' mandate from their communities to provide open access to collections, libraries license access to content in exchange for restrictions on types of use, users, and access.

To reduce time and effort for the library and the vendor, the licensed relationship requires some level of standardized expectations for both parties. Collaborative groups of professionals best formulate these expectations, and success comes from learning from each other how license provisions affect all areas of responsibility in a library, as well as how the provisions affect customers and vendors. The best licensing relationship creates clear expectations within the library before negotiations start and strives to clarify the vendor's needs so that provisions mutually benefit both parties. Only through collaboratively creating a clear understanding of desired license provisions and continuous learning will library professionals protect access for their service communities, protect library budgets and protect themselves from being overwhelmed by the licensing process.

References

Association of Research Libraries (ARL). "Licensing review and negotiation." ©2003. *Online Lyceum.* ARL. Office of Leadership and Management Services. URL: http://www.arl.org/training/licensing.html (Accessed September 17, 2004).

Bailey, Charles W., Jr. *Scholarly Electronic Publishing Bibliography.* ©2004. University of Houston Libraries. URL: http://info.lib.uh.edu/sepb/sepb.html (Accessed September 17, 2004).

Counting Online Usage of Networked Electronic Resources (COUNTER). "COUNTER: Counting online usage of networked electronic resources." ©2003. COUNTER. URL: http://www.projectcounter.org/about.html (Accessed September 17, 2004).

Elsevier Science. "Response to ICOLC Statement." ©1998. *Statements and Documents.* ICOLC. URL: http://www.library.yale.edu/consortia/elsevier.htm (Accessed September 17, 2004).

Harris, Lesley Ellen. 2002. *Licensing digital content: A practical guide for librarians.* Chicago, IL: American Library Association.

International Coalition of Library Consortia (ICOLC). "Guidelines for statistical measures of usage of web-based information resources." ©2001 *Statements and Documents of the International Coalition of Library Consortia.* ICOLC. URL: http://www.library.yale.edu/consortia/2001webstats.htm (Accessed September 17, 2004).

Jewell, Tim. *A Webhub for Developing Administrative Metadata for Electronic Resource Management.* ©2001. Cornell University Library. Central Technical Services URL: http://www.library.cornell.edu/cts/elicensestudy/ (Accessed September 17, 2004).

Library of Congress (LC). Copyright Office. "The Digital Millennium Copyright Act of 1998: U.S. Copyright Office Summary." © 1998. *Copyright.* United States Copyright Office. URL: http://www.copyright.gov/legislation/dmca.pdf (Accessed September 17, 2004).

NESLI2. "Press release: JISC announces its new partner for NESLi2." ©2002. *NESLI2, The National e-Journals Initiative.* JISC. URL: http://www.nesli2.ac.uk/press_release.htm (Accessed September 17, 2004).

U.S. Government Printing Office (GPO). "Title 17: Copyrights, Chapter 1: Subject matter and scope of copyright." ©2003. *GPOAccess: United States Code.* GPO. URL: http://www.access.gpo.gov/uscode/title17/chapter1_.html (Accessed September 17, 2004).

Yale University Library and the Council on Library and Information Resources (CLIR). "Definitions of words and phrases commonly found in licensing agreements" ©2000a. *Liblicense*. Yale University Library. URL: http://www.library.yale.edu/~llicense/definiti.shtml (Accessed September 17, 2004).

———. *Liblicense: Licensing digital information, a resource for librarians.* ©2000b. Yale University Library. URL: http://www.library.yale.edu/~llicense/ (Accessed September 17, 2004).

———. "Licensing Terms & Descriptions" ©2000c. *Liblicense*. Yale University Library.   URL: http://www.library.yale.edu/~llicense/table.shtml (Accessed September 17, 2004).

Further Reading

American Association of Law Libraries, American Library Association, Association of Academic Health Sciences Libraries, Association of Research Libraries and Medical Library Association. "Principles for licensing electronic resources." ©1997. *Office of Scholarly Communication*. ARL.   URL: http://www.arl.org/scomm/licensing/principles.html (Accessed September 17, 2004).

Americans for Fair Electronic Commerce Transactions (AFFECT). *AFFECT: Americans for fair electronic commerce transactions.* ©2003 AFFECT. URL: http://www.affect.ucita.com/ (Accessed September 17, 2004).

Brennan, Patricia, Karen Hersey, and Georgia Harper. "Strategic and practical considerations for signing electronic information delivery agreements." ©2002. ARL. Office of Scholarly Communication. URL: http://www.arl.org/scomm/licensing/licbooklet.html (Accessed September 17, 2004).

Canadian National Site Licensing Project (CNSLP). "Licensing principles." ©2000. *Canadian National Site Licensing Project*. CNSLP. URL: http://www.cnslp.ca/about/principles/ (Accessed September 17, 2004).

Cox, John. *Licensingmodels.com: Model standard licenses for use by publishers, librarians and subscription agents for electronic resources.* ©2000. Catchword. URL: http://www.LicensingModels.com (Accessed September 17, 2004).

Giavarra, Emanuella. "Licensing digital resources: How to avoid the legal pitfalls." ©2001. *European Copyright User Platform (ECUP)*. The European Commission and the Netherlands: European Bureau of Library, Information and Documentation Associations (EBLIDA). URL: http://www.eblida.org/ecup/docs/licensing.htm (Accessed September 17, 2004).

Haavisto, Tuula. "Libraries and licensing in Central and Eastern Europe" ©2002. The European Bureau of Library, Information and Documentation Associations. Central and Eastern European Licensing Information Platform   (CELIP).   URL: http://www.eblida.org/celip/documents/celipstate_final.pdf (Accessed September 17, 2004).

Harper, Georgia. "Software and database license agreement checklist." ©2002. University of Texas System. Office of General Counsel. URL: http://www.utsystem.edu/OGC/intellectualproperty/dbckfrm1.htm (Accessed September 17, 2004).

Harvard University Library. "DigAcq Web: Information for vendors." ©2004. *DigAcq Web*. President and Fellows of Harvard College. URL: http://hul.harvard.edu/digacq/vendors.html (Accessed September 17, 2004).

International Coalition of Library Consortia (ICOLC). "Statement of current perspective and preferred practices for the selection and purchase of electronic information: Update No. 1, new developments in e-journal licensing" ©2001. *Statements and Documents*. ICOLC. URL: http://www.library.yale.edu/consortia/2001currentpractices.htm (Accessed September 17, 2004).

———. "Privacy guidelines for electronic resources vendors." ©2002. *Statements and Documents*. ICOLC. URL: http://www.library.yale.edu/consortia/2002privacyguidelines.html (Accessed September 17, 2004).

International Federation of Library Associations and Institutions (IFLA). "Licensing principles." ©2001. *IFLANET, IFLA Publications*. IFLA. URL: http://www.ifla.org/V/ebpb/copy.htm (Accessed September 17, 2004).

NESLI2. "JISC model licence for journals." ©2002. *NESLI2, The National e-Journals Initiative*. JISC. URL: http://www.nesli2.ac.uk/model.htm (Accessed September 17, 2004).

Pace, Andrew. 2003. *The ultimate digital library: Where the new information players meet*. Chicago, IL: American Library Association.

Pike, George H. 2002. The delicate dance of database licenses, copyright, and fair use. *Computers in Libraries* 22 (5) URL: http://www.infotoday.com/cilmag/may02/pike.htm (Accessed September 17, 2004).

Rosenblatt, Bill, Bill Trippe, and Stephen Mooney. 2002. *Digital rights management*. New York: M&T Books.

Stanford University Libraries. *Copyright and fair use*. ©2003. Stanford University. URL: http://fairuse.stanford.edu/index.html (Accessed September 17, 2004).

University of Texas Libraries. "Licensing and libraries." ©2004. *Collection Issues in Libraries*. University of Texas at Austin. URL: http://www.lib.utexas.edu/admin/cird/issues/license.html (Accessed September 17, 2004).

Yale University Library, Digital Library Federation (DLF), and the Council on Library and Information Resources (CLIR). "CLIR/DLF model license." ©2000. *Liblicense*. Yale University Library. URL: http://www.library.yale.edu/~llicense/modlic.shtml (Accessed September 17, 2004).

CHAPTER 7

Cataloging and Access

The online public access catalog (OPAC) and its precursor, the library card catalog, have been the primary access points through which library customers discover what a given library collection has to offer. Professional cataloging produces a catalog record that contains descriptive data (author, title, issue last received) and pointers to location (*call number*, building, floor number), both of which help customers find a single item in what would otherwise be an overwhelming collection of information resources. Whether the library collection contains a thousand or a million items, the idea that one can walk through the doors of a library and within minutes stand in front of a desired resource is extraordinary. Serendipity, such as in the pleasant surprise of a researcher who finds the perfect book sitting next to the one originally sought, is a second and equally important path into our collections, which catalogers also professionally engineer through the selection of call numbers and subject headings. Professional catalogers contribute the intellectual work of this system, consciously ordering and describing each new acquisition into a library collection so that the library patron may quickly find useful information within a large collection. Ordered, accessible library collections are a powerful resource for self-directed learning in a community, and more than a century of professional cataloging standards have contributed to this powerful service.

This chapter will not to explicate these current cataloging practices in any detail. Excellent introductions to cataloging practices and the MARC format abound (Intner and Weihs 2001; Furrie 2003; Taylor 2000). I wish, instead, to show how the advent of electronic resources have changed the cataloger's domain of responsibility, and how advances in electronic management and presentation of information have begun to affect cataloging practices. Indeed, I hope to plant a seed of curiosity within my reader that will grow into a desire to explore and contribute to advances that allow cataloging to continue into this century the meaningful service it has performed during the past century.

This chapter will review how catalogers around the world are working to adapt cataloging rules, practices, and the structure of MARC to the new demands of cataloging electronic resources. Then the chapter will explore relational database design and show how library subject guides are using this tool to build dynamic, Web-based catalogs of electronic resources. Finally, the chapter will look into a future in which the promise of relational database design, XML, and dynamic Web delivery will bring adaptive library online catalogs back to the center of a typical information user's research universe. Permeating these practical activities is the reality that no one person can ever know enough about all of these endeavors, or about the ongoing change inherent in each, to make independent decisions. We therefore need to expand our professionalism from the lone expert making independent decisions into the skills of working with groups of professionals, each expert and each willing to accept collaborative leadership responsibilities.

An Overly Brief Introduction to Cataloging

During the first three-quarters of the twentieth century, catalogers typed descriptive data onto paper index cards and filed them in the library card catalog. The example catalog card in Figure 7.1 is filed by author name. A cataloger would create at least two other cards for this work, one card with the title on the first line and one with the subject, Economics, on the first line, so that descriptive cards could be filed by title and subject, respectively.

The catalog card has since matured into the digitized MARC record. Catalogers type the data elements describing an item into a MARC record and then store the record in the library OPAC (online public access catalog) database. The cataloger now need only type the data once, one data element (for example, author) per field (for example, MARC field number 100), and the computer can display the record sorted by author, title, or subject as the need arises. Note that the author's name appears twice in the record, once in the 100 field and once in the 245 field. This chapter will discuss why the data is not recognized as "author" and recorded once. The example MARC record in Figure 7.2 does not contain all the elements of a MARC record, only those necessary to illustrate this chapter's discussions.

Figure 7.1
Catalog card. An example card catalog entry filed by author.

HB 161 .S66 2000	Smith, Adam, 1723 – 1790. An inquiry in to the nature and causes of the wealth of nations. By Adam Smith . . . New York, New Publishers, 2000. Economics.

Great effort has gone into the standardization of the library catalog record. On a paper catalog card, data elements such as title, author, or subject occupy standard locations. Similarly, the title of the same work cataloged in a MARC record occupies subfield "a" of the 245 field (the field designated for the title and statement of responsibility). Because each MARC field and subfield have specialized meanings on which catalogers have universally agreed, standardization allows the catalogers to share the effort of cataloging new items with fellow members of networks called *bibliographic utilities*, for example, *OCLC* and *RLG* (Tang Sha 2002). Standardization also keeps library customers' experiences as uniform as possible between libraries.

This accomplishment is staggering. With the standard language of MARC encoding, OPAC records can describe and point customers to library holdings as diverse from each other as a video recording is from one hundred years' worth of a journal. With MARC, libraries as diverse as a corporate special library is from a metropolitan public library can describe and direct users to any item in their collections. In the pursuit of providing useful access to the library's holdings, catalogers contribute to the library customer experience. The cataloger's professional expertise is the fitting of descriptions of each new acquisition into a set of predefined MARC fields. This dexterity has met with challenges in the past, but electronic resources are proving to be the ultimate contest.

Electronic resources are rarely physical objects held in one's hand and, therefore, rarely fit smoothly into a MARC-format catalog record. The tactile nature of print items in a library collection informed the development of the three-by-five index card and by extension the MARC record. When the tactile nature of print dissolves into the virtual dimensions of electronic resources, the current assumptions of cataloging run afoul of the fluid space and time that electronic resources occupy. Electronic resources can expand and divide at the whim of the vendor of the product. Electronic resources do not, as print items do, occupy the same package of pages as when originally cataloged. Electronic resources can alter content and configuration over time, usually within radically short time spans relative to the time a print item could spend on a shelf unchanged and unchanging.

For catalogers to provide access to items in a collection with a MARC record, they must describe the content of the items in a data record of fixed scope. Catalogers must demonstrate, through the data in the record, the usefulness of a product to the library customer. The MARC record in Figure 7.2 stores many types of information that help a customer decide whether the book is a promising prospect. Catalogers must also provide a pointer that leads the user, not close to, but exactly to the resource in question. Call numbers point exactly to the location of a specific item in even the largest collection.

The nature of the titles of print and electronic resources demonstrates the differences between fitting a print resource or an electronic resource to a MARC record. A print resource has a title page with a standard format from which publishers rarely deviate. Cataloging practice uses this standard to guide catalogers to the title page for the title of a work, and have developed responses to variations from this practice. In Figure 7.2, the work is known by two titles. The title on the book's title page is *An Inquiry in to the Nature and Causes of the Wealth of Nations,* and this is recorded in subfield "a" of MARC field 245. However, the popular title by which many know the book is the *Wealth of Nations,* and this fact is recorded in MARC field 246, the field created for variant titles. By contrast, electronic resources have no standard presentation of descriptive data and no fixity to the format a designer of an electronic resource may choose to present descriptive data at any given time. When determining the title of an electronic resource, however, the cataloger must find some semblance of a common data source in order to observe the standards on which cataloging relies. Is the data source of the electronic resource the title on the homepage, the shorter title on the initial search screen, or the longer marketing title on the brochure? If catalogers use a search screen to describe one resource, they should use the search screen to consistently describe all resources. The passage of time compounds the difficulty. If the vendor, for marketing reasons, changes the title twice in one year, is the cataloger supposed to manually change the MARC record to keep pace? The cataloger must then keep track of changes that may occur to any one of the electronic resources recorded in the OPAC.

Figure 7.2
An abridged MARC record.

```
050 00 $a HB161 $b .S66 2000

100 1_ $a Smith, Adam, $d 1723-1790.

245 10 $a An inquiry in to the nature and causes of the
           wealth of nations / $c Adam Smith.

246 30 $a Wealth of nations

260 __ $a New York : $b New Publishers, $c c2000.

300 __ $a 504 p.

504 __ $a Includes indexes.

650 _0 $a Economics.

856 __ $a http://www.wealthofnations.com/
```

For example, Gale, the publisher of a popular series of print literary criticism compendiums, including *Contemporary Literary Criticism, Twentieth Century Literary Criticism,* and *Contemporary Authors,* combined the series into a single online product under the title *Literature Resource Center.* The uninitiated first-year student, looking for the suggested *Contemporary Literary Criticism,* gains nothing from the product's title in the OPAC, *Literature Resource Center.* The cataloger must decide, within the rules set forth for determining title, which title will lead the library customer to this expensive resource.

Add to this the question of whether the library can verify that the online version is an exact replica of the print. As of 2002, the online version of *Literature Resource Center,* for reasons of copyright, did not contain all the entries one would have found in the print versions of the series represented by the online product. The online product was different from the print in substance. Does the cataloger call these two items by the same title? How does the cataloger inform the customer that content in the print version may be more complete than the electronic? How will the library know if, five years later, the electronic version is more content-rich than the print (short of believing the marketing brochures)? Multiply these and similar questions times the number of electronic resources for which the cataloger is responsible. When a library's collection of electronic resources, including electronic journals, grows in a decade from 25 to 40,000, one can see the overwhelming nature of the task that lies before catalogers, that of providing access for library customers to the resources.

The need for internal materials-management descriptions compounds the difficulties of describing the resource for the library customer. The library staff must track many data elements describing an electronic resource in order to purchase and maintain it, including, all variations of title, cost and contractual payment details, licensed restrictions on means of access, and all variations on means of access (URLs). The list of purchase and maintenance data is long and complex. With the advent of computerized integrated library systems (ILSs), librarians have been able to include in MARC records, and in a database surrounding the MARC records, technical and management data necessary for acquiring and warehousing large and growing collections. Since the 1970s, ILSs have expanded the data of their predecessor card catalogs to include materials-management information for such activities as collection development, acquisitions, claiming receipt of an item, and circulation.

Cataloging is probably experiencing the most profound shift in the processes and skill sets required to perform a day's work. Catalogers must describe new library resources well enough to attract use, and they must provide enough access information to connect the interested customer with the chosen resource. The descriptive nature of cataloging remains the steadfast guardian of library customer access to the collection, one of the core missions of the library profession. Electronic resources create a demand in library customers and library professionals alike for immediately connecting library customers to expensive, and often complex, electronic products, whose access methods are in constant flux.

Difficulties of content description, such as the title in the example above, pale in comparison to the new complexities of providing access. Just as the library customer expects a call number to point to the exact location of a resource in a collection, the library customer expects an electronic resource to be one click away from the hyperlink in a MARC record. Catalogers would have to manually update an exponentially growing number of fixed MARC fields to provide always-on and always-correct online access to electronic resources. To solve this untenable expectation, MARC practitioners are beginning to take advantage of advances in computerized information access—most notably, relational database design, XML markup, and dynamic Web delivery. Before taking up these topics, this chapter will first discuss how electronic resources have impacted the rules catalogers use to create descriptions of items in a library collection and the standards that catalogers use to record these descriptions in a MARC record.

Cataloging Rules: *AACR2*

A cataloger describes the potential usefulness of items in a library collection to the customers and smoothes the access to these items in a way that saves the customers' time and efforts. The library customer uses a library collection to create knowledge and learning, either within themselves or through a creative product such as a research paper. Libraries invest money in costly information resources and invest time connecting our customers to these resources. The more time that library professionals spend streamlining access, the less time the customers must spend navigating toward the library's resources. The less time customers spend navigating access, the more time they have to spend creating and learning. Cataloging lies at the crossroads of this endeavor.

Catalogers achieve the monumental task of describing and providing access not just within one library but also uniformly throughout many libraries in the world. Standards make this achievement possible. Standards create a set of understood practices that, if followed, allow the descriptive catalog record created by one cataloger in Des Moines, Iowa, to be useful in the catalog of a library in Sydney, Australia. Local practices may customize parts of the catalog record to fit local circumstances, but the basic elements remain compatible across libraries.

The *Anglo-American Cataloging Rules*, 2nd edition, known as the *AACR2* (ALA 1978) governs the cataloging of items in library collections throughout the West and in much of the rest of the world. In December 2002, the Joint Steering Committee (JSC) for Revision of Anglo-American Cataloging Rules published the 2002 Revision (ALA 2002). This revision reflects more than a decade of discussions in the cataloging community concerning, among other things, the impact of electronic resources on accepted cataloging practices. The JSC did not overturn accepted cataloging practices, but simply broadened and reconceptualized the rules to attempt to encompass the iterative and mutable nature of electronic resources. The 2002 revision is not the final word. Discussions among library professionals continue as electronic resources grow and change in design and delivery.

The two chapters of the AACR2 to receive the most attention regarding electronic resources were Chapter 9 and Chapter 12. The title of Chapter 9 changed from "Computer Files" to "Electronic Resources," and the title of Chapter 12 changed from "Serials" to "Continuing Resources" (Hawkins and Hirons 2002). Before the revision, the *AACR2* divided bibliographic resources into two primary types, *monographic* or serial. Monographic resources are self-contained with discernable beginnings and endings. One expects serial resources to continue to grow in content with no discernable end. The 2002 revision adds to these distinctions two new categories: finite and continuing, along with the concept of integrating content. Figure 7.3 illustrates how the finite and continuing categories contain the concept of integrating resources. The figure also shows which *AACR2* chapters address which concepts.

Finite resources are the bibliographic resources that are, or will be, complete and self-contained, with no new content expected. Continuing resources, on the other hand, incorporate additional content into the existing resources with no foreseeable cessation. These two definitions sound like the traditional definitions for monograph and serial; however, electronic resources have added a new reality. In instances where electronic resources diverge from print resources, and become variable rather than fixed, the revisers created a category called *integrating*. Bibliographic resources are integrating if they receive new content, but the additions are incorporated into the larger whole without distinct separation.

Figure 7.3
Finite and continuing resources. The categories of finite and continuing resources each contain the concept of integrating resources and are addressed by different chapters of the AACR2. Adapted from Hawkins and Hirons (2002).

Bibliographic Resources			
Finite **Is or will be complete**		**Continuing** **New content added indefinitely**	
Monographic	**Finite** **Integrating**	**Continuing** **Integrating**	**Serial**
Complete. No new content expected. May receive occasional errata.	Will become complete in time. New content is not discrete from existing content.	Added content is expected, but is not discrete from rest of product.	Added content remains discrete from existing content, usually numbered.
Examples: Online dictionary with no scheduled updates; a CD-ROM.	Example: Web site of an ongoing project with an enddate.	Examples: Online database of journal articles; a typical Web site.	Example: An electronic journal with numbered issues.
Chapter 9, Electronic Resources	**Chapter 12, Continuing Resources**		

If a finite electronic resource receives only insignificant additions of errata, catalogers consider it monographic in nature and treat it with the attentions of Chapter 9, Electronic Resources, in the *AACR2*. Examples of monographic resources are online dictionaries that will only receive occasional errata, or electronic products in a fixed medium, like CD-ROMs. If an electronic resource is self-contained (or finite) but its additions and deletions will make the work noticeably different over time, it is considered integrating and treated as a finite integrating resource. Chapter 12, Continuing Resources, guides cataloging efforts of finite integrating resources.

Much of the original text of Chapter 12 dealt with the variability of serials, and the revised chapter is now helpful for describing not only serials and continuing integrating resources, but also provides major assistance in cataloging finite integrating resources. The primary advantage of the treatment of finite integrating resources within Chapter 12 is that the strict practices for monographic cataloging can be relaxed to include the practicalities developed for serials cataloging.

Bibliographic resources that are continuing in nature will receive new content into the foreseeable future. Because integrating resources receive new content that, once added, is not discernable from the existing content, the category *continuing integrating* includes most online article databases and most typical Web sites considered as a whole. For example, one cannot explicitly locate in an article database all the recently added articles, although one knows that the database content changes from month to month. A serial is a continuing resource in which new content comes in discrete packages, preferably numbered much like a print journal issues. Continuing integrating and serial bibliographic resources receive the attentions of Chapter 12.

Integrating content persists in its challenge to catalogers. When new content does not remain discrete and numbered but is incorporated into the main body of the resource, the item first cataloged changes its essential nature over time. The cataloger must keep pace with when the original catalog record no longer accurately describes the item in its current state. When should the cataloger create a new catalog record because the resource has abandoned its old self and regenerated a new existence? Where is the point of demarcation between the "old" product and the "new"? If the old product is not archived, and is not available, should the cataloger discard its record from the OPAC?

The adaptive nature of electronic resource delivery methods compounds the descriptive difficulties of cataloging electronic resources. Most electronic resources are not fixed in a medium, like CD-ROMs, but instead are available at a vendor's site remote from the library, a site under the control of a third party who may at any time and without notice change, add, or remove descriptive data (for example, title, creator, dates of coverage), content, or methods of access. The possibility of these unannounced changes undermines a central principle of cataloging–the idea of the "item in hand." This principle holds that the cataloger should follow established standards and create a catalog description solely on the evidence visible in or around the item at hand. This principle assumes that the item in hand will not change once it is cataloged and placed on the shelf. With electronic resources, we cannot but assume otherwise.

Catalogers are still resolving these and other issues of electronic resource variability. I will argue below that the difficulty lies with the fixed structure of the catalog record itself, particularly when MARC is used to contain the record, not necessarily the adaptability or application of cataloging rules.

Cataloging Structure: MARC

Even with revisions, the custodians of *AACR2* are still struggling with how to describe the fluid world of electronic resources while retaining the trusted rules of cataloging tradition. Catalogers must also try to fit these cataloging practices into the predefined, standardized structure of the MARC record. Let us return to the previous example of a product's title to demonstrate the conflict between MARC and electronic resource management. Vendors exhibit an almost willful propensity to repeatedly change the titles of their electronic products. Vendors change titles when a new user interface is unveiled, when a company is bought or merges with another, or when the vendor wants to change its marketing strategy. Titles mutate within a product depending on where the users find themselves in the interface. Titles may be contract-specific, displaying one way for one library and in an entirely different way for another library, although the content is the same.

The *AACR2* revisions stipulate that, when creating the main title entry, one may use the current version of an electronic product, and the *AACR2* allows this entry in the MARC record to change over time. An important change in the *AACR2* revision allows the cataloger to record superceded titles in MARC 250 notes fields (Figure 7.2). If cataloging describes an item for access, and if a library customer knows an electronic product by one name–one no longer present in the OPAC–then the customer may assume the content to have disappeared from the library's collection. In the example of the Gale collection of literary criticism discussed above, the record for *Contemporary Literary Criticism* will indicate no paper issues received after 1999. How will the user know to use the online Literary Resource Center? MARC fields begin to take on tasks for which they were not designed, and every new permutation of product description and product access must find a place within the fixed MARC record.

Whereas the fixed MARC record limits description, it multiplies the work of keeping that description current. In practical terms, the task of keeping up with just the title changes for the increasing tide of electronic resources added to collections every year would quickly overwhelm any cataloger. The fixed nature of MARC multiplies work within a library. Because the MARC record has only one primary field for title, a cataloger must manually empty and refill that field at every change, and must know that a change is necessary. The fixed nature of MARC multiplies work among libraries. A typical library cataloger downloads copies of MARC records from a bibliographic utility (for example, OCLC or RLG), and uses these downloaded records to create local records in a local database. Any changes in description that occur after a download become the responsibility of each individual library. Electronic resources change not just in title but also in holdings, content, access points, responsible creators, licensing provisions, and incorporation with other resources. The list of possible changes is almost endless. Once a MARC record exists in a local database, the library must make changes to MARC records when changes occur. One title change in one product prompts the manual entry of that change by tens of thousands of catalogers to tens of thousands of local records.

On a 3- × 5-inch catalog card, space and standardization are at a premium. Catalogers can add a few notes fields for title variations. Catalogers can find creative uses for certain unused MARC fields, but this must occur within strict limits and certainly not to the extent of creating entirely new fields, at least not without lengthy debate across the profession. Because libraries share records and customers, standardization is all important, and the makeup of a 3 × 5 card, or its heir, the MARC record, cannot accept new situations with pronounced agility.

Collections of data elements on a catalog card, or on a predefined MARC record, are flat files. Pieces of descriptive information (elements) about any given resource are collected within a predefined MARC record, and all elements are listed together as one long list. Change to a resource may take place over the course of its lifetime, but the stability of MARC standards ensures high-quality data, data organization, and data access across libraries. However, when fundamental change happens every eighteen months, the slow response of standardized flat files cannot maintain accurate descriptive and access data, and alternative cataloging methods begin to meet the need for the library to provide for its customers access to valuable products.

These alternatives use the relational database as a foundation to create a dynamic response to the fluidity of electronic resource description and access. A relational database is not a flat file, and this chapter goes into more detail in a later section. Relational databases provide the underpinnings of many Web-based library services that library professionals have developed separately from the OPAC to describe and provide access to resources for library customers. Two of these services are the PURL (persistent URL) server and the Web-based electronic resource guides.

Escape from the Fixed MARC Record

Catalogers concerned about the difficulty of nailing down descriptions of electronic resources concentrate these, and other cataloging standardization efforts, within the Program for Cooperative Cataloging (PCC) and its member organizations, including CONSER (Cooperative Online Serials; LC 2004b) and BIBCO (Bibliographic Record Cooperative Program; LC 2004a). These organizations are internationally influential in interpreting the Anglo-American Cataloging Rules and in setting cataloging standards for electronic resource cataloging. The standards these catalogers promulgate allow flexibility for local policies and customs around a set of core standards accepted by all who join.

Catalogers both inside and outside these organizations remain uncomfortable with the tension between fixity of local MARC records and the variability of electronic resources and have begun to explore relational data, the idea of maintaining data elements, such as title, outside the confines of a fixed MARC record, but accessible to the standardized information delivery afforded by a MARC-like record. In one example, PCC members seek to add flexibility to MARC through the use of the OCLC/PCC PURL Server (LC 2003c; OCLC 2004). A PURL server acts as an intermediary between the local, fixed MARC record at an institution and the ever-changing world of product URLs. Libraries may create PURL servers within their own technology infrastructures. This subsection will discuss a PURL server designed to meet the needs of the world-wide members of the PCC cooperative.

Figure 7.4 demonstrates how the PURL in a MARC record resolves through a PURL server to retrieve the current URL for the resource.

A URL (uniform resource locator) is the World Wide Web address of an electronic product; URLs are often placed in the 856 field of a MARC record (see Figure 7.2). With the services of a PURL server, instead of a URL, a cataloger can record a persistent URL in the MARC record for a resource. The PURL contains the address of the PURL server along with a unique identification number for the resource in question. The PURL will direct itself to the PURL server and use the unique identifier to retrieve the up-to-date URL and to link through that URL to the product. As we will see in the next section,

Figure 7.4
How a PURL resolves for the current URL.

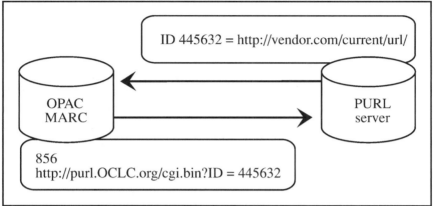

ID 445632 = http://vendor.com/current/url/

OPAC
MARC

PURL
server

856
http://purl.OCLC.org/cgi.bin?ID = 445632

the unique identifier is the secret key into the PURL server's relational database.

In the example in Figure 7.4 (the URLs are not real), the OPAC record displays a link to the product that contains the PURL http://purl.oclc.org/cgi.bin?ID=445632. The link points to the OCLC PURL server (http://purl.oclc.org/...) and carries with it the unique identification number of the resource in question (.../cgi.bin?ID=445632). The PURL server sees the ID number 445632 in the incoming PURL and sorts through its records for the record that matches the ID number. In that record, the current URL is http://vendor.com/current/url/.

The user of the MARC record (presumably a user of the library's OPAC) travels seamlessly from the link in the OPAC record to product's correct destination URL. The user selects the link in the OPAC, waits a few seconds, and then sees the product's welcoming screen.

Participants in the OCLC/PCC PURL server cooperative work together to maintain correct URLs on the PURL server. This resource sharing has the effect of distributing the work of maintenance across all participants thereby reducing the work of maintenance for any one participant. If one member somewhere in the cooperative notices a URL change, that one person makes the change one time on the main server. In any member library's MARC record, the PURL will point to the PURL server, which will always have the correct URL. The PURL entered in the local MARC record is persistent because it will never need changing by local catalogers; it will always point to the up-to-date data in the central PURL server.

The PURL in the local OPAC will provide the always-correct, one-click access from MARC record to the resource, continuing the cataloging tradition of call numbers leading a customer directly to a resource.

Just as catalogers give more than the floor number to help a customer locate a book, the PURL allows the MARC record to lead the user directly to an online resource. The PURL solves the need for constant URL management and demonstrates how library professionals can circumvent the limitation of the fixed MARC record with relational data.

Another example of a relational database escape from the confines of MARC is the development of Web-based electronic resource guides. Library by library around the world, library professionals are essentially recataloging electronic resources into Web-based delivery systems like subject guides and electronic journal finders. *Research Central,* designed by the University of Georgia Libraries (2004) is an example of a dynamic Web site that offers both a subject guide to electronic resources and an introduction to the research process. Many institutions share the *Journal Finder* service (Brandsma et al. 2003), as exemplified at the University of North Carolina at Greensboro (UNCG 2004).

Locally developed Web-based subject guides and lists of electronic journals dynamically display available electronic resources within subject-browse or keyword-search features. These features use special metadata syntax within Web pages to communicate the requests of a Web page user to an underlying relational database. The relational database searches through its thousands of data elements to find appropriate responses to the request. The special syntax then translates the response of the database to dynamically form a Web page of use to the library customer.

Cataloging provides description and access to library holdings. Subject guides have encroached into this domain because the MARC record (Figure 7.2) is not relational. The MARC record is indivisible, and in all its complexity, is the smallest unit within an OPAC. The title of a resource is always stored in the same MARC record as all other descriptive elements for that resource. We will see when we explore the advantages of relational data how this flat-file indivisibility limits the MARC record's ability to "serve up," or deliver, data in a flexible, dynamic manner and in a fashion that reflects the current circumstances of the data user and the data environment.

Paradoxically, for the same reason MARC records can rely on outside databases to store and deliver current URLs by way of PURLs, the valuable descriptive information of MARC records built by years of professional intellectual effort can begin to contain multiple and conflicting data and can begin to respond to queries with the same flexibility as services such as subject guides and citation linking. With relational databases, libraries will again be able to offer the library catalog as a single point of entry through which our patrons discover the knowledge libraries contain for them. The new world of relational databases, dynamic Web design, and metadata, particularly XML, may contain the answer.

The next section will explore how the relational database will be the key to describing and providing access to library resources.

Relational Databases

Beginning in the 1960s, librarians were among the first professionals to take advantage of computerization. Librarians already used data banks (card catalogs) to manage and provide access to large collections. From this existing system, librarians cooperatively developed the MARC standard. Not only did these developers identify numbered fields as containers for the information originally entered on the cards, but they also took advantage of the computerized coding system to create new identifying characteristics, such as format and location.

The developers of MARC continued to use the quite logical standards of the card catalog and are not at fault for being unaware of the concept of relational database design. This database design was not introduced until the early 1970s (Codd 1970; Lonsdale Systems 1999; UT 2004). It began its ascendancy in the 1980s, by which time libraries had accepted the MARC flat file as their established standard for the new computerized card catalogs, or OPACs, coming online all over the world.

Most data banks experience the same set of difficulties that hinder MARC's ability to manage and deliver electronic resources to library customers. The problems with using a single index card, or a single MARC record, in which to store description and access information are the same problems that relational databases were designed to solve. The textbook *Modern Database Management* (Hoffer et al. 2000) describes the following difficulties with flat file data systems:

- Data is redundant. Different people repeat a single piece of information in different places in order to use it for different purposes. The URL of a resource may be stored in the MARC record, but the acquisitions librarian also files the URL in a file drawer with the license and a reference librarian adds the URL to a Web-based list of electronic resources provided for patrons from the library's Web site.

- Data is inconsistent. Data banks isolate information and do not reflect changes that occur in other data banks, even those contained within the same organization. For example, libraries purchase many electronic resources, especially electronic journals, through third-party purchasing agents who keep their own data banks describing these items. If the agent finds that a resource is sold through a new vendor, meaning that the resource has a new URL, then this information is not automatically reflected in the library's own MARC record as a changed URL. Or, for example, a licensing librarian may keep in a file cabinet information about the URL that is never reflected in the ILS.

- Data sharing is limited. Because data can become redundant, the system relies on human intervention to transfer data, data changes, and new data from one existing system to another. When the licensing librarian learns of a title change, she must notify the cataloger maintaining the MARC record and the reference librarian maintaining the Web list. All three manually change the same piece of information in three different locations.

- Standards are unenforceable. Data copied into many different data banks can be changed at each locality and can diverge from its original form. Each library replicates a copy of the MARC record from a bibliographic utility into its own system, and local custom and policy usually prompt the cataloger to make some changes to the record, rendering it unique from its existence in other library's databases. The initial MARC record recorded the URL for the product's home page, but the library downloading the MARC record prefers to send customers to a search screen within a product. The MARC record must be manually changed at time of download and is now different from the standard version.

- Design is inflexible. In a flat file, data fields are limited to a preconceived purpose and number. For example, recording all possible URLs, including home page, instructions page, search screen, advanced search screen, holdings lists, license agreement, and contacts page for an electronic resource would require the creation in advance of a large number of separate MARC fields. The URLs listed for a record are limited by MARC convention with the result of limiting the number of helpful URLs available for a resource.

- Productivity is lowered. The manual entry of changes and the manual transfer of these changes from data bank to data bank create work for an expanding circle of library professionals. The nonrelational nature of a flat file record also makes display from multiple data sources close to impossible. Dynamic Web display supported by relational database design would allow MARC and non-MARC data to display in ways appropriate to the user need: by subject for instance, or by class assignment, or in partnership with other databases such as citation linkers. When the MARC record cannot support the type of flexible Web access necessary for library customers, another set of librarians have to devote time to the design of a new data bank and interface to group electronic resources in new ways, such as subject guides, electronic journal finders, and license management databases.

A flat file data storage system lists all descriptive information in one place. A modern example is computer spreadsheet software, like Microsoft Excel®. One can continue to add columns, each containing a new type of descriptive information, but eventually the spreadsheet gets unwieldy, and viewing the data or understanding how the data describe an item becomes difficult. Relational databases, like Microsoft Access®, separate the long list of data pieces (elements) describing a single item into small, interrelated collection of data (tables). For example, all titles for an electronic resource are collected in one table, all URLs in another, all license provisions in another, and so on. The database attaches unique identifiers to each set of elements and to the item being described, allowing each to be linked together in a myriad of ways to describe that same resource, depending on need and circumstance.

Figure 7.5 is a representation of how a relational database stores data within tables and links these tables together with unique identifiers to create a single description of a resource.

By its nature, a relational database is not bound by the space requirements of an index card, or even standardization of data, to a certain extent. Any number of tables can describe aspects of a resource. In Figure 7.5, for example, these are resource description, vendor description, and access URLs. The tables each hold like data (for example, titles, contact phone numbers, or URLs) that are connected together through unique identifiers. The database designer has the flexibility to design as many tables, with as many data elements, as are necessary to adequately describe the resources the database is supposed to describe.

In the example in Figure 7.5, the same vendor, DB Resellers, sells a library the electronic resources Quick Journals and Maps Galore. In a computerized spreadsheet (flat file), each resource would reside in its own row. Each row would contain all information relevant to the resource, including information about the vendor telephone number, search page URL, etc. This means that the same vendor information would appear twice, once in each row for each product, and a change to the vendor telephone number would require two manual changes.

In the relational example, data is split into tables. In the example in Figure 7.5, one table contains resource description and another the vendor description. If the vendor's phone number were to change, one would only need to make the change once, in the vendor table. When one calls up the record for either resource, the unique identifier, Vendor ID V00001, will link from the Resource record to the Vendor record and automatically pick up the new, correct telephone number.

With list of descriptive data organized into tables and connected by unique identifiers, the operator could have the database make changes based on a complex set of criteria. For example, in Figure 7.5, if a vendor

Figure 7.5
Relational tables. A relational database is constructed of tables linked through unique identifiers to describe resources.

Resource Table

Elements	Resource ID	Title	Author	Vendor ID	Access ID
Entities	R00001	Quick Journals	State University	V00001	A00001
	R00002	Maps Galore	John Americus	V00001	A00002

Vendor Table

Elements	Vendor ID	Name	Contact	Telephone
Entities	V00001	DB Resellers	Emily Smith	800-123-4567

Access Table

Elements	Access ID	Remote URL	Search Page URL
Entities	A00001	http://remote.quickjnl.com/	http://www.quickjnl.com/search/
	A00002	http://remote.maps.com/	http://www.maps.com/srch/

changed a license agreement to allow remote access, the user of a database could use the Vendor unique ID to find the resources sold by that vendor, follow each Access unique ID to the Remote URL field in the Access record, and automatically update every record where appropriate. The relational database allows data manipulation relevant to the task at hand.

Because of the connecting unique identifiers, each piece of data is available for display on a Web page in a dynamic fashion. For example, a Web page editor can choose among all the data elements only those relevant to the circumstances at hand and display them in a format appropriate for the current use. If a display system (like a library OPAC) needs a MARC-like record, these elements are available. If another display system (like a subject guide to electronic resources) needs current URLs, these elements are available. The storage of the data behind the scenes is no longer governed by the fixed elements of MARC, for example. Nor is it governed by geography. As long as the unique identifier is known, data is also available from remote databases. A description of a library resource has information available from the MARC-like elements in a local OPAC-like relational database along with the current URL from the OCLC PURL server around the world.

Taken one step further, the journal holdings of a resource, for example, could be stored in a central source trusted for its accuracy and the list accessed by libraries around the world. If the central source also knows the subscription circumstances of individual libraries (like a serials agent), the list would be personalized to the library. No more downloading and storing electronic journal lists library by library. Relational databases allow one to efficiently manage chunks of data. A single library professional (at a vendor, for example) touches the data once, keeping it consistent and allowing infinite ways to share the data with libraries around the world. Vendors are making advances in this area (for example, EBSCO 2004), but complete coordination across vendor platforms is to come in the future.

The preceding discussion of relational database concepts is the barest of introductions, and I suggest taking at least one-semester-long class in database design and management to develop an adequate understanding of data modeling and relational databases. These concepts are fundamental to any discussion of database-driven dynamic Web sites, and database-driven dynamic Web sites will be fundamental to most virtual library services in the near future. What relational databases mean for the MARC record is that the data describing a resource is not limited by what is standard in a MARC record.

A powerful example of database-driven functionality is the metasearch capability recently introduced into the library customer's research experience. Through a database designed to make intelligent decisions in response to a single keyword search string, a library customer can simultaneously search many electronic resources from diverse vendors. To take an example from the dot-com realm, Amazon.com's "OPAC" now allows keyword searching at the textual level, within the full text of books that the company has loaded into its servers (Amazon.com 2004). In an example of available library products, library vendors now provide full text metasearching across a library's subscribed databases from diverse vendors (for example, Ex Libris 2004a). Complete integration of these innovations is not a reality, but in the near future the library customer could finally have a single interface from which to access all library content—print and electronic, monographic and serial.

Integrated library systems also demonstrate the utility of relational databases. Software companies have for thirty years created database systems that contain the MARC record and attach to it, through unique identifiers, tables of data not allowed into the MARC proper, such as purchase history, circulation status, and issues received. Although the ILS systems that formed around the MARC record have acquired the advantages of relational design, MARC itself has remained fixed. In an ILS, an acquisitions staff member can attach one payment to multiple products, and in circulation, a single patron can use a single personal ID to borrow multiple items from the library's collection. Within MARC itself, however, reconciling the fluid nature of electronic resource descriptors–the multiplicity of appropriate URLs, for example–has become a thorny problem.

Although the inflexible nature of the MARC record does not lend itself to describing and providing access to the mutable electronic resources, the descriptive and standardized nature of the record may be its saving grace. Later in this chapter we will discuss metadata and extensible markup language (XML). Metadata and XML can break down a description of an item into an almost infinite number of useful pieces and intelligently rearrange those pieces to describe and provide access to that item in an almost infinite number of situation-specific ways, providing the information needed and providing it in ways elegant to the computer operator's needs.

Metadata and Extensible Standards

The library community worldwide has begun to explore ways to incorporate metadata and relational database design in current cataloging practices. Metadata is "data about data." The title of a book is data, but what in that data indicates a book title? Metadata shares information about the data itself. If resented with the words *Benjamin Franklin* without accompanying metadata explanation, a computer does not know whether it is seeing the title of a biography, the author of the *Almanack of Poor Richard the Second*, or the first two words of Chapter 1 of a book on early leaders of the United States. The metadata, or data about the data that indicates these distinctions, would be important to a search engine (seeking words in author, not title) or to the automatic formatting of a Web page (increasing the font of a title versus bolding the first two words of a chapter).

Metatags provide this metadata for communication across the Internet, such as within Web pages. Metatags allow Web-based applications to appropriately interpret data, display it to Web users and refile it into local data banks. Hypertext markup language (HTML) transports digitized objects (text, images, programmed instructions, etc.) across the Internet for display or execution on a local user's screen. HTML tells interpreting software like Web browsers how to display these objects by surrounding them with instructions called *tags*. For example, the "bold" tag, <B>, and the "end bold" tag, </B>, placed around the title of a book will cause the title to display in a Web browser on another's machine as boldface text. HTML tagging uses a standard set of tags understood by all web browsers, regardless of computer operating systems or browser software. Only "<B>" means to bold text, not <BOLD> or <BO> or any other combination, and this convention creates "cross-platform" utility, or the ability for any type of computer, from

Macintosh to UNIX, to use an HTML interpreter to understand and use electronic objects.

The eXensible Metadata of XML

Figure 7.6 shows an example of XML tagging using the Dublin Core metadata set (DCMI 2004). This example presents an abridged version of XML tagging and uses the Dublin Core metadata set to display the descriptive information found in the catalog card (Figure 7.1) and MARC record (Figure 7.2) used as examples at the beginning of this chapter. The Dublin Core metadata set is meant to closely follow the data set in a MARC record. Other metadata sets (see Table 7.1, p. 159) go much further in comprehensiveness and flexibility.

Metatags containing metadata wrap around digital objects and describe what that object should "mean" to the receiving computer program. The receiving computer program, knowing the conventions accepted for the metatags, can translate the meaning of the metatag into metadata for the end user. Notice, for example, that in Figure 7.6, line 5, the title of the book is surrounded by the tags <dc:title> and </dc:title>. If the metatag <dc:title> is the accepted convention to denote title data, and the receiving computer program knows this convention, the receiving computer sees the tag and executes special actions for the title. The special instructions can accompany the tag or exist in the interpreting software. For example, based on instructions already given the Web browser, the <dc:title> tag would tell the browser that the words to follow are title words and that the browser needs to put the word "Title:" in front

Figure 7.6
XML tagged record. An XML tagging using the Dublin Core metadata set.

```
1   <?xml version="1.0"?>
2   <!DOCTYPE rdf:RDF PUBLIC "-//DUBLIN CORE//DCMES DTD2002/07/31//EN"
        "http://dublincore.org/documents/2002/07/31/dcmes-xml/dcmes-xml-
        dtd.dtd">
3   <metadata xmlns:dc="http://purl.org/dc/elements/1.1/">
4
5   <dc:title>An inquiry in to the nature and causes of the wealth of
        nations</dc:title>
6   <dc:creator>Adam Smith</dc:creator>
7   <dc:publisher>New Publishers</dc:publisher>
8   <dc:date>2000</dc:date>
9   <dc:subject>Economics</dc:subject>
10  <dc:descriptor>Includes indexes</dc:descriptor>
11  <dc:identifier>http://www.wealthofnations.com/ </dc:identifier>
12
13  </metadata>
```

of the phrase and bold the words in the title. Other instructions could include special placement in a bibliographic citation sequence; storage in a certain field in a relational database; or hyperlinked as an "anchor," or base, for a hypertext link to the full text elsewhere on the Web.

Just as HTML is a set of standard tags recognized by any Web browser, metadata tags also need standardization if they are to be understood by interpreting software. The common standard for metadata tags is XML, or eXtensible Markup Language, (W3C 2004a). The XML standard is interesting in that it does not specify tags per se. Instead it creates a standard for extensibility. As long as one conforms to a generally accepted standard of formation and display, one can create an infinite, or extensible, number of metadata tags. The XML standard describes how to create tags, not the tags themselves.

XML tags are arbitrary. The first advantage of XML is that a person creating a relational database with unique fields can also create unique metadata tags denoting each field in that database. Because the same person is creating both the database and instructions for the Web display page, the tags in the display page can accept and understand the data from the database, understand the metadata meaning, and understand what to do with the metadata. This closed system, however, is not interoperable with other systems on a network or on the Internet. A separate system designed by another developer would not understand the unique tags created by the first developer.

The second advantage of extensibility relies on a standard way to share the unique metatags between systems. The Document Type Definition (DTD) follows XML standards to describe the XML elements in use. An XML document gives its DTD at the beginning, and points to the defined list of the metatags in use within that Web page. The closed system above would point to a self-published DTD. The DTD of figure 7.6 is on line 2, along with more information on lines 1 and 3 about the XML in use, points to the Dublin Core DTD at dublincore.org.

For the sake of interoperability, a growing number of special interest groups, from genealogists to commercial purchasing agents, have agreed on standard DTDs for use with the data unique to their field of interest. For example, the mathematics community has developed MathML, used to display the special mathematical symbols. With an accepted DTD, a community can share information simply by referencing the accepted DTD at the beginning of an XML document. Communities as diverse as commercial suppliers and ornithologists have been developing and improving DTDs since the late 1990s. Table 7.1 provides a selected list of DTDs relevant to the library community.

Table 7.1 Selected XML Document Type Definition (DTD) Initiatives		
DTD Schema	**Community**	**Purpose**
arXiv	Physics	Repositories of physics research (arXiv 2003).
ARIADNE	Education	Create and disseminate pedagogical documents and teaching environments (ARIADNE 2003).
CIMI (Consortium for the Computer Interchange of Museum Information), VRA (Visual Resources Association), and CDWA (Categories for Describing Works of Art)	Art and Museum	Describe works of art (J. Paul Getty Trust 2000).
Dublin Core	Library Cataloging	Set of 15 cataloging fields based on MARC and chosen for widest interoperability (DCMI 2004).
EAD (Encoded Archival Description)	Archivists	Deliver archival finding aids (guides to collections) in digital form (LC 2003a).
GEM (Gateway to Educational Materials)	Education	Create and disseminate pedagogical documents and teaching environments (GEM 2004).
GILS (Government/Global Information Locator Service)	Government Documents	Provide access to publicly available government information resources (GILS 1997).
MARCXML	Catalogers (Library of Congress)	Provides a metadata framework for flexible use of MARC data (LC 2004c).

METS (Metadata Encoding Transmission Standard)	Archivists and Catalogers (Library of Congress and Digital Library Federation)	Administrative and structural metadata (technical requirements, linking of disparate items, rights management, etc.; LC 2004d).
MODS (Metadata Object Description Schema)	Library Cataloging (Library of Congress)	Cataloging fields more akin to the MARC record fields (LC 2004e).
OAI (Open Archives Initiative)	Digital Libraries and Digital Archives	Describe collection and enable cross-collection searching (OAI 2004).
OASIS, DocBook	Publishers (initially of computer manuals)	Originally book elements, both literary and technical (figures, programming code, etc.). Now expanded to include many types of business transactions. (OASIS 2004).
ONIX, EDItX	International Publishers	Elements of commercially published works including serials subscription information (NISO and EDItEUR 2004; EDItEUR 2005).
TEI (Text Encoding Initiative)	Humanities and Publishers	Literary elements of published works (title, paragraph, page number, etc.; TEI 2003).
Resource Description Framework (RDF)	W3C Semantic Web, Libraries, Other collections	"Support the exchange of knowledge on the Web" (W3C 2004b).

MARC and Metadata

MARC is itself metadata. By placing text in the field designated for title information, rather than the field for author, one determines the meaning of that text as it is displayed in the OPAC user interface. MARC is not interoperable. Systems outside of ILS OPACs usually cannot understand MARC. XML makes the connection between the insular MARC record and the relational databases and dynamic Web sites that will return the OPAC to the center of a researcher's experience.

With XML, the MARC record is divisible. MARC fields can be dispersed throughout a relational database and reshaped into dynamic Web pages responsive to user needs. Data in MARC fields can be stored centrally, retaining data integrity, and at the same time manipulated locally to reflect local circumstance.

As new as XML is (development began in 1996 [Connolly 2003]), library professionals are creating and improving XML DTDs for application in a growing variety of library operations. Their aim is to expand access to library collections outside the confines of closed library systems into the world of dynamic delivery and interoperability.

Dynamic Delivery and Interoperability

Compare the library OPAC closest to you with Amazon.com's "OPAC," or the opening search screen of Google. Library OPAC interfaces are typically more complex than the initial user needs, presenting all possible searches instead of, for example, Google's one search field. The search results are less precise than the advanced user would prefer, understanding only "Smith, Adam" and not "Adam Smith" in an author field search, or worse, not displaying works by Adam Smith at the top of the list. Results lists are less useful, not, like Amazon, taking advantage of linkages inside the database to serve up books also purchased by buyers (borrowers) of the book currently on display, or review synopses, or complete tables of contents. Vendors of ILSs are beginning to incorporate elements of these advances into interface designs, yet such companies as Google, Amazon, and eBay far outpace in subtlety and richness any available OPAC interface.

Commercial interfaces reflect the millions of dollars that the companies spend annually on usability research, but library OPACs do not reflect the years of experience librarians have had at helping researchers. The one element missing from the commercial services and OPACs is the trained library professional, dedicated to giving personal, experienced, and human depth to the customer's unique research experience. If librarians could incorporate the strengths of Google (search algorithms), Amazon (description), eBay (self-organizing chaotic behavior),

AOL (community), and Yahoo (organizing) with the selecting, organizing, archiving, and human-help ethics of professional librarians, then libraries would again take their rightful place at the center of our communities' information seeking and delivery.

Roy Tennant (2002, 2004) is a very lucid proponent for the shift in librarianship away from inflexible descriptive structures toward flexible, need-specific relational databases and metadata upon which interfaces-of-the-day can be built and rebuilt over time. A dynamic Web page, a Web page with programming instructions designed to interpret and respond to the data retrieved, would form a list of results unique to the data and to the search behavior. The extensible XML metadata standard encapsulates descriptive information in a language understandable by incompatible computers. Relational database systems flexibly store this data and metadata in a nonhierarchical, expandable system that can grow and change with no obsolescence of structure. Dynamic Web design creates Web pages on-the-fly by responding to the data and metadata with programmed instructions to create Web pages of immediate relevance.

Let us return to our example of a resource's title. In a fixed MARC record, the superceded title, still recognized by the library customer, has few places to go for shelter—a notes field possibly not searched by the OPAC interface, for instance. A relational database, with its special table reserved just for titles, will store any number of different titles, with accompanying metadata describing the significance of each title (superceded, current, subtitle, acronym, nickname). When Web-based user interfaces (from the OPAC to an instructor's syllabus) receive data from that database table, XML metadata tags tell the user's interface how to display the data so that it is clearest within the context of the interface and the search based on the user's current searching behavior. With XML, the titles would be listed on a dynamic Web page with labels, such as "Current Title," "Superceded Title," "Series Title," "Sub-part Title," "Abbreviated Title," and "Nickname"; be sorted based on expressed logic; and be hyperlinked with certain titles based on another logic. Creators of the interface could augment standardized XML DTDs universally understood outside the local system with customized XML tags created specifically for a unique, local implementation, and understood by the local system. The dynamic display of flexibly stored relational data is simultaneously standardized, interoperable, and customizable.

I am attracted by the eBay model, the idea of a centrally housed and internationally available database (or databases) maintained by all participants, including the customer, in which all participants could record title changes, and, in the next second, libraries around the world would reflect that change in their own relational database and then use XML to display the change, in the language of their choice and according to the tastes of the local population. As with eBay, each local library can choose which changes to trust and which to ignore. In this environment, descriptive elements can reflect both global and local characteristics for data such as URLs, license provisions, product holdings lists, citation linking, or personalized library interfaces. For example, interfaces could be personalized to support academic fields of study, academic courses, corporate engineering research projects, or 10-year-old students collaborating from London and Tokyo.

Think of the implications for serials librarians tracking dates of coverage through a library's link directly into a serials agent's database, for acquisitions librarians linking between sibling products from a single vendor to track purchasing and inventory management, for reference librarians creating subject relevance relationships between resources of fractal proportions, and for researchers seeking citation management through the linking of citations to full text anywhere it exists. As young as relational databases and XML are relative to the history of bringing content to library communities, professionals are working collaboratively to create building blocks from accepted cataloging practices, relational database environments, and the almost infinite responsiveness of XML applications in dynamic Web interfaces (Tennant 2002; CDL 2004). The few examples that follow do not do justice to the amount of activity under way. I hope these act as prompts for the reader to seek out other projects and start original ones, if only to learn how these powerful tools can work together to increase the value of libraries within the communities they serve.

- *The Logical Structure of the AACR2 and the Functional Requirements for Bibliographic Records (FRBR).* The Joint Steering Committee (JSC) for the Revision of the *AACR2* commissioned a visual data model, a Logical Structure, of the principles of current cataloging rules. The International Federation of Library Associations and Institutions (IFLA) commissioned the FRBR, which creates a graphical structure of metadata for information resources, an Entity-Relationship (ER) data model useful for the design of a relational database (Delsey 1998; IFLA 1998; Lonsdale Systems 1999).

- *OAIster.* The University of Michigan Digital Library Production Services created a search engine that provides access to digitized archival material housed in distributed parent institutions worldwide, a search engine that uses the Open Archives Initiative Protocol for Metadata Harvesting (DLPS 2003).

- *Dublin Core, MARCXML, MODS.* The Library of Congress's Network Development and MARC Standards Office is developing a set of schemata that expand MARC into an extensible universe of metadata schemata that allow libraries to provide description, access, and technical management of all information resources, digital and nondigital (LC 2003b).

- *DOI and the Open URL Framework.* A NISO (National Information Standards Organization) standard that enables the transport of resource- and circumstance-specific metadata, using packages within the standardized syntax of an OpenURL (NISO 2004). Using digital object identifiers (DOIs), electronic resources can be uniquely identified to any remote database, the key requisite to creating relational databases recording information about the various incarnations of a resource (DOI Foundation 2003). Examples of these kinds of relational databases are link resolvers like SFX (Ex Libris 2004b).
- *RedLightGreen.* The RLG (Research Library Group) consortium of research libraries is using the FRBR (Functional Requirements for Bibliographic Records) structure to present the best list of editions available for the work. With the data-mining capabilities of a commercial product, RLG is putting a relational database to work through XML to present search results of the RLG union catalog in a rich, but easy-to-use, interface (RLG 2003).
- *The European Library Project (TEL).* The European Library Project uses a Dublin Core model to create seamless access to major European national libraries (TEL 2004).
- *Additional examples.* See others listed in the *IFLANET Digital Libraries: Metadata Resources* Web site (IFLA 2003).

Cataloging as a Group Effort

Currently, in most libraries, the OPAC competes for the customer's attention with other finding aids. This section uses the examples of the electronic resource subject guide and the journal finder, but many others exist in a typical library. Take, for example, an undergraduate looking for documentation to support a term paper. If asked, a reference librarian would advise this undergraduate to include reference works, books, and journal articles, but the student is likely to include a plethora of other information resources of varying degrees of quality. This particular undergraduate is lucky because she has asked a reference librarian to help her navigate the research process. At the undergraduate's fingertips are the OPAC, the print reference shelves, the library's subject guide of online databases, several article databases relevant to her search, the library Web-based list of electronic journals, a separate list of paper journals in the OPAC, a product that links a citation to a publisher's full-text journal Web site, the myriad free Web search engines, the online and print course reserves, universal book catalogs like WorldCat and Amazon.com, and interlibrary loan. By herself, the student would likely have missed a large portion of these resources. Depending on her tenacity, she may have become discouraged and stopped at the easiest to use (Google.com) rather proceeding to the most rewarding–the library's subject list of databases, behind which were over $1 million worth of online databases. What is likely is that she may have skipped some resources simply because she was not aware of their existence.

Even with the librarian's help, our researcher has a difficult library experience because all these resources are in disparate systems with little or no interconnectivity. How much easier for the student if the OPAC could once again become the gateway, a way to simplify this array of services. At present, it is difficult if not impossible to combine inside most OPACs both a single-search description and one-click access to the library print and electronic collection of books, reference works, journals, online article databases, and Web resources along with the library services of reference, instruction, interlibrary loan, reserves, and citation linking. Only by rethinking library structures from flat file to relational and from MARC-only to XML-enabled can we meet our communities where they need us to be, in environments dynamic and responsive to their research needs.

As we can see from the examples in this chapter, current projects combine the power of XML and relational databases with the standardization of MARC and *AACR2*. Many inside and outside the cataloging specialization are making the possibilities a reality. This new frontier means that for catalogers the required skill set has dramatically shifted. Catalogers still contribute talent and intellect to creating useful description and access. This art form has picked up new tools, complex tools that require extensive training and experience, not just in relational database design and XML but also in the programming languages of dynamic Web sites (Java or PERL, for example), user interface design, and its cousins the studies of human–computer interaction and information-seeking behavior.

Catalogers cannot and should not be expected to learn all these fields with the depth necessary to remain as an independent function within library management. Catalogers and their colleagues can, however, learn enough about these fields to ask insightful questions and be part of a collaborative group of creative experts, and this collaboration within groups of professionals can return the library to its role as central provider of information. One could see a day when, at the American Library Association annual conference, the cataloging cooperatives BIBCO and CONSER host a joint meeting with MARS (Machine Assisted Reference Service), ASIST (American Society for Information

Science and Technology), and ALCTS (Association for Library Collections & Technical Services) to mutually direct the future of MARC and the *AACR2* within an XML framework.

Those who are expert at cataloging would ask experts in customer experience, user interface design, systems design, dynamic Web delivery, and the management of electronic resource collection development to contribute to the vision of cataloging for ease of access. The collaborative combination of catalogers, reference librarians, systems librarians, information architects, and library acquisitions managers would be a potent combination in designing a system seamless for both library staff and library customers. Add to this team library professionals from ILS vendors and electronic resource vendors, and the results would be revelatory. Within the microcosm of the single library, all these professionals can collaboratively share the learning and risk-taking. Only through groups can service quality improvement efforts on this scale take place.

Conclusion

Catalogers and their colleagues are in a position to rescue the library profession from obscurity. Catalogers are the library profession's experts at describing and providing access to our collections. Through delivery systems imbued with the flexibility of relational databases and the extensibility of XML-informed interfaces, the true wealth of library resources will reach our communities, including print, media, electronic, archival, and formats not yet invented along with human research assistance, the professional selection of "free" resources, and the professional organization of this universe of knowledge. When a cataloger learns enough XML and relational database theory to have in-depth conversations with experts in these fields, the opportunities for providing correct, current electronic access information become vast.

Fixed MARC and OPAC user interfaces will neither contain the changing nature of electronic resources nor create a seamless environment for the confused researcher. Catalogers, along with a team of professionals who combine expertise in relational database design, XML interoperability, and dynamic Web delivery, could not only help libraries better manage electronic resources within their own collections, but also create a simpler research environment of more value to the library's community.

References

Amazon.com. "amazon.com." ©2004. Amazon.com. URL: http://www.amazon.com/ (Accessed September 17, 2004).

American Library Association (ALA). 1978. *Anglo-American cataloging rules, 2nd edition*. Chicago, IL: American Library Association.

———. 2002. *Anglo-American cataloging rules, 2nd edition, 2002 revision.* Chicago, IL: American Library Association.

ARIADNE. ©2003. ARIADNE Foundation. URL: http://www.ariadne-eu.org/ (Accessed September 17, 2004).

arXiv. *arXiv.org e-Print Archive.* ©2003. Cornell University. URL: http://arxiv.org/ (Accessed September 17, 2004).

Brandsma, Terry W., Elizabeth R. Bernhardt, and Dana M. Sally. 2003. Journal Finder, a second look: Implications for serials access in today's library. *Serials Review* 29 (4):287–294.

California Digital Library (CDL). *eScholarship.* ©2004. The Regents of the University of California. URL: http://www.cdlib.org/programs/escholarship.html (Accessed September 17, 2004).

Codd, E. F. (Ted). 1970. "A relational model of data for large shared data bases." *Communications of the ACM* 13 (June):77–387.

Connolly, Dan. "Development history." ©2003. *Extensible Markup Language (XML).* W3C. URL: http://www.w3.org/XML/hist2002 (Accessed September 17, 2004).

Delsey, Tom. "The logical structure of the Anglo-American Cataloging Rules–Part 1, Introduction (including key issues and recommendations)." ©1998. *Joint Steering Committee for the Revision of the Anglo-American Cataloging Rules.* JSC. URL: http://www.nlc-bnc.ca/jsc/aacrint.pdf (Accessed September 17, 2004).

DOI Foundation. *DOI: The Digital Object Identifier System.* ©2003. DOI Foundation. URL: http://www.doi.org/ (Accessed September 17, 2004).

Dublin Core Metadata Initiative (DCMI). *Dublin Core Metadata Initiative.* ©2004 DCMI and OCLC Research. URL: http://dublincore.org/ (Accessed September 17, 2004).

EBSCO. *EBSCOhost Electronic Journal Service.* ©2004. EBSCO. URL: http://ejournals.ebsco.com/ (Accessed September 17, 2004).

EDItEUR. ©2003. EDItEUR. URL: http://www.editeur.org/ (Accessed September 17, 2004).

Ex Libris. "Metalib: The library portal." ©2004a. Ex Libris. URL: http://www.exlibris-usa.com/metalib.htm (Accessed September 17, 2004).

———. "SFX: Context-sensitive reference linking." ©2004b. *SFXit.* Ex Libris. URL: http://www.sfxit.com/ (Accessed September 17, 2004).

Furrie, Betty. 2003. *Understanding MARC bibliographic: Machine-readable cataloging.* 7th ed. Washington, DC: Library of Congress. URL: http://www.loc.gov/marc/umb/ (Accessed September 17, 2004).

Gateway to Educational Materials (GEM). *GEM Project Site.* ©2004. U.S. Department of Education. URL: http://www.geminfo.org/ (Accessed September 17, 2004).

Global Information Locator Service (GILS). *Global Information Locator Service (GILS).* ©1997. GILS. URL: http://www.gils.net/ (Accessed September 17, 2004).

Hawkins, Les and Jean Hirons. 2002. Transforming *AACR2:* Using the revised rules in Chapters 9 and 12. Paper presented at North American

Serials Interest Group (NASIG) Conference, June 22, 2002, in Williamsburg, VA. URL: http://www.loc.gov/acq/conser/aacr2002/A2slides.html (Accessed September 17, 2004).

Hoffer, Jeffrey A., Mary B. Prescott, and Fred R. McFadden. 2000. *Modern database management.* 6th ed. Upper Saddle River, NJ: Prentice Hall.

International Federation of Library Associations and Institutions (IFLA). "Functional requirements for bibliographic records: Final report." *IFLANET Activities and Services: Cataloguing Section, FRBR Review Group.* ©1998. IFLA. URL: http://www.ifla.org/VII/s13/wgfrbr/finalreport.htm (Accessed September 17, 2004).

———. "Digital libraries: Metadata resources." ©2003 *IFLANET Electronic Collections.* IFLA. URL: http://www.ifla.org/II/metadata.htm (Accessed January 15, 2004.)

Intner, Sheila S. and Jean Weihs. 2001. *Standard cataloging for school and public libraries.* 3rd. ed. Englewood, Colo.: Libraries Unlimited.

J. Paul Getty Trust and the College Art Association, Inc. *Categories for the Description of Works of Art.* ©2000. JPGT. URL: http://www.getty.edu/research/conducting_research/standards/cdwa/ (Accessed September 17, 2004).

Library of Congress (LC). 2003a. *EAD: Encoded Archival Description, version 2002.* ©2003a. Library of Congress. URL: http://lcweb.loc.gov/ead/ (Accessed September 17, 2004).

———. *MARC standards: The Library of Congress, Network Development and MARC Standards Office.* ©2003b. Library of Congress. URL: http://lcweb.loc.gov/marc/ (Accessed September 17, 2004).

———. *OCLC/PCC PURL Service.* ©2003c. Library of Congress. URL: http://lcweb.loc.gov/acq/conser/purl/main.html (Accessed September 17, 2004).

———. *BIBCO Program for Cooperative Cataloging.* ©2004a. Library of Congress. URL: http://www.loc.gov/catdir/pcc/bibco.html (Accessed September 17, 2004).

———. *CONSER Cooperative Online Serials.* ©2004b. Library of Congress. URL: http://www.loc.gov/acq/conser/homepage.html (Accessed September 17, 2004).

———. *MARCXML: MARC 21 XML Schema.* ©2004c. Library of Congress. URL: http://www.loc.gov/standards/marcxml/ (Accessed September 17, 2004).

———. *METS: Metadata Encoding and Transmission Standard.* ©2004d. Library of Congress. URL: http://www.loc.gov/standards/mets/ (Accessed September 17, 2004).

———. *MODS: Metadata Metadata Object Description Schema.* ©2004e. Library of Congress. URL: http://www.loc.gov/standards/mods/ (Accessed September 17, 2004).

Lonsdale Systems. "Entity relationship models." ©1999. *Lonsdale Systems.* Lonsdale Systems. URL: http://members.iinet.net.au/~lonsdale/docs/erd.pdf (Accessed September 17, 2004).

National Information Standards Organization (NISO). *The OpenURL Framework for Context-Sensitive Services: Standards Committee AX.* ©2004. NISO. URL: http://www.niso.org/committees/committee_ax.html (Accessed September 17, 2004).

National Information Standards Organization (NISO) and EDItEUR. *Joint Working Party for the Exchange of Serials Subscription Information.* ©2004 NISO and EDItEUR. URL: http://www.fcla.edu/~pcaplan/jwp/ (Accessed September 17, 2004).

Online Computer Library Center (OCLC). *PURLS: A Project of OCLC Research.* ©2004. OCLC. URL: http://purl.oclc.org/ (Accessed September 17, 2004).

Open Archives Initiative (OAI). *Open Archives Initiative.* ©2004. Digital Library Federation and the Coalition for Networked Information. URL: http://www.openarchives.org/ (Accessed September 17, 2004).

OASIS. ©2004. Organization for the Advancement of Structured Information Standards (OASIS). URL: http://www.oasis-open.org/ (Accessed September 17, 2004).

Research Library Group (RLG). *RedLightGreen.* ©2003. RLG. URL: http://www.redlightgreen.com/ (Accessed September 17, 2004).

Tang Sha, Vivianne. "Bibliographic Utilities." ©2002. *Internet Library for Librarians.* InfoWorks Technology Company. URL: http://www.itcompany.com/inforetriever/util.htm (Accessed September 17, 2004).

Taylor, Arlene G. 2000. *Wynar's introduction to cataloging and classification.* 9th ed. Englewood, CO: Libraries Unlimited.

Tennant, Roy, ed. 2002. *XML in libraries.* New York: Neal-Schuman.

———. 2004. *Managing the digital library: A library journal book.* New York: Reed Press.

Text Encoding Initiative Consortium (TEI). *Text Encoding Initiative.* ©2003. TEI Consortium. URL: http://www.tei-c.org/ (Accessed September 17, 2004).

The European Library (TEL). *The European Library (TEL): The Gate to Europe's Knowledge.* ©2004. The European Library. URL: http://www.europeanlibrary.org (Accessed September 17, 2004).

University of Georgia Libraries. "Research Central." ©2004. *University of Georgia Libraries.* University of Georgia. URL: http://www.libs.uga.edu/researchcentral/ (Accessed September 17, 2004).

University of Michigan. Digital Library Production Services (DLPS). *OAIster.* ©2003. DLPS. URL: http://oaister.umdl.umich.edu/o/oaister/ (Accessed September 17, 2004).

University of North Carolina, Greensboro (UNCG). Jackson Library. *Journal Finder.* ©2004. UNCG. Jackson Library. URL: http://journalfinder.uncg.edu/uncg/ (Accessed September 17, 2004).

University of Texas (UT). Information Technology Services. "Introduction to data modeling: Overview of the relational model." ©2004. *Windows Services.* UT. ITS. URL: http://www.utexas.edu/its/windows/database/datamodeling/rm/overview.html (Accessed September 17, 2004).

W3C. *Extensible Markup Language (XML) 1.0.* ©2004a. W3C. URL: http://www.w3.org/TR/REC-xml (Accessed September 17, 2004).

———. *Resource Description Framework (RDF).* ©2004b. W3C. URL: http://www.w3.org/RDF/ (Accessed September 17, 2004).

Further Reading

Delsey, Tom. "The logical structure of the Anglo-American Cataloging Rules–Part 2, Introduction (including key issues and recommendations)." ©1999. JSC. URL: http://www.nlc-bnc.ca/jsc/aacrint2.pdf (Accessed September 17, 2004).

Gilmour, Ron. 2003. *XML: A guide for librarians.* Chicago, IL: American Library Association.

Gibbons, Susan and Brenda Reeb. 2004. Students, librarians, and subject guides: Improving a poor rate of return. *portal: Libraries and the Academy* 4 (1):123–130.

Herold, Ken, ed. 2004. *The philosophy of information.* Library Trends vol. 52, no. 3 (Urbana Champaign: University of Illinois).

International Federation of Library Associations and Institutions (IFLA). "Digital libraries: Cataloguing and indexing of electronic resources." ©2003 *IFLANET Electronic Collections.* IFLA. URL: http://www.ifla.org/II/catalog.htm (Accessed September 17, 2004).

Library of Congress (LC). "2002 revision of AACR2: Impact on integrating remote access electronic resources." ©2002. *Program for Cooperative Cataloging.* LC. PCC. URL: http://www.loc.gov/catdir/pcc/ir/AACR2rev_dr02.htm (Accessed September 17, 2004).

———. "MARC and FRBR." ©2004. *MARC Standards.* LC. Network Development and MARC Standards Office. URL: http://www.loc.gov/marc/marc-functional-analysis/frbr.html (Accessed September 17, 2004).

Miksa, Francis L. 1998. *The DDC, the universe of knowledge, and the post-modern library.* Albany, NY: Forest Press.

Miller, Dick R. and Kevin S. Clarke. 2003. *Putting XML to work in the library: Tools for improving access and management.* Chicago, IL: American Library Association.

Svenonius, Elaine. 2000. *The intellectual foundation of information organization.* Cambridge, MA: MIT Press.

Tillett, Barbara B. *Principles of AACR.* ©2001. JSC. URL: http://www.nlc-bnc.ca/jsc/docs/prin2001.pdf (Accessed September 17, 2004).

———. "2002 revision of *AACR2* and LC implementation: December 1, 2002." ©2002. Library of Congress. URL: http://www.loc.gov/catdir/pcc/ir/AACR2rev_ovrvbt02.html (Accessed September 17, 2004).

Torok, Andrew G., ed. 2003. *Organizing the Internet.* Library Trends vol. 52, no. 2 (Urbana Champaign: University of Illinois).

"XML Sub Categories." ©2004. *Hotscripts.com.* iNET Interactive. URL: http://www.hotscripts.com/XML/ (Accessed September 17, 2004).

CHAPTER 8

Technology Infrastructure

The library is no longer a place; it is also an activity. The library as an institution remains a physical structure that stores data, information, and knowledge for use by a community, but, with computerization, the library also becomes an infrastructure of technology and professional effort through which these commodities flow from vendor networks to computer users. Collaborative management of this technological infrastructure requires expertise in one's own job and enough knowledge of systems architecture and systems design to communicate with those who implement the infrastructure along with you. Collaborative management of the technological infrastructure of libraries also requires conscious and conscientious management of professional elements, including adaptive decision making through informed maintenance and improvements within the technological infrastructure, continuous training of decision makers at all levels, and seamlessness in the customers' experiences through an attention to the fit between human and technology.

This chapter seeks to give a broad overview of the technological infrastructure necessary to deliver library services to customers. I find this infrastructure easier to understand as levels of technology, one supporting the next to create a technological environment within which library professionals and library customers do their work. These levels are more a matrix of interrelated capacities than layers separate from each other, and the levels I present here are my own invention serving only to clarify my discussion of what is, in reality, an intricate whole.

Despite the fact that each level affects the performance of all other levels in complex ways, expert knowledge of all four levels is difficult, if not impossible, to attain. For this reason, managing this infrastructure through a collaborative group approach is as important to the management of the library technological infrastructure as is any concrete set of technical skills. Only through groups can libraries hope to integrate the expertise necessary to provide a seamless environment for us as professionals and for our customers.

The four levels of library technology infrastructure that I will use in my discussion are as follows.

1. Hardware, including computers, servers, and peripherals
2. Connectivity, or the information conduits between hardware components
3. Software, or the operating instructions for the hardware
4. User interface, or the point at which Levels 1 through 3 encounter the human users who have work to do

If one considers hardware to be physical containers through which library customers receive information, libraries have always been in the hardware business. Libraries have developed efficient processes necessary to warehouse and lend paper-based containers and have perfected the shelving, binding, and classification of book-like resources and nonprint media that come in physical packages. The delivery of electronic resources, however, requires the management of an additional infrastructure of connectivity, software, and interface within the library building and out onto library customers' desktop computers. Electronic resources add to the responsibilities of the library as a physical space for storage and community service the responsibilities of the library as a conduit of activity between vendors of information and the library's customers inside and outside the library's walls.

Information delivered as an electronic resource is stored in bits and bytes, a form unreadable by humans. The bytes need translating machines (Level 1, Hardware), conduit between these machines (Level 2, Connectivity), manipulation (Level 3, Software), and human-ready display (Level 4, User interface). All of this activity is virtual, meaning that participants do not handle physical items—books—instead, they handle virtual replicas of these items, pages on a computer screen. As with print resources, the library is still the intermediary purchaser of content for a community of consumers, but in addition to physical shelving the library must now purchase, network together and maintain the appliances, conduits, and interfaces within which this virtual content resides, flows, and displays. To manage this flow of virtual content, the library must form relationships with other organizations that make up parts of this network, including vendors, parent institutions, and library customers' Internet service providers (ISPs) and other connecting networks. And library professionals must forge collaborative working relationships across lines of expertise and responsibility to form adaptive learning networks that turn routines into responsive decision making.

The advent of technology infrastructure changes the skill set required of every library professional. No library professional, administrator, librarian, paraprofessional, support staff member within any library department is exempt from the need for a basic understanding of all levels of the library's technological infrastructure. Each level works with the others in a sensitive relationship, and a basic understanding all four levels is crucial to supporting effective decision making for oneself and one's colleagues and creating a high quality library experience for the customer.

The task of encapsulating a discussion of library technological infrastructure within the pages of a single book chapter is daunting. In such a small space, important information will be summarized to the point of obfuscation, glossed over, or just plain left out. I am tempted to let the section on Level 4 stand as my final word. If all your technology learning has as its goal the creation of a seamless experience for the library customer, then your learning, and your library, will be used to its highest purpose. I will, however, brave the task of illuminating in some small way the other three levels and in the process I hope to provide enough of an outline for the reader to begin, or continue along, what will be a career-long adventure of learning about technology in libraries.

Accompanying what can only be a brief introduction to each level of library technology infrastructure will be an examination of how each level takes its ideals for success from the ideal of success at Level 4, the user interface. Because the user interface is pivotal to successful management of the other levels of a library's technology infrastructure, I begin this chapter's discussion at Level 4. I hope that the habit of placing the needs of the user above the needs of the technology will remain with you throughout your learning adventure as a library professional.

Level 4: User Interface

Level 4 is the interface between the technology of Levels 1 through 3 and the human users' accomplishment of work. Successful management of Levels 1 through 3 happens only with a consistent attention to Level 4. Library professionals can be tempted to ignore or procrastinate with their attention to Level 4 because the elements of human behavior inherent in interface design do not respond to planning in the same way as the relatively predictable mechanics of the first three levels. Attention to

Level 4, however, is crucial for any discussion of the other levels to take place. When observations about use start with, "If only they [the users] would . . ." or "They [the users] will just have to . . .", the system designers have made technological decisions about the infrastructure that put the user second to the needs of Levels 1 through 3 and are now bemoaning the user's inappropriate handling of a system that was designed without primary reference to the user. Designers of successful systems, systems that users like to interact with, have always started, revisited, and ended their Levels 1 through 3 design work with constant reference to Level 4.

Seamlessness is a computer-use experience during which the user completes tasks intuitively, with consistency and without interruption from the computer system. The Level 4 ideal relies on a computer experience that is uninterrupted by technological difficulties. In a sense, the computer user should be aware of completing the primary task, finding an article, for example, not the secondary task of using the computer. Connections between servers do not break down. Peripherals respond as directed. The user's computer does not "crash" or lock up. Searching occurs from the smallest number of entrances to the largest array of resources (e.g., metasearching). By extension, the Level 4 ideal requires that the computer ask the human user to complete tasks related only to the human's work, not the computer's. For example, the user should not have to reenter the same data again and again (e.g., passwords), should not have to provide instructions for server-to-server communication (e.g., remote access protocols), and should not have to solve task problems internal to the computer (e.g., choose which printer to send printing jobs to). The Level 4 ideal, lastly, asks that the computer respond to the user as an individual with unique work habits and goals. The Level 4 ideal sets a high standard, and we are at present not in a world of the seamless computer experience. The modern library professional's task in the library-as-activity environment is to continuously strive through collaboration, learning, and innovation to bring the library customer's experience closer to this seamlessness.

Computers and computer use are advanced forms of communication. Allow me to use one of the most fundamental forms of human communication to illustrate seamlessness. In storytelling, the author is not supposed to interrupt the "dream" of the listening or reading experience. Hackneyed plot, stereotypical characters, or implausible events snap the reader/listener out of participation in the experience of the story and into questioning the story mechanics. This break in experience causes the magic of the story to flee and with it the entertainment and instruction that the author had hoped to impart.

A technology infrastructure that works seamlessly will not interrupt the experience of its use. A technology infrastructure that works seamlessly will have reliable physical components, will effortlessly and quickly transport data from where it is stored to where it can be used, will allow intuitive and barrier-free use by humans, and will put the concerns of the human before the concerns of the machine. In other words, a user will not notice a library technology infrastructure that works seamlessly. What the user will notice is that they enjoy "visiting" the virtual library.

I repeat my assertion that our customers' primary responsibility within our walls, real or virtual, is the retrieval of existing knowledge to support the creation of new knowledge either for themselves or for others. Library customers should not also be burdened with navigating technical difficulties within the library's information retrieval infrastructure. The responsibility for solving these infrastructure difficulties is that of the library through its values and the library professionals through their dedication to smoothing the way of the researcher. Even if parts of the infrastructure lie outside the library's control, in the hands of others in our organization, other institutions altogether or vendors selling us a product, library professionals are responsible for setting expectations for these third parties and for contributing to standardization efforts, always with the goal of creating a seamless electronic service environment. Chapter 9, Customer Services, will explore design of the user interface in more detail. In the present chapter, hardware, connectivity, and software create an infrastructure on which successful customer services rely.

Level 1: Hardware

The basic unit of electronic resource delivery is the appliance called a *personal computer.* The two most common forms of personal computer are the Macintosh and the PC. The PC generally uses a Microsoft operating system and the Apple, or Macintosh, computer uses a Macintosh operating system. Some refer to all personal computers, PC and Macintosh, as *PCs.* For clarity, I will use "personal computer" to refer to both operating systems and "PC" to refer to computers using Microsoft.

The library often provides personal computers for its service community. With these public personal computers, library customers access electronic content and perform computerized tasks such as word processing. A library also provides personal computers to all staff to complete the work required to run a library. Library customers also access virtual library services from outside the library, through personal computers and other devices such as PDAs (personal digital assistants), which are usually not under the care of the library. Both the managed hardware inside the library and the unmanaged (by library professionals) hardware outside the library play a role the library's creation and management of its infrastructure.

Instead of hardware, I would like to be able to use the word *appliance.* This expresses the desire for a "plug and play" design, for which an intimate knowledge of the machine is not necessary. The design of personal computers is improving, reducing the need for the user to figure out the system to get it to work. Personal computer vendors are combining components in ways that reduce the amount of tinkering required to achieve smooth operation.

Take the modem as an example. I remember trying to install an internal modem in the late 1980s. After I barked my knuckles on the computer housing and got the dial-up codes wrong because the owner's manual had a typo, I finally heard that high-pitched squeal that meant that the modem had connected with the outside world and that I was in business. Last year my factory-ready computer connected to my ISP right out of the box and I got right to work. The less time library professionals, and library customers, need to spend on the technology, the more time they spend on creating knowledge.

As library professionals, we should guide our expectations toward the use of our skills as professional knowledge managers and away from the use of our time as appliance tinkerers. Trained library professionals should make purchase, maintenance, and security decisions always with an eye toward the reduction of tinkering, but because library professionals will be computer system troubleshooters for the foreseeable future, an understanding of the personal computer is required knowledge of any library professional.

A personal computer is made up of six basic segments:

1. Input, or information sent from an external peripheral device to the personal computer.

2. Output, or information sent from the personal computer to the external peripheral.

3. Memory, also called *RAM* (random access memory), or the staging area where information from input devices awaits processing by the personal computer and where processed information awaits transmission to an output device.

4. Processor, or the central processing unit (CPU), the manager of the flow of information through the arithmetic and logic unit (ALU), into and out of memory, and to and from input/output (I/O) devices.

5. Storage, usually high-capacity, long-lasting memory units (for example, hard drives, floppy disks, CD-ROMs, DVDs, and Flash devices)

that store information not currently in use by the processing unit or waiting in memory.

6. Peripherals, devices that send information to human users, for example, monitors and printers, and also receive information from human users, for example, keyboards and mice. Peripherals also include devices designed to communicate with other pieces computing equipment, for example, a synchronization cradle for a handheld PDA.

Instead of describing the inner workings of the hardware within a library infrastructure, for which classes abound, I will discuss the management principles important to the creation of a high-quality library customer and library staff experience. These principles are training, selection, maintenance, and ergonomics. These issues are complex and should be managed by collaborative groups of library professionals, never by an individual with only one vantage point.

Training

From the administration to the front line, library professionals must be familiar with how components of the library technology infrastructure work. Library professionals in public service will need these basic skills to understand and troubleshoot the personal computers provided to the public. All library professionals need these skills to optimize the use, reliability, and security of what are likely their central and most expensive work tools.

If the library invests in only one form of training for its library professionals, the library should invest in creating in its library professionals a comprehensive understanding of computer operation. This training need not be highly technical, but library professionals do need to understand the basic concepts, operation, and consequences that arise from interaction with a computer. The cost of training is always smaller than the combined benefits of the staff time saved (in salary dollars), reduction in equipment failure (in salary dollars and capital expenditure), and happy library customers (in approved budget increases).

Hardware is the first level of the library technology infrastructure and is the foundation on which all other library technology is built. Library professionals benefit from training in the basics of the use, maintenance, and security of computers and their peripherals. Many libraries have technical experts either on staff or within the library's parent organization who can respond to technical difficulties. Investing in computer training across the library, however, allows these experts to concentrate their efforts on more effective, higher-level work. Library professionals who are knowledgeable about computer users not only manage their own and public workstations more reliably, but they also suffer less work disruption and save money, both in terms of avoiding the loss of staff time in salary dollars and avoiding the loss of customer esteem for library services.

Each of the aspects of managing hardware requires ongoing training. Seek training at local community colleges or technical institutes, in online teaching environments, and in a rich collection of user manuals. The best learning occurs when we teach to others. Establish regular in-house training sessions in which those who have attended training can share what they have learned with others in the library. Create a culture of banishing computer failure through continuous learning.

Some argue that concentrating knowledge in the hands of a few ensures that these few will have a better grasp of the technical nature of computer maintenance. Now that libraries are saturated with computer technology, a few cannot handle the volume of maintenance tasks. Attention to tasks an educated computer user could accomplish draws these experts away from more substantive work within the library technology infrastructure, and because the increasing complexity of library infrastructure takes more of these experts' time, the "less important" tasks languish and slow the work of the library overall. Distribute the understanding of and responsibility for technology throughout the library and the library more successfully fulfills its purpose within the community.

Selection and Purchase

Personal computers will be one of the largest annual investments the library makes. Neither the capital outlay for hardware nor the cost of staff time for installation and maintenance are ever trivial within a library budget. Plan purchases based on projected timelines that take into account capacity, replacement, maturation, peripherals, and depreciation.

Fundamental to computer selection is processing speed and memory size. A large memory is not useful if the processor or the I/O devices are not fast enough to efficiently handle the flow of data. Conversely, a large processor is not useful if the RAM cannot hold a sufficient amount of data while the data is processed. Both processing speed and memory increase the cost of a new computer. Choice of capacity will influence and be influenced by the desired replacement schedule.

If the replacement of computers will happen all at once, several years in the future, then the best choice is to purchase the highest levels of memory and processing speed possible. Always plan to replace computers on cycles of less than five or six years. In a world of rapid technological change, older computers cost the library more in staff time (and customer goodwill) than it would cost to replace them.

A more advisable strategy is to plan to replace half of all computers every two years, or, to keep annual budgets stable, replace one-fourth of all computers every year. With that pace, you will not have to invest in the most expensive equipment. The library can choose mid-range size and speed knowing that the pace of change in the marketplace will increase the efficacy of computers for which you will pay mid-range prices in four years. With replacement every year or two years, the expertise to install the new computers will fall into a regular routine, and may become a candidate for outsourcing to a local computer service firm.

Balance the purchase strategy against a second important consideration, consistency among units. Personal computers purchased within eighteen months of each other, from the same vendor, with the same basic configurations will be easier to maintain. Software goes out of date faster than hardware, and keeping all software current is a crucial component of this strategy. The cost of a computer is its purchase price, the price of software and software upgrades, *plus* its lifetime cost of staff time and customer convenience. As customer convenience degrades, the costs of the computer increases, both in terms of library efficiency and the library's value within in the community.

As part of the purchase strategy, consider rotating newer and older computers between locations in a library. Prioritize the placement of the computers. Make the newer computers available to certain users and give the older computers to other groups deemed less in need of processing speed and memory. For example, place newer computers in public service area reserved for researchers and place older computers in an e-mail-only or an OPAC (online public access catalog) queue for quick, in-and-out traffic.

Never relegate older computers to staff or allow staff computers to age longer than the purchase pattern chosen for the rest of the library dictates. The quality of most library services depends heavily on the personal computers with which library professionals perform their tasks. The quality of library service depends on every library function performing as well as possible, which means the computer on staff desktops should not bottleneck productivity.

Peripherals, and the hardware required for the connectivity discussed in the next section (Level 2), require equal consideration. In the marketplace, input devices (such as keyboards, mice, scanners, memory drives) and output devices (such as monitors, printers, storage media, and projectors) improve quickly in functionality and price. However, input devices can often be used longer with less negative impact on staff time and user experience. For example, the speed and memory of CPUs may change dramatically every two years, but monitors last much longer. Treat the CPU (the "box" that contains the processor and other components) and the monitor (the screen) as separate purchases and decide, based on planned use, whether new monitors are worth the investment. Always keep in mind interoperability, or the compatibility of computers and peripherals. Purchase the products that are most likely to conform to accepted standards and most likely to be compatible with equipment purchased in the future.

Library use of peripherals, by both staff and customers, can be much more demanding than a manufacturer envisions. Use industry reviews to select high-quality durable peripherals (type "printer reviews," for example, at Google), but balance these reviews with visits to other libraries with use patterns similar to your own and discover what they have found to work well.

Personal computers are capital and quickly depreciate in value, both in monetary and in practical terms. Consider leasing as an alternative to purchase. During the past ten years, leasing has matured to include worry-free replacement of defective equipment, as well as trained technicians (for which your library does not pay salary and benefits) who stand ready to repair or replace as the need arises. Leasing firms would compete mightily for access to a market as large and visible as a library information commons. Opening the lease contract for bid every one, two, or three years would lower price and ensure top-quality service. Technicians from the leasing firm would also free in-house library systems professionals for more specialized work of higher value to the library.

Funds for leasing usually come from an operating budget, and funds for purchase from a capital equipment budget. In some organizations, the operating budget is more variable than a capital budget. This variability can allow more discretion in spending, or more uncertainty about funds over the long term. Do, however, include an investigation into the benefits of leasing over the costs in regular budget deliberations.

Decisions concerning selection, purchase, and maintenance of hardware should in involve a wide range of perspectives. System professionals alone will not be aware of crucial information that public service professionals can contribute. Invest in training for everyone so that all library professionals can conduct a knowledgeable discourse and so that the library can provide superior electronic resource services to customers.

Maintenance

Previously, I called computers *appliances,* referring to our need as library professionals to focus on our professional work, not on grooming the computers around us. These conditions do not yet exist. We must maintain our personal computers much as we would have serviced our own cars before the age of 100,000-mile warranties. Basic maintenance includes, but is not limited to, the following activities.

- Automate backups of daily work. Store backups offsite. Protect original copies of software.
- Optimize speed and storage through Clean Disk, Defragmentation, and Scan Disk utilities included in most PC systems. Macintosh users can download shareware utilities.
- Increase security with automatic operating system and software updates. Always install and update virus protection software on every computer and server in use. One infected computer can quickly infect many others.
- Clean the surfaces of the case, fan grills, screen, keyboard, and mouse. This is not an aesthetic requirement. Dust and dirt reduce the productivity of the machine. Pay extra attention when using liquids on computer surfaces.
- Turn off at least the monitor during long hours of inactivity. Valid arguments exist for both leaving on and turning off the CPU during long periods of inactivity. Leave a CPU on to reduce the stress to the machine of powering on and off, and most computers go into an automatic sleep mode. Turn a CPU off to reduce use of power and to allow the computer to run small maintenance processes during the shutdown and boot (start up) processes.

These are only a few of the myriad tasks that optimize a personal computer. Promote good computer maintenance habits for all library staff members, and they will benefit from computers that rarely interfere with the work of the library or of library customers (Haryott 2003; Howden 2000; Google 2004).

Security

Of the maintenance tasks, security is the most crucial. Personal computer operating systems and software are susceptible to malicious programs that corrupt or destroy data. Train library professionals to recognize and avoid viruses and worms transported by e-mail and downloaded from Web sites. Investigate how to implement passwords to control access to computer operating systems and networks. Investigate how to "lock down" public computer operating systems so that vandals cannot access functions beyond those necessary to use the provided library services. Security is a never-ending process of education for everyone, not just the systems professionals.

Ergonomics

Computers injure their long-term users. Lowered productivity as a result of computer-related injury is expensive for the library and painfully disruptive for the staff member. Back injury, eyestrain, and repetitive stress injuries to tendons in the hands, wrists, and arms pose a real threat to library professionals who use computers for any length of time. Appropriate ergonomic configurations for both staff work areas and public work areas include good-quality chairs, gel wrist rests, and an optimal work flow around equipment and furniture in a room (O'Neill 1998; Bonomo and Seidler 1998). An investment in ergonomics is not a luxury. The cost of an unhealthy staff is far higher than the cost of creating a healthy environment.

Level 2: Connectivity

I have found that in most library professionals, and in myself when I began to manage electronic resources, a shallow understanding of connectivity. This part of the library infrastructure is the lifeblood of our services to our customers, and an understanding of connectivity helps us improve customer access to costly electronic products, discuss product expectations with vendors, troubleshoot access problems our customers encounter, and create better services for our customers in the future.

Understanding connectivity within a technology infrastructure is like driving with a well-designed map. With a map, the driver's perspective shifts from the confusion of knowing only the immediate surroundings to a bird's eye view of what is next and what is possible. For a library professional tasked with preserving customer access to electronic resources, a good portion of a typical day includes troubleshooting the myriad reasons why a library customer is having difficulty with the connections within the technology environment. With a map, or an understanding, of all points along the connectivity network, the library professional can resolve the myriad reasons along the connection routes, especially the issue of authentication, or why customer access to purchased electronic products has broken down. Of all the possible difficulties, solving authentication issues is the most frequent chore for the troubleshooter, and, to understand ways authentication can fail, one must first achieve a passing understanding of connectivity.

Servers and Clients

Libraries have taken advantage of computer connectivity since the seventies, when library patrons could search and view on monitors (dumb terminals) the contents of a digitized library catalog stored on a central computer in the back (a mainframe). Separating the output peripheral from the storage and processing unit was necessary because of the size of these centralized machines. A typical mainframe could take up an entire room or building floor. As the eighties progressed, the miniaturization of the processing units and the exponential increases in processing speed and memory size meant that a personal computer on a desktop could become a self-contained machine, housing both the data and the software needed to view and manipulate that data.

Dumb terminals do not contain a processing unit (CPU) or memory (RAM). Dumb terminals display only what the mainframe instructs, and cannot act alone, but they do have one advantage over personal computers. Data housed within a mainframe is a single copy accessed through the many access points of terminals. Data housed on a single desktop personal computer is isolated, and to distribute that data one must copy it into other personal computers. Changes to data on the original personal computer are not then reflected in other copies of the data on other personal computers. The mainframe computing system balanced the need for distributed access, in which multiple users simultaneously search and view central data, with the need for data integrity, in which a single, central copy protects data from diverging into copies stored in multiple locations with conflicting changes by different operators.

Today, through client-server relationships—between client software on personal computers and specialized computers called *servers*—library professionals and library customers can enjoy powerful computing on our desktops along with distributed access to centralized data. Servers are usually faster computers with more memory that have been designed to act in one of the multitude of server capacities useful within the client-server system, for example, file servers, Web servers, mail servers (for e-mail), application servers (for software), directory servers, and network servers. Servers are powerful and are capable of interacting with a distributed network of personal computers and other servers, and, with the right software and hardware upgrades, even personal computers can be converted into servers. (In a peer-to-peer network, personal computers interact without the benefit of a designated server. But for this discussion, I will concentrate on the client-server configuration.)

The word *client* can refer to one of two concepts. A client workstation, most often a personal computer, receives data and applications over a network from a connection to a central server. A server controls the network functions. The client workstation both receives information from a network and has independent applications and data.

Client software resides on a personal computer. This software receives data or applications stored on servers and translates the data or instructions into human-understandable formats. An example of client software is the Web browser that resides on a personal computer but retrieves data from remote servers across the Internet, translates display instructions within that data, and uses the instructions and data to re-create a Web page on the screen of a local personal computer.

Networks

Between client and server lies the network, a complex collection of transmission components, hardware, and software that carry data, decide how the data traffic will flow, and translate between disparate systems speaking different "languages." A typical network configuration is as follows:

- Client stations and a server station each have a unique network address, or IP (Internet protocol) address, through the TCP/IP protocol (transmission control protocol/Internet protocol).
- These stations send data transmissions in short, standardized bursts called *packets*. Packets come in standard protocols understood by all network servers, for example, FTP (file transfer protocol) or HTTP (hypertext transfer protocol). Each packet contains the TCP/IP address of the sending and receiving stations.
- These packets contain data wrapped in descriptive information, such as the originating and destination station addresses (their IPs).
- The packet travels first along an access link dedicated to only the traffic to and from the each station (for example, a phone line or an Ethernet cable).
- A router along this access link uses the descriptive information around the packet to decide how to direct the packet to other transmission links in the network.
- In larger networks, the packet can also travel along a high-capacity trunk line that carries multiple packets simultaneously.
- The packet passes through a server that makes decisions, based on its knowledge of the packet instructions and network traffic, about how to best transmit the packet along to another location.
- The packet arrives at the destination address. The destination could be a server that will process the data, for example, an OPAC (online public access catalog) server that processes a search request, or it could be

another personal computer either inside or outside the originating computer's network.

Two major components influence the efficacy of data transmission. First, the servers that control network traffic and process the data can be fast or slow depending on their processing speed, network algorithms, and systems administration. Second, transmission links between these servers can be fast or slow depending on their material characteristics and configuration. These links, whether electrical current, light, or radio waves, all must travel through some substance to reach their destination. The combination of material and method influences the speed of transmission. I will not discuss these here. The reader should take any opportunity to read and learn about data transmission because any understanding of this complex field will contribute to an ability to facilitate better customer access to library services.

Distance considerations and transmission quality give rise to different network configurations that address different networking needs:

- Peer-to-peer networks are newer than client-server networks and consist of personal computer workstations that are networked directly to each other and that share the duties usually performed by a central server or servers. In the event of network failure, the individual computers are still accessible.
- Local area networks (LANs) connect workstations and server stations (personal computers to servers and back to personal computers) within a limited geographic area, for instance, within one library. LANs usually rely on faster cabling such as Ethernet and are slowed only by the capacity of the server or servers that manage traffic.
- Wide area networks (WANs) connect separate geographical locations using the transmission services of a third party. For example, a main library and a branch each have LANs that are connected via cabling owned by a service provider.
- An internet uses routers to connect two or more networks. A router discards a packet's frame from one network and wraps it in a frame for the next network. This allows two separate networks to share information. For example, a network managed by a library can connect directly to a larger campus network yet remain distinct.
- The Internet encompasses networks and smaller internets worldwide. The Internet is a vast cooperative—most often of public service institutions, such as universities—that manages the flow of packets in much the same ways as local networks decide where and how packets travel from one station to another. Internet service providers (ISPs) provide smaller libraries

and most library customers a connection from an individual computer to the Internet. Individuals can purchase personal accounts with commercial ISPs, or the parent organization can act as an ISP for its members.

IP Addresses

Within a network, each workstation and server has a unique TCP/IP address, or IP address for short. Each workstation and server has its own IP address within a local internet. Internet protocol addresses are in four segments of numbers, each between 0 and 255, separated by "dots," or periods (for example, 100.50.125.5). Switches, routers, and network servers all understand this IP address and use it to guide packets through the network (or networks) to the correct destination IP.

All stations (workstations and servers) connecting to the Internet must have an IP address unique from all other stations worldwide. The concept of "host" simplifies this enormous task. Networks that connect to the Internet are designated hosts and are assigned a range of IP addresses (for example, 100.50.125.0 to 100.50.125.255). The first two segments of the IP are unique to an organization's network, or host, and the latter two specify a specific station within that network. A host name, or domain name, is the human-language equivalent of the IP range registered for a host (for example, xyz.com). Internet protocol addresses have a host name only when humans will need to use the IP address, for example, to specify an e-mail recipient's address. Network components understand only the dotted decimal form of an IP address, not the host name that human users type in. domain name system (DNS) resolvers are servers located on the Internet that translate the host name (xyz.com) into the host's dotted decimal (100.50.125.0) before a packet is launched into the network.

All this is to say that networks are sensitive to impediments to speed and vulnerable to failures to make a connection. The equipment (connectivity and hardware) used to create the network can speed or slow the work of the humans using the network. Systems administrators have the complex and never-ending job of maintaining networks that optimize the speed of transmission, maintain the integrity of the data, and control the cost of the network.

Added to this task is the worry of security. Networks designed to easily transmit data and instructions beneficial to its human users are also vulnerable to data and transmissions that are harmful to the network. Network security is a topic too vast for this chapter, but I will emphasize that one can never underestimate the importance of continuous learning in network security, even if one is never directly responsible for the security maintenance. Eric Maiwald (2003) has written a clear introduction. I will focus here on authentication, an issue that frequently impacts a library's ability to serve its customers.

Authentication

The weakness of network connectivity is twofold. Most data is valuable as a possession, and the owners want only authorized users to see and make changes to this data. Some data and applications are valuable as commodities, and the owners want to allow access only to those who have paid. Trust and open access were the defining characteristics of early networks and internets because the entry technology of was difficult to obtain and networks were relatively closed systems. Over time, the technology of entry to networks has become easier to obtain and networks themselves are becoming more interconnected, especially through the Internet. Security, in the sense of controlling access, has become a central issue.

Because the originating network IP address is always included in packets, this piece of information has become a common method by which some communications are allowed through and others are not. Packet filter firewalls, for instance, intercept all communication entering from outside a network and decide, based on a series of logic rules, whether to allow a packet through. The IP address is not the only key that secures networks, by far, but as libraries manage electronic resources an understanding of IP authentication takes center stage in our efforts to improve access to products that we purchase for our customers.

Most vendors of electronic resources authorize access by detecting a potential user's IP address. Vendors allow access to their products on the assumption that the user is authorized if the workstation where the user is working is located within the host IP range registered for the purchasing library's network. Security based on IP address works reasonably well when the client workstations are contained within a library or campus network, in other words, when libraries are treated as a physical space to which library customers come to use library services.

The library's customers, however, do not usually confine their work to single workstations, nor do they confine their work to the library or to other locations within the IP range, such as offices or computer labs. Often, customers wish to access library electronic resources from home using a commercial ISP or while traveling and working from within another organization's network. In these cases, the customer becomes a remote user, and the vendor will not recognize the IP address of the user's workstation. In a world of seamless service, libraries must be able to provide access for their customers not because they are standing in front of the correct workstation, but because they are customers of the library. Methods to ensure access regardless of location include the following.

- *Proxy server*–Libraries can install a proxy server that overwrites the customer's actual IP, if it is remote from the authorized network and unrecognized by the vendor, with the IP of the proxy server from within the library's recognized IP range. A popular proxy server software is EZProxy (Useful Utilities 2004).

- *Password*–Some vendors still rely on password authentication. This solution is usually not tenable for the library. Communicating passwords for more than two or three products to more than a handful of users is too complex an endeavor to which to devote staff. Not only must the passwords be stored securely and passed along to the user at the time of need, customers find passwords confusing and hard to remember. One solution is a secure environment (a Web page or Web site that only displays to authenticated users) within which to distribute and track passwords, but this is not a cost-effective solution in most cases. Password-only access makes a product expensive in terms of staff time, and is a valid reason to avoid purchasing a product.

- *Attribute*–Authentication not by place (e.g., the right workstation) but by attribute (e.g., a valid member of the organization) is the optimal security configuration for library service to customers. The Shibboleth project is part of Internet2 and in July 2003–released Version 1.1. Shibboleth allows the user who is authenticated within an authorized network to communicate with remote networks that recognize that authorization (Internet2 2004). For example, the university faculty member connects to the university from home using a commercial ISP (under the commercial ISP's IP address) and authenticates into a personal account on the university network. Vendors of the library's electronic resources accept as authentication the faculty member's personal authentication into the university network rather than the IP address of the commercial IP.

The day has passed when vendors, library professionals, and library customers can treat the library solely as a physical location. The library is now a virtual service for library customers whenever and wherever they need it. Professionals within both libraries and vendor organizations can work together to create a seamless experience for their mutual customers.

Outsourcing

The creation and maintenance of a network, both traditional and wireless, requires specialized expertise. Libraries often include such an expert or experts on staff, or rely on such experts from within the parent organization. Effective libraries carefully budget how they spend the valuable time and expertise of these library professionals. Network management tasks not unique to a library's circumstances may benefit from outsourcing, leaving the in-house professionals to focus on activities unique to the library that improve the library's service to its customers.

Networking and other systems technicians from local outsourcing companies provide three staffing advantages:

- These experts receive continuous training in the recent technologies.
- If service is unsatisfactory, the library can change experts and firms.
- The library's systems professionals are freed to focus on projects unique to the library's environment.

One important point when contracting is to contract through a single source. Multiple contractors can develop the habit of "finger-pointing," and time spent managing their relationships is time away from library work. Similarly, the library and contractors will benefit from a single, technically knowledgeable library professional through which the library–contractor relationship is managed.

Network hardware and software may also be outsourced. Service providers on the Web also allow use of their own hardware dedicated to your purposes, for example, Web hosting (Lunarpages 2004) and shared drives (Xdrive 2004). Service providers network shared access to software, for example, courseware (Blackboard 2004) and forums (Snitz 2004; Thinkofit 2004). These service providers appeared on the horizon only a few short years ago, so continue to investigate this new market to learn how these services can save your library time and money (Matthews 2002).

When a broad cross-section of the library, from library management to the front line, understands the basics of networking connectivity and use of the network, then conversations with network experts are more informed and effective. Library professionals trained in basic communications technology can combine a knowledge of the network they use daily with an understanding of how that network can affect their own tasks and service to the library customer.

Level 3: Software

The last link between data storage, communication, and use is software. The term *software* is defined as any data or set of instructions stored electronically, but it more commonly means the instructions telling a computer how to manipulate, transport, and display data to and from other computers or for human users. Some software is systems software, which operates the systems or utilities that interact directly with a computer, such as Microsoft's Windows. Other software is application software, through which computer users complete tasks, such as Microsoft Word.

The Object-Oriented Perspective

To create applications, programmers must encode the infinite gray shades of human needs into instructions understood and efficiently executed by the binary intelligence (on/off, ones and zeros) of computers. Programmers from the 1960s through 1980s used procedural programming, creating long sets of step-by-step instructions encompassing an entire task, start to finish. The result is a single monolithic construction within which programmers must foresee all possible situations in advance, and in which shades of gray are inconveniences, not the final goal.

Beginning in the 1980s and blossoming in the 1990s, programmers adopted the concept of object-oriented programming. Object-oriented programming breaks computer instructions down into sets of distinct, reusable "objects" that are saved in "libraries" and used where needed. Object-oriented programming creates software that is

- Clearer to those not its original creators
- More efficiently organized for use by a computer
- Easier to correct, evolve, and maintain over time

Object-oriented programming represents a shift in worldview as programming shades of gray begins to move toward the infinite variety of human activity.

Programming no longer begins each task with a blank slate. Programmers can now create software components that are reusable and easily adapted by new programmers to new situations. This psychological shift no longer treats programming as insulated, individually owned projects designed by a programmer for a computer, but as an open activity relying on common standards that must incorporate and be incorporated by other programming projects. Within this worldview, the programmer can more easily meet the customer's experiential imperatives.

Pete McBreen (2002) characterizes this as a shift from software engineering (programmers create a blueprint to build a structure not easily changed) to "software craftsmanship" (programmers build their learning from other programmers, and from use and testing, to take iterative steps toward a final product). In this new view, programming is no longer a closed system that seeks a final correct answer (blueprint) before creating a product but an open system built around an assumption of continuous adaptability during the programming process. Programmers are no longer expert technicians solving a problem from start to finish to create a final product, but are now master craftspersons whose primary relationship is to the customer and to building products that will adapt as customers adapt. This is a different perspective than that held by some within the programming community, particularly because closed systems lend a sense of stability and control over the work of programming whereas open systems must be flexible enough to adapt to environmental changes, but I would like to explore here what this new perspective would mean for library services provided to our customers.

Seamlessness

A user does not start up a piece of software to *use* the software. A user calls on the software to accomplish a task. In the Level 4 ideal, a computing environment is one that does not intrude on the user's experience as they accomplish this task. When software works together to create a seamless work environment, the user can concentrate effort on the task at hand, not on tasks the software throws up on the way to accomplishing the task.

In a typical OPAC (online public access catalog), a searcher must make decisions about fields (such as title, author, date of publication), syntax (such as last name before first name in the author field, but not in the subject field), and Boolean operators (such as narrowing with the Boolean AND or expanding with the Boolean OR). These decisions are essential to create clean results that reflect only what the searcher seeks. The reason the single Google search box is so powerful is that the searcher does not have to make these decisions. The Google software, that combination of search algorithm and search execution, takes care of all those decisions behind the scenes. As librarians, we can quibble over the effectiveness of the Google software, but library customers are voting with their feet. Google uses the preferred interface. (See Chapter 9 for more.)

The most influential, and expensive, pieces of software for any library are the ILS (integrated library system), which contains the OPAC, and the interfaces of the electronic resource products that libraries purchase from vendors. The ILS is the staff interface to data recorded for purchasing, processing, and classifying functions, and within the ILS the OPAC is the public interface to this same data, giving the content and location of items within our collections. The ILS software must, therefore, integrate the work flows of product purchase, classification, storage, and delivery to the customer. If a library's ILS software is to rise to the new expectations of adaptability, it should be open to fast and flexible programming improvements that respond quickly (in months, not years) to advances in the library profession. Examples of rapid change that affect ILS performance abound:

- Over the course of an eighteen-month period, electronic-only journal subscriptions that were rare in Library A become commonplace and require ILS functions radically different from those used to manage paper journals. Library A cobbles together programming efforts from members of the staff to augment the proprietary ILS systems.

- Updates from the ILS vendor allow Library A to personalize its OPAC interface. User tests still show a low level of understanding of the fields and Boolean operator decisions necessary to search the MARC records. Some in the library pine for a one-field search screen that brings back accurate results. Others scoff at the possibility of such a thing.

- Library A is contributing to the Digital Library Federation initiative (Chandler and Jewell 2003; DLF 2003), which is creating a standard structure for administering electronic resources in a system that is similar to the current ILS systems. Library A would like to be able to capture and manage the hundreds of data elements necessary to track electronic resource licensing, funding, delivery, maintenance, and customer access and is investigating a programming effort by Library A staff members, but are daunted by the task.

- The OpenURL standard (NISO 2003) that allows the transport within a URL of citation metadata from a vendor's article database through a citation linker server to a publisher's article repository. This URL is smart enough to follow the trail from a citation in one vendor's citation database to the article in the journal publisher's database, allowing a user one-click access from article citation to article full text. Library A is investigating SFX (Ex Libris 2004).

- Since the mid-1990s, Library A has continuously improved its dynamic Web-based electronic resource subject guide and its searchable list of electronic journals using increasingly complex Web development tools. They have chosen Cold Fusion® and Dreamweaver® (Macromedia 2004) to provide a development environment that allows Web design for display, through HTML, XHTML, CSS, and JavaScript; for dynamic delivery of data from MySQL (2004) and Microsoft SQL Server (Microsoft 2004) databases to Web browsers through PHP, SQL, ASP, and XML; and for the delivery of applications, including Java, PERL, CGI, and .NET. Many staff hours have gone into creating a unique environment for Library A's customer base.

- But professionals at Library A know that their environment is still confusing to the average researcher. Customer Relationship Management (CRM; CRMguru.com 2004) uses technology to integrate all an organization's services into a single, highly refined relationship with the customer. Library A dreams of a time when a CRM-like online environment could take the form of a seamless library customer experience that wraps into a one-step, personalized interface such services as always-on authentication, cross-*platform* searches of multiple electronic resources (for example, Metalib [Ex Libris 2003]), professional human help and electronic document delivery.

Growing out of late 1990s' work with such standards as XML and SOAP, W3C formalized Web services (W3C 2004) that allow software-to-software transactions across the Internet with the effect of smoothing a user's task objectives between diverse software entities. Web services allow interoperability between diverse and proprietary applications without interrupting the user's higher-level task completion. Through Web services, functionality proprietary software is rendered more profitable because, whereas its internal code remains a unique and marketable product, the Web services standards allow the software to blend its work with the work of software from other companies without interrupting the user.

A library professional's objective is to not do the work of vendors (for example, tracking journal title changes) along with his or her own work (creating a collection useful for the library's customers). A library user's objective is to not do the work of the library (figuring out how to pass through the access hurdles into electronic resources) along with his or her own work (to walk away with useful information). Ideally, Web services would integrate the management and use of all the various print and electronic library resources into a single task environment that assists the user from topic definition to document delivery, even bibliographic citation management. Vendor products that remain closed systems, distinct and separate from other systems, cannot adapt to the fast pace of change and are less valuable within the central purpose of libraries. Vendor products that become open systems will contribute to the central purpose of libraries, that of providing a community with seamless access to the best resources in support of each community members' creation of knowledge.

First-generation library Web sites listed electronic resources separate from electronic journals, and separate from the OPAC. Second-generation library Web sites create portals that attempt to dynamically pull these lists together and present them in an understandable way. Creators of third-generation library Web sites are attempting to integrate these disparate applications and other library services in order to present them to the user as a single, seamless application.

The OPAC used to be the single public interface into ILS holdings; OPACs cannot, however, effectively manage and deliver databases, electronic books, electronic journals, and other electronic resources in a seamless environment. At the simplest, a library Web site must help a researcher decide between an OPAC, a database subject guide and an electronic journal finder. Not only must library customers choose between these library interfaces, often they must then confront the interface of a vendor's electronic resource to gain access to content. Because of this lack of seamlessness, the time and effort of both library professionals and library customers is drained away from core activities of research to address software deficiencies. For example, a typical fifty-minute library-use instruction class must, in order to teach the technical aspects of interface searching, sacrifice attention to information competencies such as research methods and information evaluation.

Proprietary software has remained closed to protect revenue through the sale of a unique product. Standards such as XML allow cross-platform interoperability without opening proprietary programming to the public. With such standards, ILS vendors and vendors of other electronic resources are beginning to incorporate into their products the ideals of adaptability and local customer control.

Although library customers will soon consider integrated Web services a standard online experience, many libraries are limited by staff size and expertise and cannot engage in the programming required to provide these types of services. This type of programming, accomplished library by library, means that wheels are invented and reinvented. Local programming efforts are invaluable in the learning they contribute to the profession as a whole. However, library professionals, both in libraries and in vendor organizations, also have the responsibility to press forward toward the possibilities of adaptable, standards-based, open-system programming. The goal of library professionals is to acquire vendor products that achieve expectations for seamlessness and productive work for library staff and library customers.

Conclusion

If one considers hardware to be the physical containers through which library customers receive information, libraries have always been in the hardware business. Libraries have had over a century to develop and improve the processes necessary to purchase, warehouse, and lend paper-based physical containers. Information delivered as an electronic resource, however, is stored in bits and bytes in a form unreadable by humans. To deliver this information in virtual form, the library needs to create and maintain a technology infrastructure between vendors of electronic content and the library's customers. Electronic resources, therefore, diverge from the treatment of a library as a print warehouse. The library is still the intermediary purchaser of content for a community of consumers, but as intermediary the library must now also purchase or create, maintain, and continuously improve the technological infrastructure within which this content resides, flows, and displays. Library infrastructure is no longer just the building, attendant shelving, and other furniture. The infrastructure is now also a technological service that takes physical and virtual form to better deliver content to library customers.

These virtual resources need storage and translating computers (Level 1, hardware), conduits between these computers (Level 2, connectivity) and human-ready display with which the user can read and manipulate the data (Level 3, software). Most importantly, however, the library needs to create a seamless environment (Level 4, user interface) within which the library customer completes the tasks of research. When the technology infrastructure is seamless and does not intrude on the work of the user, the user can achieve the library's primary purpose to its community, the provision of entertainment, research, and learning resources.

Beginning in the 1990s and continuing into the current century, the technological skill set required for productive contribution to our profession has increased dramatically. No library professional is exempt from needing a basic understanding of the library's technology infrastructure, from hardware to connectivity to software, and because the skill set is so large, collaborative groups will become the required standard of interaction. When library professionals within library organizations create adaptive decision-making relationships with colleagues in neighboring departments and neighboring libraries the library will more easily succeed in its service to its community.

Library professionals from vendor organizations and libraries must work together to create technological infrastructures that can keep up with change. These library professionals can work toward standardization that will allow interoperable interaction between disparate electronic resources and create a seamless research environment for library customers. A well-managed electronic resource infrastructure will save library professionals time and, therefore, money, but most importantly, a well-managed electronic resource infrastructure will make the library its community's first choice for the activities of research and learning.

References

Bonomo, Perry and Daniel Seidler. 1998. *ErgAerobics: Why does working @ my computer hurt so much?* New York: ErgAerobics, Inc.

Blackboard. *Blackboard.* ©2004. Blackboard, Inc. URL: http://coursesites.blackboard.com/ (Accessed September 18, 2004).

Chandler, Adam and Tim Jewell. *A Webhub for Developing Administrative Metadata for Electronic Resource Management.* ©2003. Elicensestudy. URL: http://www.library.cornell.edu/cts/elicensestudy/ (Accessed September 18, 2004).

CRMguru.com. *CRMguru.com.* ©2004 CustomerThink Corporation. URL: http://www.crmguru.com/ (Accessed September 18, 2004).

Digital Library Federation (DLF). "DLF Electronic Resource Management Initiative deliverables." ©2004. *A Webhub for Developing Administrative Metadata for Electronic Resource Management.* Elicensestudy. URL: http://www.library.cornell.edu/cts/elicensestudy/dlfdeliverables/home.htm (Accessed September 18, 2004).

Ex Libris. "Metalib." ©2003. *Ex Libris Products.* Ex Libris. URL: http://www.exlibrisgroup.com/metalib.htm (Accessed September 18, 2004).

–––. "SFX: Context-sensitive reference linking." ©2004 *SFXit.* Ex Libris. URL: http://www.sfxit.com/ (Accessed September 18, 2004).

Google. "Google Directory > Computers > Education > Hardware." ©2004. *Google Directories.* Google. URL: http://directory.google.com/Top/Computers/Education/Hardware/ (Accessed September 18, 2004).

Haryott, Jim. "The top 21 essential PC skills–Part 1." ©2003. *vnunet.com.* VNU Business Publications. URL: http://www.vnunet.com/Features/1143749 (Accessed September 18, 2004).

Howden, Norman. 2000. *Buying and maintaining personal computers: A how-to-do-it manual for librarians.* New York: Neal-Schuman.

Internet2. *Shibboleth Project.* ©2004. Internet2. URL: http://shibboleth.internet2.edu/ (Accessed September 18, 2004).

Lunarpages. *Lunarpages.* ©2004. Add2Net, Inc. URL: http://www.lunarpages.com/ (Accessed September 18, 2004).

Macromedia. *Cold Fusion Developer Center.* ©2004. Macromedia. URL: http://www.macromedia.com/devnet/mx/coldfusion/ (Accessed September 18, 2004).

Maiwald, Eric. 2003. *Fundamentals of network security.* New York: McGraw-Hill Osborne Media.

Matthews, Joseph R. 2002. *Internet outsourcing using an application service provider.* NY: Neal-Schuman.

McBreen, Pete. 2002. *Software craftsmanship.* Boston, MA: Addison-Wesley.

Microsoft. *Microsoft SQL Server Home.* ©2004. Microsoft. URL: http://www.microsoft.com/sql/default.asp (Accessed September 18, 2004).

MySQL. *MySQL.* ©2004. MySQL AB. URL: http://www.mysql.com/ (Accessed September 18, 2004).

National Information Standards Organization (NISO). "The OpenURL framework for context-sensitive services: Standards committee AX." ©2003. *NISO Standards.* National Information Standards Organization URL: http://www.niso.org/committees/committee_ax.html (Accessed September 18, 2004).

O'Neill, Michael J. 1998. *Ergonomic design for organizational effectiveness.* Boca Raton, FL: Lewis Publishers.
Thinkofit. *Conferencing on the Web.* ©2004. Thinkofit. URL: http://www.thinkofit.com/webconf/ (Accessed September 18, 2004).
Snitz. *Snitz Forums.* ©2004. Snitz Communications. URL: http://forum.snitz.com/ (Accessed September 18, 2004).
Useful Utilities. *EZProxy.* ©2004. Useful Utilities. URL: http://www.usefulutilities.com/ (Accessed September 18, 2004).
W3C. *Web Services Activity.* ©2004. W3C. URL: http://www.w3.org/2002/ws/ (Accessed September 18, 2004).
Xdrive. *Xdrive: Secure Online Storage.* ©2004. Xdrive. URL: http://www.freedrive.com/ (Accessed September 18, 2004).

Further Reading

Breeding, Marshall. 2004. The trend toward outsourcing the ILS: Recognizing the benefits of shared systems. *Computers in Libraries* 24 (5): 36–38.
Center for Internet Security (CIS). *The Center for Internet Security.* ©2003. Center for Internet Security. URL: http://www.cisecurity.org/ (Accessed September 18, 2004).
Drew, Bill. "LibWireless discussion group." ©2004 *Wireless Librarian.* Bill Drew. URL: http://people.morrisville.edu/~drewwe/wireless/ (Accessed September 18, 2004).
California Digital Library (CDL). *eScholarship.* ©2004. The Regents of the University of California. URL: http://escholarship.cdlib.org/ (Accessed September 18, 2004).
Indiana University. *Knowledgebase.* ©2004. The Trustees of Indiana University. URL: http://kb.indiana.edu/ (Accessed September 18, 2004).
Lycos. *Webmonkey: The Web Developer's Resource.* ©2003. Lycos. URL: http://www.webmonkey.com/ (Accessed September 18, 2004).
Mann, Bill. 2003. *How to do everything with your tablet PC.* New York: Osborne/McGraw-Hill.
Microsoft. *Microsoft Knowledge Base.* ©2004. Microsoft. URL: http://support.microsoft.com/ (Accessed September 18, 2004).
Singer-Gordon, Rachel. 2003. *The accidental systems librarian.* Medford, NJ: Information Today.
Rosch, Winn L. 2003. *Hardware bible.* 6th ed. Indianapolis, IN: Que.
Webopedia: Dictionary of Computer and Internet Technology. ©2004. Jupitermedia. URL: http://www.pcwebopedia.com/ (Accessed September 18, 2004).

CHAPTER 9

Customer Services

At long last, the library profession can use electronic resources to take a library's services to the customer. We need no longer wait as professionals ensconced in a groomed collection for members of the communities we serve to walk through our doors. A physical collection and its attendant responsibilities will still exist into the foreseeable future, but much of what we have learned about customer services during the past century is undergoing a major shift in perspective. As libraries move away from collection-centered decision making toward customer-centered decision making, the implications for our profession and our professional expectations are enormous. From library architecture to information-seeking behavior, from accessibility standards to marketing, the library profession's founding ethicists, like S. R. Ranganathan, would be amazed and most likely pleased by the changes electronic resources have wrought in library science. Ranganathan is best remembered as a diligent evangelist of getting information to people who needed it, and with electronic resources libraries can take the library to customer desktops.

Collection-centered library management often divides responsibilities for a collection between technical services and public services. Professionals in the technical services group are concerned with managing the collection, such as acquisitions, serials, cataloging, and systems administration. Professionals in the public services group typically serve customers through reference, library instruction, circulation, reserves, interlibrary loan (separate from or integrated with document delivery), and special collections that requiring special handling, ranging from serials, media services, and government information to the more locally unique archival, museum-quality, or special-interest collections. In traditional library management, technical services and public service are collection-centered and typically shape services, and the administrative departments formed around them, to address the needs of a collection, not to support the arc of a customer recognizing and fulfilling a need. Cataloging professionals, for instance, provide the specialized service of creating catalog records and do not typically help library customers interpret the catalog records at the reference desk.

When library professionals become customer-centered the entire library is reconceptualized as responsible for customer services. For example, a reference librarian acts as an intermediary who teaches search techniques and call numbers but who has not created the library catalog record itself. From an open systems perspective, because the next person to view a catalog record is meant to be a user, the cataloger is much closer in virtual proximity to the library customer than the reference librarian. While library professionals in reference consider themselves "public service," professionals in "technical services" may not perceive themselves as engaging in a direct interaction with the library's customers.

An open systems viewpoint breaks open the functional divisions between technical services and customer services to create a more collaborative work environment. In a closed system, library professionals apply a specialized expertise to the assembly line of collection maintenance then "ship it down the hall" to the next functional group of experts. In an open system, a system focused first on the expectations of the customers, all specialists come together over the unified task of creating and improving (or jettisoning) service after service in response to external and internal changes over time. Specialties do remain. Some library professionals will always prefer helping a student through the intricacies of a research project, while others will revel in the intricacies of cataloging. To create the best services, these specialists will rely on a constant flow of external and internal information between themselves. This flow is possible only through collaborative groups networked throughout the library and beyond its walls. This information flow serves to integrate their specialized knowledge sets into a decision making adaptive to the changing ways the library community values library services.

Collaborative organizations relinquish functional divisions for library-wide collaborative systems. If most departments still meet in their own weekly meetings, separate from other departments, the library is not engaged in collaborative decision making. To create a collaborative system, department heads transform from functional taskmasters into whole-system organizational visionaries. Value-conscious library budgets refocus from the directed logic of closed-systems resource allocation (for example, the logic that a department that processes more books needs more staff) to an open, customer-oriented system of allocation (for example, not a logic of "my" department needs more staff than "your" department, but whether "our" library service receives appropriate staff and monetary support to create the level of book processing necessary to meet customer expectation, within the priorities set by the library).

As an interim step toward open systems collaborative work, library management and staff professionals are beginning to achieve project successes by forming grass roots, cross-functional collaborative groups from within libraries, consortially among libraries, and even across professional lines into other realms of expertise to create collaborative groups that tap a wide array of professional skills and creativity. Prescient library professionals ignore functional divisions to create and re-create collaborative groups that include not only specialists from many library departments, but also experts from other fields, customers, vendors, and members of funding authorities to design solutions for identified customer needs.

For example, instruction librarians teach users how to perform research within a collection. Reserves librarians create a specialized collection-within-a-collection of high-use items with shorter circulation periods. In an open-systems library creating customer-centered services, these two professionals can use electronic resources (digitized electronic reserves and Web-based instruction) to create a course-specific Website that delivers high-use items within an instructional platform that prompts research learning among students. Further, the Web sites' services can change each semester to reflect the needs of the course's faculty and students.

This chapter will investigate how the burgeoning of electronic resources creates a greater need for customer-centered principles in the innovation of services that treat the library as a whole system directed toward high-quality public service. Therefore, when I refer to public services in this chapter, I include in that group all professionals in the library whose work affects a customer whether or not they see customers in their daily work.

I have divided public services into three degrees of customer contact in order to lend structure to a complex and expanding array of services. This three-tier structure does not reflect any real stratification used consciously by practicing professionals. Looking at customer service through the lens of degree of customer contact, one senses a shift of priority from how the customer interacts with the library's collection to how the constellation of library services, including, for example, the collection, the interfaces, the interactions with library professionals, and the physical layout of the library building, serve the customer at the customer's point of need.

The first order of customer service is personal assistance by a library professional to a library customer. Traditionally this service occurs at a

service point, or "desk." Direct service is rapidly expanding into the virtual worlds of chat and e-mail reference, electronic reserves, electronic
document delivery and the digitization of special collections, yet the
direct contact between library professional and customer remains an
important factor in delivery of the service. Because electronic resources
go to the customer, instead of the customer coming to a collection,
library professionals must also abandon the "fortress" desk to move into
the physical spaces of the library customer both inside and outside the
library.

The second order of service is indirect service, or creating an environment within which the library customers help themselves. Customer use
of electronic resources requires two forms of indirect service: (1) a clear,
intuitive self-help environment that allows customers to use a library
without direct service, but the creation of which requires a significant
investment of time and expertise by library professionals and (2) library
professionals also impart information literacy skills that allow customers
to continue to be productive users of libraries throughout their lives.

The third order of service is the assistance professionals provide
library customers by appropriately managing the technological environment and thereby creating seamlessness through an accessible, usable,
useful environment. Creating an accessible and usable environment
takes the form of providing technical assistance directly to the customer,
liaising with vendors to solve access issues or enforcing standards of reliability and ensuring accessibility within the library's online environment
and within the online environments of the products that the library purchases. Library professionals create a useful environment through marketing and public relations. Marketing and public relations not only
attempt to make the customer aware of the existence and benefits of
library resources and services, these activities help the library conform
its services more closely to customer expectations and needs.

Each order of contact—direct service, indirect service, and technological environment—relies on the collaborative contributions of those from
both traditional public services and technical services, and I hope to
show how group learning, assessment, and adaptive planning can make
the library a valued service within the community it serves.

First Order of Contact: Direct Service

At least one service desk dominates the entrance to a typical library.
Behind this desk sit library professionals waiting for the library's community members to patronize the services of the library. Service desks
are helpful if the library customer has made a trip to a physical building
to make use of a physical collection. These desks lose prominence for

customers making their way in a virtual world, and when asked to choose between print and electronic, library customers (from professional researchers to grade-school students) reveal a reasonable and logical preference for the convenience of electronic access to information services (Armstrong 2001; CSU 2001; Tenopir 2003). If library customers cannot, or perceive that they cannot, conveniently obtain information services from libraries, they will go to libraries' next closest competitors, Google, for example.

Because of electronic resources, library professionals in customer services have experienced a fundamental shift in the way they think about service structure and delivery. A recent special issue of *Reference Services Review* (Vol. 31, No. 1, 2003) presented papers on the future of reference that cautioned library professionals to go out and meet customers where they are. The authors explored how electronic resources allow library professionals to think of service as coming out from behind a desk to stand next to the customer, to experience research from the customer's perspective. This spatial shift has implications for how professionals approach service design for both our own services and the services we purchase from vendors, for how our understanding of customers' information-seeking behavior influences our interactions with them, for how libraries' physical environments influence customer use of virtual services, and for the tenor of our customer relationships.

Service Design from an Open-Systems Perspective

In a closed system, one designs a technology and then presents it for use. Designers use their own training and professional experience to create a technological environment judged to be the most appropriate for its customers. Great effort then goes into training the customer to fit into the system. Print library collections are closed systems because they are self-sustaining and have boundaries relatively impermeable to external influence. A print collection regularly gains new materials, but the process by which the new materials are acquired, classified, shelved, circulated, and reshelved is standard procedure and is rarely influenced by external forces. For example, the Library of Congress Classification System will never undergo rigorous usability testing with the aim of fundamentally changing the practice to better reflect current information-seeking behavior. The mind boggles at the disruption that would be caused by this opening of the classification system to external influence.

External forces do exist for print collections. Budget funds, won annually from a funding authority external to the library, would be one exception to the model of print collections as closed systems, but only if members of the funding authority were aware of and responded to customer information. Usually, however, the budget system is influenced mostly by considerations internal to the library's parent organization, not by direct pressure by customers. Chapter 4, Budgeting and Planning, suggests ways to change that insularity through value-conscious budget planning. Another exception would be the collection development process, if it were directly informed by customer input. However, in most libraries, professionals make collection development decisions without direct assessment of customer expectations (discussed in Chapter 3, Assessment).

The closed system of the print collection uses acquisition and classification to prepare for the approach of a patron, and this is a good thing. While I do think that processes like budget planning and collection development would benefit from a deeper response to the customer, I am not advocating opening library collection management processes to external influence at a fundamental level. Instead, what I would like to make clear is the importance of not treating the design of library services with the same closed-systems expectations we bring to collection management. Library professionals, in pursuit of libraries that are valuable to their communities, are in the difficult position of simultaneously maintaining a closed, stable collection and maintaining adaptive services open to influence from the customer. In essence, it is as if we were learning to ride a bicycle all over again, this time under the influence of new laws of physics.

Researchers in information science (for example, Nardi and O'Day 2000) conclude that the world of technology design cannot be a closed and hierarchical system. Design efforts are successful because the eventual users define the project from the beginning.

With the advent of electronic resources, libraries can no longer act as closed systems focused on building a collection for a community to use. Successful libraries work to become open systems focused on creating services continuously responsive to community needs. In an open, customer-centered system, a collection is one supporting component of an array of services created in response to customer need. Library professionals begin all service design activities with attention to customer expectations. From the foundation of current customer experience, professionals determine what to create, improve, and relinquish in order to meet the expectations of service communities at the customer's point of need (in the library, at home, in the office, or on a trip) and at the customer's time of need (all-day-every-day availability supported by task-relevant assistance).s

Designer attention to customer expectations creates an open system with a structure noted more for permeability, and adaptability, to outside influence than for the setting of boundaries through library procedure and the experience of library professionals. Designers who treat technology design, and the larger field of service design, as an open system consider the people using the technology to be as important to the design process as the technology itself. Library professionals who consider successful service design as central to successful library performance will hold their own and their vendors' service products to this principle of open adaptability.

Perceptions of Information-Seeking Behavior

Information-seeking behavior is the psychology users exhibit as they sift through the myriad information resources available to them in pursuit of some goal for the use of that information. The information-seeking behavior of library customers is affected by the expectations created in an information environment much larger than that created by the library profession. An environment that contains, for example, barrier-free instant access, the algorithmic relevance of Google, and the dynamic and localized delivery of XML and other Web services standards (discussed in Chapter 7, Cataloging and Access).

Library solutions, therefore, respond to the placelessness of distance learning, virtual work teams, online information delivery, and the World Wide Web with seamless remote access, virtual professional help, library adherence to usability and accessibility standards, and protection of universal access to information. A library's external environment is no longer a separate concern of the customer but not the librarian (method of access), of the librarian but not the customer (the price of electronic resources), or of one department in a library (reference) but not another (cataloging) or vice versa. In an open system, all participants must come together to respond to each new disturbance (change) within a system, and within a system's environment, with an integration of expertise, experience, and intelligence.

The philosophies of a service desk and direct service differ in their perceptions of information-seeking behavior. Standing behind a desk, one assumes that the customers want help bridging the gap between an information need and the appropriate choice and use of an information resource to fulfill that need. When I work behind a reference desk, the task that requires the most skill is that of resolving the patron's inability to give me an adequate description of the information need. How to perform the "reference interview," or the ability to elicit such information from a library patron, is a base competency for any reference librarian (Bopp and Smith 2001).

Research in information-seeking behavior, for which Simon Attfield, Ann Blandford, and John Dowell (2003) give an excellent review, however, contradicts this linear model of proceeding from information need to fulfillment. Uncertainty, which is the bane of any service interaction over a desktop, is in reality the central and defining experience of typical information-seeking behavior. In a state of uncertainty, the researcher cannot clearly define the information need for which a helpful library professional suggests resources. The original idea that prompted the researcher's investigation provides a vague focus, but its very instability leads the seeker to deeper understanding through a process of passing from uncertainty to clarity back to uncertainty and eventually to a final clarity. Discoveries of a better definition, a new perspective, a contrasting opinion, and a valuable side-topic all lead the researcher in a different direction than anticipated at the beginning. Indeed, the process of defining the information need may have as much influence on the final definition as any preconceived notion with which the researcher started the process. Through the research process, the researcher gradually resolves the uncertainty, progressively identifies the problem, and successively builds a creative process of research that contributes to a personal knowledge and understanding of the topic.

The reference desk, or any library service desk, relies on the model of the supplicant with a prepared request (for example, an assignment, a thesis statement, or an article citation). Reading Attfield et al. (2003), I finally understood the profound hesitancy exhibited before the reference desk by otherwise intelligent, thoughtful people. These people were hesitant to approach the resource of experience and tenacity that my colleagues and I represented behind that reference desk, even when the same person had worked with us before, because we stare out at them waiting for The Question. They look back at us and picture the confusing, back-tracking, impulsive, divergent, and enlightening learning process upon which they are about to embark, and they wish they had a partner for the journey, not an authority behind a desk (Reenstjerna 2001).

Library professionals are beginning to use electronic resources to make this partnership a reality. Chat, e-mail, and phone reference; electronic document delivery and digitized special collections accessed from anywhere; and online circulation and electronic reserves—all are services that deliver content directly to the customer through channels ranging from the computer to the postal service. When library professionals develop a successful electronic environment for library customers, we travel alongside them at every step with seamlessness, advice, instruction, and resources delivered when and how the customer needs them.

With context-sensitive assistance, the system would recognize a user as an individual with unique research needs and would be smart enough, through an array of relational databases and a rich lexicon of metadata, to pick out the resources from the universe available to the library that are pertinent to that individual and display these resources in ways relevant to the user's current context. For example, in a dynamic environment, a high school media center Web site could know that the person currently accessing the system is a 10th-grader enrolled in certain set of classes. The dynamic environment would create an opening screen with the following.

- General resources pertinent to the student's current classes
- Resources similar to resources used during the few months
- On- and off-topic learning resources suggested by the student's teachers
- New items the library has cataloged in the past week that may help with various assignments the student is currently completing
- The bibliography of the student's current World History paper; and, based on a text analysis of this running bibliography
- Suggested resources not yet used
- A few document delivery items recently received and ready for download
- A discussion board of other high-school students worldwide completing a paper on a similar topics
- A notice to renew a few books
- A message about an interesting direction for the paper's research that the librarian–research partner thought of while driving home from work yesterday

This all sounds a bit over the top in light of the programming and staff time this environment would require of a beleaguered sole librarian in a rural high school. Recent strides in commercial portal design may make this a reality yet (Antelman 2002; JISC 2003). What I am suggesting to this sole librarian, or to any library professional with more ideas than time, is to use what is important to the customer to focus innovative efforts. Treat innovation as a process in which one starts small and learns, along with the customer, what works and what does not. Treat innovation as a group effort and gather together as many partners as possible, ranging from fellow colleagues in the same state to colleagues around the world to vendor developers seeking to improve products.

Library professionals can focus service design projects on open electronic resource environments that treat our researchers as the decision makers and their research paths as nonlinear. Library professionals need to create dynamic Web environments governed not by linear structures (for example, hierarchical subject trees) and functional processes (for example, dividing the Web site by library department) but by dynamic structures. Library technology environments need to contain processes that follow alongside the potential actions of diverse users.

Design of Physical Space

When we imagine public service, do we imagine delivering it from behind a desk in an environment that library professionals control, or do we imagine ourselves accompanying library customers into environments they control? The configuration of the public service spaces in libraries will reflect the perspective we choose. According to library designers Richard Bazillion and Connie Braun (2001), space formulas currently used to design new library environments inadequately account for the flexibility required to house customers, volumes, and furniture (including technical equipment). In a survey of recently renovated libraries, Scott Bennett (2003) found that by the end of the project the single most important element of the redesign was flexible space. Bennett found that many of the libraries surveyed took advantage of flexible design to almost immediately undo and reconceptualize recently completed renovations.

Furthermore, in Bennett's view, successful design efforts focused less on information management tasks as defined by the library professionals and more on the customers' evolving learning tasks (collaborative group work and active, experiential learning). The physical space of a library becomes an information commons that is responsive to customer activities, not governed by library procedure. "The greatest challenge in designing a learning commons is to ensure it is conceptually 'owned' by learners, rather than by librarians or teachers" (Bennett 2003).

Information commons (MacWhinnie 2003; Ramsey 2002) support kaleidoscopes of knowledgeable library staff, equipment, technology services, meeting spaces, communal spaces, and (collaborative not lecture) teaching spaces. Information commons have the potential to maintain, even advance, the library's place as a center for learning and research within library communities of any type: corporate, academic, school, public, or special.

Service Relationships

Beyond flexible architectural design, the best way library professionals may follow our customers through evolving modes of learning and work is to regularly leave the library building. In academic libraries, liaison work builds a relationship between a library subject specialist and the academic departments (faculty and students) this specialist serves. In nonacademic libraries, the liaison relationship exists in many different forms, from the relationships between a librarian and the constituency served with the purchase of the materials unique to the customers' special needs, to the relationships that develop between savvy researchers and the librarians they call on a regular basis. Surveys of liaison work completed in 1994 (Wu 1994) and today (Glynn and Wu 2003) demonstrate a dramatic shift in emphasis within liaison work. Library professionals have moved away from collection building toward building effective relationships, particularly through electronic channels of communication. The latter survey also found that effective relationships are not generic communications, but are characterized by personalized, focused intent that recognizes the receiver's unique needs.

Service relationships that strive for efficient attention to the widest audience do not give return equivalent to the energy expended. For example, a study of personality types found faculty members to be most receptive to one-on-one conversations relevant to immediate research needs and least receptive to large-group presentations (Scherdin 2002). In another example, students consistently respond better to library service and instruction that is specific to immediate task requirements and that fits the students' current curriculum needs. Students do not use, to the degree expected, subject guides designed to serve an entire library community (Armstrong 2001; CSU 2001; Tenopir 2003).

When library professionals use a working knowledge of their customers' interests and previous work to create new services, these services become the catalyst for library services of great impact. A public library could, for example, use the personal relationships built around its Business reference desk to create a dynamic Web site for its business community. The creators of the Web site would pull together and continuously refine resources of global and local importance to everyday business life, while also creating pockets of resources targeted at particular business interests, business skill sets, or specific industries. The Web site would dynamically respond to the habits and expressed needs of each user, treated as an individual.

Close relationships are time and resource intensive. A subject guide built by library professionals with the intent of best serving the widest possible audience saves the professionals' time as well as the customers'. The designers can, through educated guesses, create lists of resources organized in a way that we think will support engineers' research initiatives, or teachers' curriculum plans, or the personal experiences of a community of business people. The subject guides, however, will be underutilized (Armstrong 2001). Time spent creating a service that does not get used is not cost effective. When we use dynamic Web sites, based on relational databases and metadata (discussed in Chapter 7, Cataloging and Access), and informed by twenty minutes in the offices of several business leaders, the service will develop into an environment that fits the researcher's activities.

The value of time spent personalizing customer services returns to the library in unforeseen ways:

- The business resources become so valuable to library customers that a friend of the mayor could comment on the value of the library in her daily business life just when municipal budgets are under review.
- Engineers brag to a vice president about "their" information center's support of a successful research project, and the center's reputation goes up a notch in the executive suite.
- Twenty minutes of conversation in the offices of ten faculty members generates positive changes among the views that these faculty members hold in regards to library resources. Over the next five years these faculty members, who teach an introductory composition class, affect the research habits of 10,000 students: (2 semesters × 5 years) × (10 faculty × 100 students per class).

Service relationships between librarian and library community that are efficiently wide in scope do not accomplish effective service delivery. Service relationships that are focused on individual needs create powerful engines of change in customer perceptions of the library and in the usefulness of the library in the customers' research efforts. Electronic resources and the technology of dynamic Web delivery allow, and with future innovations will allow, the library professional to design personalized service across the scope and diversity of the library community.

Assessment of Direct Service

In order to know the dynamic structures and processes of the potential user, whether in building design, liaison work, or research assistance, assessment needs to be a central factor of all service design projects. The library must know customers in all their variety well enough to provide the right services within the right environments. The library must know the impact of these services well enough to engage in the continuous improvements that keep these services in tune with changing research needs and resources.

Scott Bennett's survey (2003) of space planning decisions finds that most planners relied on assessment of library operations and included little or no direct assessment of modes of library customer research and learning. Jo Bell Whitlatch (1995, 2003), surveying a decade of customer services, finds that libraries create most public services with a focus on the cost of a service to the library, either in time or money and not the cost to the customer of using the service (through measurement of customer expectation, usability testing during development, and feedback during use). Whitlatch found that the libraries focused on the number of transactions and not the success of transactions from the customer's perspective, and that decision-makers consistently had minimal contact with customers, set few if any continuous improvement standards and required no feedback with which to improve a service once it was launched.

Search behavior, customer expectations, and researcher needs vary widely among disciplines and between user population demographics (Tenopir 2003; CSU 2002). We cannot rely on professional assumptions about what is best for the library's customers and about what is an appropriate physical or virtual research environment. To provide successful direct service, we enter the fray. Library professionals picture the library's services from the customer's perspective. The professionals leave library offices to create personal contacts and use current measurements of customers' expectations to make design and service decisions. Through all of these activities, professionals meet customers at every turn with innovative services that the customers will use and that will make the professionals' work worthwhile.

Second Order of Contact: Indirect Service

Library professionals provide indirect service for library customers by creating research environments that get out of the way of research. Library professionals provide indirect service when we create an intuitive self-help environment and when we work as hard as we can to make a researcher's work a seamless experience. The profession is making great strides toward this ideal, but we are still just beginning to discover the possibilities.

A revolutionary aspect of electronic resources for libraries is that, at last, library services are freed from the limitations of physical presence. Finely wrought classification systems create an elegant way to lead a layperson to a single volume in a million-volume collection, and library professionals can now embark on the search for elegant, yet unobtrusive, virtual environments within which to deliver electronic products and services. Using seamless design of responsive environments and constant attention to customer information literacy, library professionals can weave the library into a research experience that customers will turn to as their first choice for information.

Responsive Research Environments

At present, library electronic environments are not library customers' first research resource, and frequently users who do find themselves in a vendor's database or a library-created information environment are likely to not obtain the content sought either because they use the resource appropriately or they become confused and exit early (Armstrong 2001; CSU 2002; Tenopir 2003). A library professional's primary task for the survival of libraries in the near future is to create virtual environments conducive to customers' information-seeking behavior. We must create an environment based not on our professional perception of an appropriate research methodology, but instead on the customers' perception of what kind of environment is conducive to task efficiency. If the customer feels the library's environment is not efficient to use, they will walk away.

Attfield et al. (2003) conclude that information-seeking behavior is not a linear process that begins after a researcher outlines a problem statement. Rather, research (or on a larger scale, knowledge creation or learning) is an iterative process during which defining the problem is as much or more a part of the process as reaching a final conclusion. The authors make a connection between the psychology of design (Nielsen 2000; Norman 1990) and the psychology of information-seeking behavior. System design must support the uncertainty essential to the search. "To support this fluid process [of problem evolution] one needs to enable the user to have a seamless conversation with the materials of the situation, and to enable the continuous interplay between exploration, experimentation, creative insight, commitment and review" (Attfield et al. 2003; 451).

Compare, for example, a search for information resources in a typical library electronic resource subject guide and the Web search engine Yahoo! (2004). A subject guide is created with the expectation that a researcher will be able to find a research topic's place in a hierarchy of knowledge. The designers of a typical subject guide organize electronic resources by topic for the researcher who has defined a research problem and seeks its fulfillment.

If the user is already familiar with the name of a useful electronic resource, an additional alphabetical listing provides the appropriate link to the database. If the user is not familiar with an appropriate resource, the subject guide presents the library's resources organized in a subject hierarchy that will, presumably, create a match between the researcher's problem and a set of resources grouped (by a library professional) around topics appropriate to possible research problems.

Yahoo!, on the other hand, starts with the user's initial guess at a definition of a research problem in the form of a single search box. Using powerful algorithms to rank the relevance of resources stored in Yahoo! 's lists, a dynamic results list represents Yahoo! 's best guess at meeting that problem's stated need. A promising entry will have a link to the entry's subject category in Yahoo!, allowing the researcher to explore and refine the problem scope. At the top of the search screen, Yahoo! also provides a list of typical keyword combinations similar to what the searcher typed, further branching from the initial search into promising areas of inquiry. Yahoo! understands the importance of working with the researcher, rather than presupposing researcher requirements.

One can argue with comparing the effectiveness of Yahoo! 's algorithms with those of a library subject guide. Yahoo! researchers work full time on refinements to the underlying search algorithms. Library professionals do not have that level of expertise, or staff resources. One could argue that a library subject guide and Yahoo!'s subject guide are not comparable. Yahoo! can search within Web sites for keyword matches, whereas libraries cannot create a search mechanism that goes into a vendors' proprietary electronic resources for best matches to keywords.

The ideal would be DIALOG's DIALINDEX, File 411 (2004), which searches across almost all DIALOG databases to discover the best resource for a set of keywords. Several vendors sell products that execute cross-platform searches across diverse vendor database platforms (or proprietary environments). One example is MetaLib by ExLibris (2004). These products must create agreements with each electronic resource vendor and can only search a fraction of the electronic resources that libraries purchase. The field of cross-platform searching is young and support from library professionals in libraries and in vendor organizations can bring the promise closer to meeting the expectations library customers develop after they use Yahoo! to find information.

In more than one committee meeting in more than one library, I have participated in the discussion of how to bring the specific subject of a freshman-level paper (for example, global warming) into the broad-topic subject trees our guides must adhere to in order to retain any semblance of control. How do you channel an assignment on global warming into the correct online article databases? If the subject guide focuses only on the science, the customer will not see links to the political resources. Where, except in an entry created specifically for global warming, will a subject tree list BIOSIS and the *Congressional Record* together on one screen? The number of subject groupings must either remain general, and therefore small and manageable (for library professionals), or an effort to meet the need every conceivable paper topic becomes an infinite fractal.

What if, instead of trying to group resources based on a user's problem statement (chosen topic), we created environments that supported the uncertainty and creativity of problem definition? A user study (CSU 2002) discovered that student researchers used search engines like Yahoo! to create a pool of "gateway" resources through which they sifted, branched out, changed course, and discovered satisfying results. Library professionals wince at this, not just because of the paucity of the resources on which students rely within Yahoo!, but because the process would be difficult to support with the proprietary databases we purchase from vendors. The mind reels at the computing power and programming dexterity required to create such responsive environments within the hundreds, growing into thousands, of electronic resources and services that libraries manage today.

Virtual library environments operating at this level of responsiveness will not likely come out of in-house creative committees within a single library. Library professionals will need to do what we do best and collaborate across lines of profit, expertise, and geography to create standardization (for example, XML, OpenURL metadata transport, ILL [interlibrary loan] Protocol standards); cooperative ingenuity (OAI [Open Archives Initiative], ILL peer-to-peer networks); and commercially supported innovation (Google algorithms, SFX citation linking, BlueAngel cross-database searching).

Libraries already have at their disposal the elements of a seamless research experience:

- Direct service from trained reference staff through chat, e-mail, and the telephone
- Personalized care through electronic reserves and course- or project-specific gateways
- Metasearch interfaces that search multiple databases at once both within a single vendor's product list or across vendors' offerings
- Direct Open-URL linking of citations between articles and their full text, either within a single vendor's product list, or across vendors' offerings
- On-demand document delivery and distributed circulation of materials either through OpenURL protocols, ILL protocols, or vendor pay-per-view options
- Intercollection searching and access to digitized objects from special collections around the world, including archival materials and government publications
- Constant professional attention to information literacy

The question before us is how to vault over the walls of functional specialization, bridge the gap between profit and nonprofit, close the geographic distance between libraries to create environments within which the library offers all these services as one service: a self-help environment that envelops the researcher in elegant simplicity.

Information Literacy

Offering an elegant research environment to library customers requires complex networks of cooperative ingenuity on the part of library professionals. A seamless electronic resource environment frees the researcher from entangling technical issues to focus on issues of satisfying a research problem. A seamless environment also frees library instruction from technological details to focus on the intellectual skills required for research. These self-help environments will support library customers' research experiences and will contribute to the fulfillment of library professionals' second responsibility, that of promoting information literacy.

The Association of College and Research Libraries' Information Literacy Competency Standards (ACRL 2003) makes a distinction between information literacy and information technology skills. Current information literacy efforts teach the cognitive abilities of information literacy with which the researcher can:

- Determine information need
- Access information effectively
- Evaluate information resources critically
- Incorporate information into one's own sphere of knowledge
- Use information to accomplish a defined purpose
- Understand the consequences of the use of information

Current information literacy efforts also teach the technical skills required to navigate library, vendor, and Internet information resources, for example:

- Remote authentication procedures unique to the library's virtual environment
- Search procedures unique to a vendor's unintuitive interface

A seamless environment would reduce the need to teach technical skills and increase the time library professionals and library customers could devote to cognitive research skills.

A responsive research environment would also support current developments in pedagogy toward student-centered, experiential learning. We have already seen that information-seeking behavior is more iterative than linear (Attfield et al. 2003) and that searchers seek out research environments that respond to their task at hand (CSU 2002). Studies are also finding that learners gain the most from instruction that is task-specific and experiential (CSU 2002). This type of instruction creates a safe environment within which to exorcise fears of incompetence (Baron 2002) and uses cooperative learning (Conger 2000) to create a peer-supported atmosphere of experiment, experience, and success. The ACRL cites the report from the Boyer Commission on Educating Undergraduates *Reinventing undergraduate education: A blueprint for America's research universities* (1998), which strongly ties a successful education with student-centered learning.

Experiential learning happens through discovery, through the student's direct experience, trial, error, and discussion with fellow students and guiding teachers. Experiential learning is founded on the cognitive skills of information literacy, and these cognitive skills must themselves be taught in an experiential environment. Creating information literacy cognitive skills in a linear, teacher-focused environment leads to a classroom of students who, for example, sit transfixed while a library instructor runs through the databases and Boolean searches and access requirements and rules and regulations required to complete that semester's biology paper. The library instructor is in control of the class and the material. At the reference desk the next day, the instructor notices that only a fraction of the material covered less than twenty-four hours before made any impact on the confused student who had the courage to approach the desk. The instructor wonders what will happen to the students who chose not to ask for help.

In an experiential learning environment, students do not need to be in an expensive computer lab. Experiential in this case means thinking through for one's self. Students, with guiding questions from the instructor accomplish the following:

• Discuss the best way to develop a paper topic
• Think through and create criteria for acceptable sources
• Figure out the implications of the term *Boolean* together
• Work in pairs helping each other search a particularly important and difficult database

The instructor is still working very hard but this time as a "guide on the side, not sage on the stage (Wallace 2002)." The instructor behaves thus:

- Asks the right questions
- Answers questions that arise from a student's experience of a failed search
- Ensures that the student's conversations cover a few important points before the class concludes

The student is the central figure in this classroom and absorbs knowledge by experiencing the thought process, and can use this experience to begin to figure out more of the research process as time progresses. Much of the research on experiential learning involves students and faculty in K–12 schools and postsecondary colleges and universities. Experiential learning is life-long learning, however, and nonacademic libraries benefit, too, from a shift to a customer-centered learning atmosphere (Knowles et al. 1993).

Assessment of Indirect Service

For indirect service through seamless research environments and information literacy instruction to have lasting impact, all efforts must flow from and respond to a steady stream of assessment and feedback. Designers of library services create with the understanding that even the best efforts of today will need to change and evolve to meet the customer needs of tomorrow. The best research environments come under constant user testing and feedback (as discussed in the next section).

The best instruction programs are experiential learning laboratories for both the students and instructors. Assessment of learner competencies will help instructors calibrate programs to these learners' preexisting skill sets (Lener 2003a). Assessment of the quality of learning experience and outcomes will provide the feedback necessary to keep the learning relevant (Lener 2003b). Assessment of outcomes and impact on life-long learning skills will provide proof of the library's value to the community (NCSU 2004).

Third Order of Contact: A Usable Environment

The more effort a library customer puts into the work of research, particularly the work of navigating library information environments, the less time and energy is available to that customer for the work of learning and creating. The library profession's fundamental ethos is to provide access to knowledge without interfering with the research process. In electronic resource management, this translates into usability and accessibility.

As library professionals we have a choice. If libraries remain linear, closed systems, library professionals can push the work of access onto library customers, expecting them to learn the complex systems of information delivery that currently characterize library information environments. If library professionals choose to adapt through open systems, we can take on the work by streamlining our environments into seamless, nonintrusive delivery systems that release our customers to their creative work. For library professionals, this work is difficult–even grubby. We must become initiated into an array of technology, design, and assessment skills not normally associated with the typical library professional's training or experience. Within the choice to take on the work of streamlining access, however, lies the relevance of the library profession to the succeeding generations within library communities because through seamlessness the library creates for itself a central role in community research habits.

The two sections above, Direct Service and Indirect Service, show how choosing the path of seamlessness can influence the physical and virtual workspaces through the collaborative relationships that library professionals create with colleagues and customers. Libraries' information delivery systems can, with dynamic portals, chat reference, information commons, and technologies not yet in use, meet researchers at their points of need rather than waiting for them to come to us. Library instruction efforts shift from a focus on step-by-step technical skills (needed for a difficult-to-use information environment) to a focus on the cognitive skills of the research process (problem definition, search strategy, and source evaluation).

Library professionals influence three components of the nexus between the customer's experience of the environment and the structure of the environment itself: the usability and accessibility of technical equipment and online interfaces; the design and delivery of electronic resources by vendors; and the marketing activities that create within library communities an awareness of high-quality library services that are different from typical Internet fare. Assessment plays an important role in each of these components.

Usability and Accessibility

The field of usability research is also called human–computer interaction (HCI; Perlman 2004) and is the study of the interface between human and computer. An electronic resource interface is the set of physical or virtual tools through which a user of a piece of technology communicates desired actions to that technology. In the physical world, an interface can be composed of touch-sensitive buttons like those on a printer. In the virtual world, the interface is usually the graphic software display on a computer screen or the graphic display of a Web page. When these interfaces attain the status of "usable," they allow a user to complete a task without hindering the interaction (Norman 1990; Neilsen 2000, 2004). Although library professionals must remain conscious of physical usability when selecting equipment and furniture, the greatest concern lies with evaluating the library's own services and vendors' products for usability.

In one sense, usability concerns itself with accessibility, or designing for the experience of users with differing abilities in sightedness, motor function, color perception, and other physical conditions. In the United States, public institutions must conform to a minimum level of accessibility described within the Americans with Disabilities Act (DOJ 2004) and the Section 508 amendment to the Rehabilitation Act (CIO 2004). Assistive technologies such as software that magnifies computer screen displays (W3C 2003) and basic design principles that support legibility within Web sites (W3C 2004) help libraries achieve these accessibility standards.

In a second sense, usability is the expectation that the design of an interface will not intrude or impede the use of a technology. Usability guidelines for Web interfaces proliferate, and the principles are too numerous to cover in this chapter. Jakob Neilsen (2000) is likely the best-known, if slightly controversial, guru of usability. Usability.gov gives evidence-based design guidelines (NCI 2004) for federally funded Web sites, but the research is so well documented, it is an excellent place to find usability guidelines for all types of Web sites. Usability encompasses the entire experience of a user and communicating with technology through design (as in Web page layout) is one part of a wide range of suggested practices. I give these references for the reader to begin an education in this important field of study.

As both a heavy user and frequent designer of Web sites, if I were to list five principles of Web design, they would be as follows:

- Artifice should not overwhelm action. A reader should be able to tell in a glance how to access content (relevant to the reader), because access to the content is not overwhelmed by fancy design. For example, many vendor Web sites obscure the "button" to (expensive) purchased content with unclear wording and humble placement within colorful, if distracting, advertising of other services.
- Artifice should not overwhelm purpose. The Web site should primarily convey useful information. If the contrast of text to background is black to white, the content is readable; otherwise, the text is decoration–

not information. Conversely, graphics should impart useful information. Graphics should not move after an initial rendition.

- Important information should be "above the fold." (Newspapers place front-page lead stories above the horizontal fold.) A user, in other words, should be able to see all the important information on a Web page without having to scroll down. A graphic rarely imparts the most important information contained within a page and should not take up major portions of the screen "above the fold."
- The Web site is focused on the user's activity and purpose—not its creator's (or organization's) structures, activities, needs, or priorities. Every page clearly answers at a glance: where am I? where have I been? where can I go? what can I accomplish on this site/page?
- An entire Web page loads in less than 20 seconds on a 56k modem. Even if all library customers use high-speed connections, this discipline keeps pages clear, uncluttered, and to the point. If the pages are dynamic and rely on an underlying relational database, learn how to design the database and queries for speed.

If I could only assert one principle, I would ask the following question. How fast are your users traveling at each point in your Web site?

- If users are in top level, introductory sections of your Web site, treat the users as if they were traveling at 70 miles per hour. Be as informative and concise as a freeway sign.
- If users have reached content relevant to their intended activity, treat them as if they have slowed to a walking pace. Be as informative, but also as concise as, a Historical Marker. (In the United States, heavy metal signs about three feet (one meter) square stand on roadside pedestals explaining why that location is of historical significance. A history of the location must fit on the marker.)
- In other words, you have exactly the speed of your users' travel to catch their attention. The faster they are traveling, the less time you have to waste placing the unimportant on a page (unimportant to the viewer). The slower they are traveling, the more information they will need, but still in a concise format. Bulleted text is magic for clarity on a Web page.

As many rules and principles as one learns, one can only attain usability and accessibility through assessment. Choose test subjects well. The designers of a site cannot adequately evaluate usability because they are too closely affiliated with the design effort. Users for whom the site was not designed cannot evaluate a Web site because they are not engaged in the same thought processes as a true user. (For example, fellow library professionals cannot adequately evaluate a Web site designed for use by students.) For most site designs, just three to five, appropriately selected users can give much needed insight into design successes and needed changes.

Allow time in the design schedule to create and test several prototypes (Gottesdiener 2002), and apportion assessment over the course of the design effort, not just at the end. Measure customer needs and expectations before a design effort starts, and repeat the testing of prototypes throughout the design process. While the Web site is in use, repeatedly monitor the design through testing and feedback. When the customer of a site is involved in its design, the site will meet the needs of that user and follow the needs of that user as they evolve.

Vendor Products

Usability is not only a concern for libraries; the vendors from which libraries purchase electronic resources also influence a large portion of the online experience of the library's community. Library professionals from both libraries and vendors will profit from close collaboration. Vendor design decisions impact library customers in two ways. First, usable vendor environments provide stable, always-on access to those trying to log in to an information product. Second, usable vendor environments present usable interfaces to a wide array of user interests and capabilities.

The first instance has the single greatest impact on the work-life of an "electronic resource manager," those library professionals dedicated by job title or by default responsibility to daily managing customer access to library electronic resources. I could find no formal studies, but in my personal experience as an electronic resource manager, and in informal discussions with such managers across the United States, these professionals devote more than half of almost every workday to resolving library customer access problems into purchased electronic resources, regardless of collection size, from $40,000 to $3 million.

When access breaks down, the customer will not know where along the path—from library computing infrastructure through to parent-organization infrastructure and into the vendor infrastructure—the process has either confused the user or faltered on unusable technology. Each new access problem spawns for the electronic resource manager a new problem-solving investigation along this path and along any number of side-paths created by situations unique to the customer (department servers), the library (authentication protocols), the parent organization (firewall configurations), the Internet connection (outages at a consortial partner), or the vendor (asking for a password when none is needed). During this complex investigation, few of the systems are within the control of the library, and the negotiation of problem description and resolution can become a protracted exchange between multiple technical assistance personnel.

Increasingly, the responsibility for this work has coalesced into a single library staff position dedicated to customer service for electronic resources. This solution is expensive and near term. As the proportion of library collections that are delivered in an electronic format reaches critical mass, we must begin to augment this "fire-fighting" with more-organized cooperation between professionals in the library and vendor worlds. Libraries can set standards for minimum product performance during one negotiation of contract that will impact negotiations of future contracts. Libraries can keep track of user access problems and present patterns to vendors during the next contract renegotiation. Libraries can calculate the salary cost of these access problems and add them to the base-line cost of a product to demonstrate the true cost of the product within the library's overall budget. (Time that an electronic resource manager spends resolving access issues is time, in salary expenditure, taken away from improving the library's own interface with its customers.)

The relationship between library and vendor relies on assessment, from counting the number of times technical problems arise to documenting in prose e-mails the positive and negative experiences of customers and electronic resource managers. A polite e-mail addressed to a vendor's "Improvements Team" about repeated difficulty with a login button allows the vendor to build a record of ways to make a product worth purchasing. This sharing of access problem (and success) data between the library and the vendor is not, and should not be, a punitive comment on quality but an overture to work together to smooth the problems.

Vendors of high-quality products open their design efforts to input from both library professionals and library customers. Software and systems development always benefits from a customer orientation by beginning design efforts with an understanding of what the customer wants, involves customer feedback at every step (not just the final roll-out) and facilitates feedback through extensive testing and ongoing product improvement. Because the library considers a product important enough to consider purchasing, both the library and the vendor have an interest in improving their mutual customers' experiences with that product.

Marketing

In the creation of a usable, and therefore used, research environment, library professionals' marketing efforts have the greatest influence on library customer's research experiences. Without this one activity, all other activities discussed in this book are for naught. Without marketing, library services disappear in the cacophony of information services vying for the attention of our service communities and the interests of our funding authorities. Marketing makes tangible the value a library's community holds for the library and for which the library receives a budget. Marketing focuses the activities of library professionals and library customers on the one paramount result of our profession's calling, customer access to information.

Marketing is not the single activity of public relations, or more narrowly promotions (explained below). Marketing is a process of interlocking activities that could also describe library management as a whole. Library management combines library work and output in such a way as to provide a set of services for which the community (through its funding authority) is willing to pay. Marketing decides which services should require what kind of professional work and convinces the community (and its funding authority) these services are worth using and therefore worth paying for. Marketing is a different shade of library management. If the library in which you work is worried about its budget next year, only marketing will ensure a desired outcome.

The marketing process directs all activities of an organization toward satisfying customer needs. Marketing (Kotler 2002; Owens 2003; Weingand 1998) can be described with the following hierarchy of activities:

- Market strategy is the creation of a positive effect on customer experience and budgetary income through a combination of marketing research, positioning (target marketing and market segmentation), advertising (public relations, promotions, and publicity), market mix (advertising, products and services, distribution, and pricing), and marketing performance.

- Marketing research discovers what the customer wants, the trends that will affect what the customer will want, how well the library's competitors are meeting the needs of customers, and how well the library is currently meeting these needs.

- Positioning takes its cue from the results of marketing research and leads to decisions, including:
  - Market segmentation, which discovers all possible types of current and potential customers the library could serve
  - Target marketing, which chooses which types of customers, customer needs, and service specializations library professionals would like to spend their limited time pursuing

- Advertising attracts current, latent, potential, and lost customers' attention to the library's ability to serve their needs such that the customer chooses the library over competing services. The library may attract attention in many ways, including:

- Public relations, which creates a positive image for the library's services through the library's own and other media communications (newspapers, Web sites, word of mouth, etc.)
- Promotions, which create a constant image of the library's services as the first choice for the customer, thus reinforcing their habitual use of the library's service (repeated mention in media, repeated reasons to return to use the service, repeated instruction in use, etc.)
- Publicity, which tries to foster an image of the library's services in third-party media that is as positive as possible
- The market mix creates an overall marketing program that makes the best use of library professionals' time and resources and that has the highest possible influence on the library's targeted customers' choices to use the library's services instead of a competitor's. The marketing program will include the advertising activities listed above and such decisions as:
  - Products and services, of which the library should offer the ones that make the best use of library professionals' skills and other resources, best meet the needs of the library's target customers, and place the library above its competitors as the first choice for a customer
  - Branding, which seeks the combination of meaning, experience, and uniqueness that causes the customer to instantly recognize the library's service as the one to choose
  - Distribution, which seeks the methods that make the best use of library professionals' skills and other resources, best meet the needs of the library's target customers, and place the library above its competitors as the first choice for a customer
  - Pricing, which determines the cost of library services to the customer in terms of time and effort, also known as *convenience*, and asks what level of cost does the library want to incur for the customers considering what makes the best use of library professionals' skills and other resources, what best meets the needs of the library's target customers, and what places the library above competitors as the first choice for a customer?
- Marketing performance regularly measures marketing effectiveness to tell the library when the marketing mix needs to evolve in order to preserve the ability to serve the customer and the ability to garner an adequate budget to support these efforts. Measurement needs to occur in regular cycles because libraries exist in open systems and are not immune to such changes as new technology, economic shifts, customer preference, and competitor innovations.
- Customer service consistently meets customer expectations and contributes to positive customer outcomes. When customer service suc-

ceeds, the library's marketing efforts have succeeded, and the management of the library is the best it can be.

This marketing terminology is used so often that definitions are hard to pin down, but in the end, marketing is a mindset. Marketing means continuous learning about the library, the library's environment, and the library's customer. Marketing is a leader's way of using the customer to define each action the leader takes in a workday, as an individual, a part of a work group and for the organization as a whole.

Marketing is not addressed with the necessary depth in most library school degree programs (Bouthillier 2002; Ferreira 2002; Webber 2002). I have also had discussions with library professionals who question the need or appropriateness for libraries to engage in any of the marketing activities listed above. Libraries do invest time in many of these processes already, either as a defined part of our jobs (for example, instructing customers in the use of our services or classifying an item so that it can be found), or as an acquired professional skill (for example, service quality assessment or following usability standards when authoring Web sites). Other processes, such as promotion or determining price, mesh less easily with our profession's ethics of noncommercial, unobtrusive interaction with patrons. From a hallway conversation with a customer in front of the cafeteria to the disbursement of our budgets, effective library professionals at all levels come to see every one of their work tasks as part of a marketing plan for the library.

The effectiveness of a library's holistic marketing process is a window into the effectiveness of a library's management strategy, its service quality, and its financial health. Every time a decision within a library (from the contents of a MARC field to the design of a new building) attracts or retains customers, that decision helps the library's future chances of serving those customers and all the friends they tell about the positive experience. When the library's service community perceives value in its library's services, this perception is reflected in the value that funding authorities place on the library within the panoply of community services they fund. With a healthy budget, libraries can provide high-quality services and live up to our core mission to provide access to knowledge.

Conclusion

Customer service, termed *public service* in many library organization charts, is the library's golden moment, the moment when all other activities within the organization come to fruition. Through customer service, the library fulfills the needs and expectations of the community for which the library was formed to serve. In collection-centered decision making, customer service is the purview of a selected number of library professionals, or library departments. The customer-centered design of customer services, however, involves every department in the library. The customer-centered decision-making model assumes that every decision by a library professional, regardless of that professional's function or specialty, will affect the experience of a customer. Under this assumption, functional divisions in a library give way to a norm of cross-departmental collaboration on improving the customer experience.

Customer service occurs at three levels of interaction: direct service, indirect service, and a usable environment. The design of direct library service does not expect the customer to fit into library processes; instead, the library professional goes to the customer either physically or virtually. The design of indirect library service creates elegant, yet unobtrusive, virtual environments that weave the library into a research experience that customers will turn to as their first choice for information. The design of useable library services applies the principles of usability, accessibility, and marketing to reduce the customers' work of navigating library information environments, so that more time and energy is available to that customer for the work of learning and creating.

The greatest of these is marketing. Marketing bends all activities in the library toward improving and communicating the library's value within its community. The effectiveness of a library's marketing process is a window into the effectiveness of a library's collaborative decision-making strategy, the library's service quality, and the ultimately library's financial health as it demonstrates to its funding authorities its value to the community it serves.

References

American Library Association. Association of College and Research Libraries (ACRL). "Information literacy competency standards for higher education." ©2003. *ACRL Standards and Guidelines.* ALA. ACRL. URL: http://www.ala.org/Content/NavigationMenu/ACRL/Standards_and_Guidelines/Information_Literacy_Competency_Standards_for_Higher_Education.htm (Accessed September 18, 2004).

Antelman, Kristin, ed. 2002. *Database-driven web sites.* Binghamton, NY: Haworth Press.

Armstrong, Chris, Jean Everett, Roger Fenton, Ray Lonsdale, Elizabeth McDermott, Rebecca Phillips, Sian Spink, Rhian Thomas, and Christine Urquhart. "JUSTEIS: JISC usages surveys, trend in electronic information services, final report." ©2001. JISC. URL: http://www.dil.aber.ac.uk/dils/research/JUSTEIS/cyc2rep.pdf (Accessed September 18, 2004).

Attfield, Simon, Ann Blandford, and John Dowell. 2003. Information seeking in the context of writing: A design psychology interpretation of the 'problematic situation.' *Journal of Documentation* 59(4):430–453.

Baron, Sara. 2002. Problem or challenge? Serving library customers that technology left behind. *The Reference Librarian* 75/76:129–147.

Bazillion, Richard J. and Connie L. Braun. 2001. *Academic libraries as high-tech gateways: A guide to design & space decisions.* Chicago, IL: ALA Editions.

Bennett, Scott. *Libraries Designed for Learning.* ©2003. Council on Library and Information Resources. URL: http://www.clir.org/pubs/reports/pub122/pub122web.pdf (Accessed January 12, 2004.)

Bopp, Richard and Linda Smith. 2001. *Reference and information services.* 3d ed. Englewood, CO: Libraries Unlimited.

Bouthillier, France. 2002. The teaching of marketing and quality management in schools of Library and Information Studies: The case of North America. In *IFLA Publication 99: Education and research for marketing and quality management in libraries.* Munich: K. G. Sauer.

Boyer Commission on Educating Undergraduates. *Reinventing undergraduate education: A Blueprint for America's Research Universities.* ©1998. Stony Brook State University of New York. URL: http://naples.cc.sunysb.edu/Pres/boyer.nsf/ (Accessed September 18, 2004).

California State University (CSU). *California State University Information Competence Assessment Task Force.* ©2002. California State University. URL: http://www.csupomona.edu/~kkdunn/Icassess/ictaskforce.html (Accessed September 18, 2004).

Chief Information Officers (CIO) Council. *Section 508.* ©2004. Chief Information Officers (CIO) Council. United States Executive Branch. URL: http://www.section508.gov/ (Accessed September 18, 2004).

Conger, Joan. 2000. Wake up that back row: Interactive library instruction without hands-on student computers. *Reference Librarian* 73:309–22.

Dialog Thompson Corporation. DIALINDEX®, File 411. ©2004. *Bluesheets.* Dialog Thompson. URL: http://library.dialog.com/bluesheets/html/bl0411.html (Accessed September 18, 2004).

Exlibris. *Metalib®.* ©2004. Exlibris, Ltd. URL: http://www.exlibris-usa.com/metalib.htm (Accessed September 18, 2004).

Ferreira, Sueli Mara. 2002. The state of marketing teaching in schools of Library and Information Science in South America. In *IFLA Publication 99: Education and research for marketing and quality management in libraries.* Munich: K. G. Sauer.

Gottesdiener, Ellen. 2002. *Requirements by collaboration: Workshops for defining needs.* Boston, MA: Addison-Wesley.

Glynn, Tom and Connie Wu. 2003. New roles and opportunities for academic library liaisons: A survey and recommendations. *Reference Services Review* 31(2):122–128.

Joint Information Systems Committee (JISC). "LibPortal: Library Portal Survey and Review" ©2003. *JISC Projects.* Joint Information Systems Committee. URL: http://www.jisc.ac.uk/index.cfm?name=project_libportal (Accessed September 18, 2004).

Knowles, Malcolm S., Elwood F. Holton, and Richard A. Swanson. 1998. *The adult learner: The definitive classic in adult education and human resource development.* 5th ed. New York: Elsevier/Gulf Professional Publishing.

Kotler, Philip. 2002. *Marketing management.* 11th ed. Prentice Hall.

Lener, Ed. "Student-centered assessment tools." ©2003a. *Instruction Initiative Clearinghouse & Resource Pages.* Virginia Tech University Libraries. Instruction and Outreach Department. URL: http://www.lib.vt.edu/services/clearinghouse/studentcentered.html (Accessed March 1, 2004).

———. "Teacher-centered assessment tools." ©2003b. *Instruction Initiative Clearinghouse & Resource Pages.* Virginia Tech. University Libraries. Instruction and Outreach Department. URL: http://www.lib.vt.edu/services/clearinghouse/teachercentered.html (Accessed March 1, 2004).

MacWhinnie, Laurie A. 2003. The information commons: The academic library of the future. *portal: Libraries of the Academy* 3(2):241–257.

Nardi, Bonnie A. and Vicki L. O'Day. 2000. *Information ecologies.* Cambridge, MA: MIT Press.

National Cancer Institute (NCI). *Usability.gov.* ©2002. United States Department of Health and Human Services. National Institutes of Health. National Cancer Institute. URL: http://usability.gov/ (Accessed September 18, 2004).

Nielsen, Jakob. 2000. *Designing web usability: The practice of simplicity.* Indianapolis, IN: New Riders Publishing.

———. *Useit.com.* ©2004 Jacob Neilsen. URL: http://www.useit.com/ (Accessed September 18, 2004).

Norman, Donald. 1990. *The design of everyday things.* New York: Basic Books.

North Caroline State University (NCSU). "Outcomes Assessment." ©2004. *Internet Resources for Higher Education.* NCSU. URL: http://www2.acs.ncsu.edu/UPA/assmt/resource.htm (Accessed September 18, 2004).

Owens, Irene, ed. 2003. *Strategic marketing in library and information science.* Binghamton, NY: Haworth Press.

Perlman, Gary. *HCI bibliography : Human-computer interaction resources.* ©2004. hcibib.org. URL: http://www.hcibib.org/ (Accessed September 18, 2004).

Ramsey, Karen M. 2002. B.D. (before digital) and A.D. (after digital): Rethinking space in a mid-sized academic library. *Technical Services Quarterly* 19(4):31–38.

Reenstjerna, Frederick R. 2001. Thinking about reference service paradigms and metaphors. *The Reference Librarian* 72:97–111.

Steckel, Mike. "Ranganathan for IAs [Information Architects]." ©2002. *Boxes and Arrows.* Boxes and Arrows. URL: http://www.boxesandarrows.com/archives/ranganathan_for_ias.php (Accessed September 18, 2004).

Scherdin, Mary Jane. 2002. How well do we fit? Librarians and faculty in the academic setting. *portal: Libraries and the Academy* 2(2):237–253.

Tenopir, Carol. *Use and users of electronic library resources: An overview and analysis of recent research studies.* ©2003. Council on Library and Information Resources. URL: http://www.clir.org/pubs/reports/pub120/contents.html (Accessed September 18, 2004).

United States. Department of Justice (DOJ) *ADA Homepage.* ©2003. United States. Department of Justice. URL: http://www.usdoj.gov/crt/ada/adahom1.htm (Accessed January 20, 2004.)

Wallace, Marie. "Guide on the Side Sampler." ©2002. *LLRX.com Guide on the Side Column.* Law Library Resource Xchange, LLC. URL: http://www.llrx.com/columns/guide64.htm (Accessed September 18, 2004).

Webber, Sheila. 2002. Teaching of marketing and quality management in schools of Library and Information Science (LIS) in the UK. In *IFLA Publication 99: Education and research for marketing and quality management in libraries.* Munich: K. G. Sauer.

Weingand, Darlene E. 1998. *Future-driven library marketing.* Chicago: American Library Association.

Whitlatch, Jo Bell. 1995. Customer service implications for reference practices. *The Reference Librarian* 49/50:5–24.

———. 2003. Reference futures: Outsourcing, the web, or knowledge counseling. *Reference Services Review* 31(1):26–30.

World Wide Web Consortium (W3C). *Evaluation, Repair, and Transformation Tools for Web Content Accessibility.* ©2003. World Wide Web Consortium (W3C). URL: http://www.w3.org/WAI/ER/existingtools.html (Accessed September 18, 2004).

———. *Web Accessibility Initiative (WAI).* ©2004. World Wide Web Consortium (W3C). URL: http://www.w3.org/WAI/ (Accessed September 18, 2004).

Wu, Connie, et al. 1994. Fostering effective liaison relationships in an academic library. *College & Research Libraries* 55 (8):254–303.

Yahoo! ©2004 Yahoo! Inc. URL: http://www.yahoo.com/ (Accessed September 18, 2004).

Further Reading

3M Library Systems. *Strategic Marketing for Academic and Research Libraries.* ©2004. 3M. URL: http://cms.3m.com/cms/US/en/2-115/czrRzFZ/view.jhtml (Accessed September 18, 2004).

American Library Association. Association of College and Research Libraries(ACRL). *Information literacy.* ©2003. ALA. ACRL. URL: http://www.ala.org/ala/acrl/acrlissues/acrlinfolit/Information_Literacy.htm (Accessed September 18, 2004).

Boxes and Arrows. ©2004. Boxes and Arrows. URL: http://www.boxesandarrows.com/ (Accessed September 18, 2004).

Chi, Tom and Kevin Cheng. *OK/Cancel.* ©2003. Tom Chi and Kevin Cheng. URL: http://www.ok-cancel.com/ (Accessed September 18, 2004).

Donham, Jean and Corey Williams Green. 2004. Perspectives on . . . developing a culture of collaboration: Librarian as consultant. *The Journal of Academic Librarianship* 30(4):314–321.

Foote, Steven. 2004. Changes in library design: An architect's perspective. *portal: Libraries and the Academy* 4 (1). URL: http://muse.jhu.edu/journals/portal_libraries_and_the_academy/v004/4.1foote.html (Accessed September 18, 2004).*Hotscripts.com.* ©2004. iNET Interactive. URL: http://www.hotscripts.com/ (Accessed September 18, 2004).

Hunt, Fiona and Jane Birks. 2004. Best practices in information literacy. *portal: Libraries and the Academy* 4 (1). URL: http://muse.jhu.edu/journals/portal_libraries_and_the_academy/v004/4.1hunt.html (Accessed September 18, 2004).

Illinois State University. Center for the Advancement of Teaching. *Active Learning Strategies.* ©2001. Illinois State University. URL: http://www.cat.ilstu.edu/teaching_tips/active.shtml (Accessed September 18, 2004).

International Federation of Library Associations and Institutions (IFLA). "Document Delivery and Interlending Section." ©2004. *IFLANET Activities and services.* IFLA. URL: http://www.ifla.org/VII/s15/sidd.htm (Accessed September 18, 2004).

Joint Information Systems Committee (JISC). *Docusend: Integrating Document Delivery Services.* ©2003. JISC. URL: http://www.docusend.ac.uk/ (Accessed September 18, 2004).

———. *Electronic Theses.* ©2004. Robert Gordon University Library, Aberdeen (UK). URL: http://www2.rgu.ac.uk/library/e-theses.htm (Accessed September 18, 2004).

Kuhlthau, Carol Collier. 2004. *Seeking meaning: A process approach to library and information services.* 2nd. ed. Westport, CT: Libraries Unlimited.

Marketing Library Services (MLS). ©2004. Information Today. URL: http://www.infotoday.com/mls/ (Accessed September 18, 2004).

Networked Digital Library of Theses and Dissertations (NDLTD). *Networked Digital Library of Theses and Dissertations.* ©2004. URL: http://www.ndltd.org/ (Accessed September 18, 2004).

Prince Edward Island Department of Education. *Building Information Literacy [In Grades 1 – 12].* ©2004. Prince Edward Island Department of Education. URL: http://www.edu.pe.ca/bil/ (Accessed September 18, 2004).

Resource Discovery Network (RDN). *ePrints UK.* ©2004. Resource Discovery Network (RDN). URL: http://www.rdn.ac.uk/projects/eprints-uk/ (Accessed September 18, 2004).

Rosedale, Jeff. *Electronic Reserves Clearinghouse.* ©2003. Manhattanville College Library. URL: http://www.mville.edu/administration/Staff/Jeff_Rosedale/ (Accessed September 18, 2004).

Siess, Judith. 2003. *The visible librarian: Asserting your value with marketing and advocacy.* Chicago, IL: American Library Association.

Glossary

For unfamiliar terms used in the definitions below, look for entries elsewhere in the glossary, or consult the index for text references. For definitions of computer terms not listed here, please see other computer reference works.

AACR2. Anglo-American Cataloging Rules, 2nd ed.

Accessibility. Designing technology interfaces with attention to the experience of users with differing abilities in sightedness, motor function, color perception, and other physical or neurological conditions.

Adaptive learning, adaptive management. The process by which individuals and groups use information from an organization's environment to make and implement decisions that keep the organization's services responsive to its environment. See **Iterative**.

Analytics. Recording in a catalog record or records the individual resources available within, or the components parts of, a larger purchased product.

Authentication. Electronic resources, when paid for, need to be provided only to the library's predetermined set of customers. Authentication assures both the library and the provider from which the resource is purchased that the customer is an authorized user. An example of authentication is the entering of a user name and password before gaining access to a Web site.

Back files. Electronically archived full-text content of the issues journals or other serial publications that were published before a chosen date. Usually sold as a separate product and often but not always beginning with volume one.

Browser. Software that interprets documents written with markup codes such as HTML and other Web standards and displays these documents in a format viewable by humans.

Call number. An identification number that organizes the items in a library collection into a subject category and indicates for a library customer the location of physical items within the library building.

Collaborative management. Responsibility for organization success is shared among organization members. These members have authority over their own work, contribute through teams to the work of others, and contribute through leadership to the decision making and overall purpose of the organization. See **Leader.**

Collection. The set of information objects that the library chooses to provide to its community. The collection includes information objects shelved in the library building and electronic resources, licensed or free, that the library provides as a service.

Collection development. Collection development is the intellectual activity of consciously adding or not adding information resources to a library collection, guided by an understanding of a library community's information needs.

Community. All of the people who a library's services are meant to serve as described within the express purpose of the library. See **Customer** and **User.**

Consortial partnership, consortia. Libraries cooperatively purchase products from a vendor, trading lower prices for libraries with a greater number of customers for vendors and gaining consistent licensing for both parties.

Customer. A view of library community members that is different from the concept of "patron." Customers can choose, or choose not, to use library services. They can choose, or choose not, to perceive that libraries have value within their communities. Library professionals go out to meet customers on the customers' terms. Customers can be active (current users), latent (aware of, but do not use, library services), potential (not aware of library services), or lost (once did, but no longer do, use library services). See **Patrons**.

Decision maker. Any library professional, from the frontline implementer to the managing administrator, who chooses to create, continue, improve, or discard a library process, product, or service. See **Implementer**, **Leader**, and **Manager**.

Digital collection. Archival material of which a digital facsimile has been made or that is itself digital, and is delivered electronically, usually over the Web.

Dynamic, or database-driven, Web site. A Web site that forms pages based on real-time information, for example, information received from the Web site user or from an associated relational database. In a static Web site, the pages appear as written by a Web designer and do not change until the designer makes a change.

Electronic resources. Information delivered to library customers through an electronic medium, as well as the infrastructure needed to support this delivery. Electronic products are purchased from third-party vendors and can be housed in the library in the form of memory devices such as diskettes, CD-ROMs and DVDs or stored on library or third-party servers and accessed across a network. The latter are online electronic resources.

Full text. That which will immediately fulfill some part of the library customer's information need. This could include the text of a written work, as well as nontext content such as raw data, images, music, or three-dimensional models.

Full text linking. By agreement, one electronic resource vendor can create a hypertext link from a citation within its own product to the full text of the cited object within a competing vendor's product.

Funding body, funding authority. The person, or group of people, who review and grant the library's budget request each fiscal period. If applicable, these funding bodies can include donors and potential donors.

Genre statement. Within a collection development or other procedural policy, states special considerations for electronic resources that would affect or augment a main policy document.

Group, collaborative group. A collection of individuals, who each act as leader for the others, in order to work collaboratively toward a solution. Used in this book instead of "teams" because of the latter's competitive connotation and diffusion of meaning through overuse.

Hierarchical management. The responsibility for organizational success is divided among a hierarchy, or pyramid, of organization members, each with increasing authority over the work of the other organization members. This organization structure is also known as *top-down management* because most of the decision-making authority resides with the organization member at the top of the pyramid.

ILS. Integrated library system. A database or series of databases purchased from a vendor that a library uses to manage its materials and purchasing and to provide an OPAC for customer use.

Implementer, frontline worker. Those library professionals whose decisions and actions directly affect the customer experience. Although these professionals do not have to come into direct contact with the customer. Implementing decisions can occur as independent professional actions or can follow from supervisory and administrative decisions. See **Leader.**

Information. In the context of external services, information is the data, information, knowledge, and entertainment provided by libraries for the benefit of a community of users. In the context of internal library decision making, information refers to the data that decision makers collect to support their decision making.

Infrastructure. That combination of computer hardware and software, communication wiring, and user interface design that allows a library staff member or customer to access the library's electronic resources. Included in the cost of infrastructure is the human expertise required to create and maintain it.

Iterative. Repeating an action, prototype, or test with the goal of learning from each repetition by adapting the action to what was learned and increasing that action's success on each repetition.

Leader. One who consciously contributes, through personal endeavor and assistance to others, to the success of an organization's expressed purpose, paying particular attention to creating positive response to change. While leaders may only manage their own work, or may manage the work of large numbers of people, they make a conscious contribution to the success of the colleagues in their sphere of influence.

Learning, or living, document. A collection of observations, agreed responses to certain situations, exceptions, and other sources of collected experience that, maintained over time through review and revision, become an adaptive representation of policy and procedure. Conversely, static, non-adaptive policies become, over time, increasingly disconnected from the experiences of library professionals and library customers.

Librarian. A library staff member with a master's degree in library and information science (MLIS).

Library professional. Any library staff member, from the frontline implementer of services to the top-level administrator, whose work contributes to the purpose of the library. Any library vendor staff member whose work contributes to the purposes of the libraries that the vendor serves.

License. With a license the library gains for those in its community access rights to content, usually online, in return for which the library agrees to terms of access that protect the library's, the library customers' and the vendor's interests.

Manager, supervisor, administrator. One who directs the actions of others, a group, or an organization. See **Leader.**

MARC. Machine-readable cataloging. A set of standards that govern the communication of bibliographic data, usually within and between library catalogs.

Materials management. The selection, purchase, receipt, and storage of physical and virtual objects within a library collection.

MLIS. Master's of library and information science. Most North American and European libraries, and many libraries worldwide, require that librarians have an MLIS.

Monograph. An item in a library collection with a defined beginning and end and no further expectation of change or augmentation of content.

OCLC. Online Computer Library Center. One of several central bibliographic cataloging services through which member libraries share prepared cataloging records through a union catalog. The OCLC is also a library research organization.

One-click access. The URL provided in a descriptive record directly accesses the content described, with no further linking by the viewer. The viewer only selects one link to access an electronic resource.

Online, online resource. Electronic resource accessed by computer over a communication network.

OPAC. Online public access catalog. The electronic interface library customers use to search or browse the contents of a database, or databases, describing a library collection.

Patrons. A view of library community members as people who approach physical or virtual service points to have an information need fulfilled. Patrons come to a library on the library's terms. See **Customer**.

Platform. An electronic resource vendor's proprietary virtual environment.

Politics, political behavior. The self-preservation in the face of change, either through protection of one's own familiar routine or protection of the routines of one's own division of an organization, even if the protective decision has a negative impact on other organization members, other divisions within the organization, or the product of the organization as experienced by the customer. See **Leader**.

PURL. Persistent, or permanent, URL; a URL that provides an unchanging link to an electronic resource. Usually this permanence is accomplished through a unique identifying code contained within the PURL that a separate database of variable URLs uses to provide the correct, current URL.

Purpose. The combination of intent and values that drives an activity. It influences the decisions of any individual, group, or organization engaged in the activity and shapes the desired result of that activity.

RLG. The Research Libraries Group. One of several central bibliographic utilities through which member libraries share prepared cataloging records.

Routine. The following of accepted practice or standard procedure. Permits standardization and congruence of activity between work groups and between libraries, but can also stifle adaptation when not coupled with collaborative management and adaptive learning.

Seamlessness. A computer-use experience during which the user completes tasks intuitively, with consistency, and without interruption from the computer system in use.

Serial. Works published in regularly or irregularly with no discernable date of completion.

Service provider, Internet service provider. A vendor of networking services. Internet service providers (ISPs) provide access to the global network known as the Internet, usually for private citizens or organizations that cannot access the Internet directly.

Scholarly communication debate. An ongoing discussion in the publishing, academic, and library communities concerning the economic and technological difficulties of supporting the free flow of scholarly discourse while protecting both the ease of access for scholars and the revenue of publishers.

Staff. All employees of the library. Includes library administration, professional librarians, and paraprofessionals. A more conventional definition limits staff to just paraprofessionals; this book does not. See **Library professional.**

System. That combination of things, people, processes, and resources that an organization brings together in special ways to produce a hoped-for result. In an open system, the organization is influenced by forces from outside, like customer expectations, advances in technology, changes in the labor pool, fluctuations in the price of resources, etc.

URL. Uniform resource locator. The address of a document, or other resource, on the World Wide Web.

User. A library customer making active use of a library resource or service.

Value, demonstrated value. The combination of assessed service quality the library provides its customers and the assessed outcome, or impact, the library has on these customers' lives.

Vendor. A commercial organization that provides electronic resources to libraries for purchase. Some vendors are the publishers of the information contained within the electronic resource. Some vendors aggregate content published by third parties. Conventional definitions distinguish between aggregators and publishers; this book refers to both as "vendors."

Virtual. An object in an electronic environment that has no physical presence but has the effect of the real. Physical shelves act to store and present physical library objects to potential readers. A library Web site, by storing links to electronic resources and presenting them for potential use, is virtual shelving. Physical meetings bring people together in the same room. Virtual meetings bring people together in an online environment, and these people need not be in the same location or contribute at the same time.

Walk-away. The decision by a library customer to stop using a library product or service before fulfilling the information need that prompted its use. Usually walk-away occurs when the difficulty or inconvenience (cost) of a product or service becomes higher that the customer is willing to pay.

Index

About the Author

JOAN E. CONGER received her BA from Smith College and her MLIS from the University of Texas, Austin. As a librarian she has coordinated electronic resource management, web development, reference, research instruction, cataloging, systems, acquisitions, assessment, and training in libraries large and small, academic and corporate. Through all of these learning experiences she become dedicated to the idea that every current library employee has the power, through collaborative effort, to successfully turn upheaval and uncertainty into extraordinary service. Preparing for this book, Joan began to find research supporting why many of her change efforts succeeded in spite of the kind pessimism of others. Through this research she discovered the field of Organization Development and is now a full-time PhD student in Organizational Development at the Fielding Institute. She hopes to give back to the library profession what she learns there.